No Popery!

No Popery!
Anti-Papal Prejudice

Herbert Thurston, S.J.

"But you don't suppose," said Michael, "that people would believe a thing like that."

"They will believe anything, my dear, that suggests corruption in public life. It's one of the strongest traits in human nature. Anxiety about the integrity of public men would be admirable, if it wasn't so usually felt by those who have so little themselves that they can't give others credit for it."

— John Galsworthy, *The Silver Spoon*

Roman Catholic Books
A Division of Catholic Media Apostolate
Distribution Center: Post Office Box 2286, Fort Collins, CO 80522

ISBN 0-912141-83-2

CONTENTS

PREFACE

In the Litany of the Book of Common Prayer, as originally printed in the reign of King Edward VI, the congregation were directed to pray : " From the tyranny of the Bishop of Rome and all his detestable enormities, good Lord deliver us." Although this particular invocation was shortly afterwards suppressed, the tradition, duly fostered in past centuries by such works as the *Homilies appointed to be read in Churches* and *Foxe's Book of Martyrs*, has lasted on to our own day. It has begotten among many excellent people an attitude of hostility and suspicion, the fruitful soil in which no suggestion of papal corruption is too fantastic to take root and propagate itself. There will always be writers and publishers who are willing to turn such conditions to their own advantage. The infamous work of Dr. Angelo Solomon Rappoport, largely advertised shortly before the War as a " best seller," has been dealt with sufficiently in the pages which follow. But even since the present volume has been in type, a work of fiction, prurient to the very verge of indecency, has come from the press, reviving in the most offensive form the scandals associated with the name of the mythical Pope Joan. In this the publishers do not scruple to state that the author, " citing such authorities as Marianus Scotus and Sevarius (*sic*), in the course of this enthralling novel, re-opens the disputed question by proving that the woman Pope did indeed exist." " The author," they go on, " gives us a vivid and outspoken history of her amazing life of amorous adventure which culminated in one of the most tragic *dénouements* in history " ! ! How far Messrs. Hutchinson and Co. have themselves been imposed upon, it is not easy to say, but two facts are certain. First that even if the passage attributed to Marianus Scotus were authentically written by him two hundred years after the supposed date of Joan's death, it consists of no more than two lines, stating that the Pope who succeeded Leo IV and reigned for a couple of years, was a woman. Not a single other detail is there furnished regarding her, and even this jejune entry in the chronicle, as every modern critic admits, is an interpolation of much later date. Secondly the reference given to Nicholas Serarius (the very name is incorrectly printed both on the cover of the novel and in the Preface) is a mere piece of *blague* ; for Serarius, so far from bearing witness to the existence of Pope Joan, published a long dissertation proving that the whole story was a myth.

The real preface to the present book is the quotation from John Galsworthy which is printed on its fly-leaf. I have wished primarily to illustrate the principle he enunciates that there is nothing which people will not believe about a public man, and moreover to show that this is particularly verified when that public man succeeds to a load of inherited obloquy such as is the case with all the Popes. To bring home this truth to the reader, it was necessary, painful as the suggestion of such scandals must be to any devout Catholic, to discuss the charges in a certain amount of detail. There is nothing, I trust, in the pages which follow which can feed a prurient curiosity ; but the mere statement that this or that Supreme Pontiff was accused of moral irregularities would not have sufficed. The reader had to be made to understand that such charges may be specific, that they may be repeated by many people and may be vouched for by politicians who among their own associates were men of a certain standing and influence, and yet remain purely calumnious, without a shadow of fact to support them. Fortunately in the instance of Pius IX, by an accident which can by no means be counted on in other similar cases, we have an absolute refutation of the scandals maliciously associated with his name, a refutation of a kind which excludes all possibility of error. It is made plain that these charges, of which no whisper was ever heard until he had been for some years Pope and Sovereign of the States of the Church, had no better foundation than the deliberate calumny of the Italian revolutionaries. The testimony of his political antagonist and fellow townsman, Nicolini, who, while denouncing his alleged tyranny in the most violent terms, bears unstinted testimony to the purity of his life, is decisive. None the less such calumnies no doubt produced their effect in poisoning the minds of the ill-disposed. On the other hand the mere fact that abominable stories were told and credited, did not prove, and does not in other cases prove, that there is even the shadow of foundation for the vile things which are asserted.

Disregarding chronological order, I have discussed the case of Pius IX towards the beginning of this little book because it seemed to me that many people do not allow for the possibility of slander so widespread and so unscrupulous. But assuredly Pio Nono was not the only Pontiff who, for political, religious or interested motives, was bitterly hated by a section of his disaffected subjects. Those who are most familiar with the conditions which prevailed in the Middle Ages will be least inclined to question the fact that the circulation of wildly calumnious reports is more likely to have occurred in the ninth, or even the twelfth century, than in the nineteenth. In some cases, those, for example, of St. Gregory VII or Pope Sylvester II, so much evidence has been preserved which is to the credit of the Pontiff in question, that historians have felt justified in dismissing as altogether worthless the scandalous stories by which they were held up to obloquy. But there are many other pontificates with regard to which for various reasons we are less well informed. It is the contention of this book that even where injurious charges have been freely made and there is little positive testimony to set against them, we are not justified in assuming that there must have been real foundation for the abuse with which the Popes were assailed. In earlier ages it was almost always the extravagant which by preference claimed attention. A humdrum life of ordinary decent conduct made no mark. Any spicy gossip of misdemeanours or irregularity in high places was

apt to be put on record by the chronicler, even when he himself
only half believed it.   It was something to enliven his narrative,
and he had no reason to be afraid of a prosecution for libel.   The
circumstances under which he wrote, the limited audience—
for the most part a sort of family circle—which he addressed, .
did not stimulate any consciousness of the duty which he owed
to historical truth.   Passions ran high in those ages of blood and
iron, and the colouring of the records which have been preserved
to us is largely a matter of accident.   On these grounds it seems
to me that we have no justification for bringing in a verdict of
guilty against the incriminated pontiffs, especially in matters
affecting moral conduct, unless the evidence is overwhelming
and unless it comes from friendly sources as well as from the
denunciations of the ill-disposed.   The tendency was not to
cloak the failings of highly-placed ecclesiastics, but rather to
drag them to light and to exaggerate.

There can, of course, be no question of maintaining that the
record of the papacy is unsullied.   There have been Popes whose
private lives and even public conduct have brought disgrace
upon the sublime office which they held.   The holy Oratorian,
Cardinal Baronius, as pointed out in the first chapter, has set
an admirable example of candour in freely admitting the facts
wherever the proof seemed adequate.   No sort of impecca-
bility had ever been claimed for the Papacy.   It is only in their
office of teachers of the Church that the Divine promise has been
made that the Vicars of Christ shall be protected from error.

Some portion of the contents of this volume has in one form
or another previously appeared in print and my thanks are due
to the editors of *The Month*, of the (American) *Ecclesiastical Review*,
and of the American Quarterly *Thought*, for allowing me to make
use of the material published in their pages.

HERBERT THURSTON, S.J.

St. George's Day, 1930.

NO POPERY

Chapter I

BAD POPES

When Christ our Lord conferred upon the Apostles, and notably upon St. Peter, the power to forgive sins, to consecrate the Eucharist, to impose hands in ordination, etc., and had appointed them and their successors to be the teachers of His Church so long as the world should last, He nevertheless left them subject to all the infirmities, of soul as well as body, which are common to our fallen nature. If the Church, in view of its origin and of its final end, may rightly be called divine, it is also a human institution in so far as it is constituted of human elements. This is a point which seems to have been emphasised in Christian tradition from the very first. St. Peter, to whom the solemn promise of indefectibility was made by Jesus Christ, and who was himself to shed his blood for his Master, began by being unfaithful to that Master, as all four evangelists record, and in the hour of trial declared that he " knew not the man." There are not many incidents connected with our Saviour's life to which such special prominence is given, but the fall of St. Peter is recounted in each of the gospels with a fulness of detail which seems rather out of proportion to its relative insignificance. The triple denial was a striking fulfilment of a prophecy, but it had no direct consequences nor any bearing upon the subsequent history of the Passion or the constitution of the Church.

Again, even after Pentecost, the head of the college of Apostles is presented to us as still subject to human foibles and imperfections. In a well-known passage of the Epistle to the Galatians, St. Paul speaks as follows :

And recognising the grace conferred upon me, James
and Cephas and John—they that were reputed as pillars—
gave to Barnabas and myself the right hand of fellowship,
we to go to the gentiles, they to the circumcised.   Only
we were to remember the poor ; the very thing that I
have been eager to do.

But when Cephas came to Antioch, I withstood him to
his face, because he was self-condemned.   For before some
came from James he used to eat with the gentiles, but after
they had come he withdrew and held aloof from them,
fearing those of the circumcision.   And the rest of the
Jews dissembled along with him, and thus even Barnabas
was led away by their pretence.   But when I saw that they
were not walking aright according to the truth of the
gospel, I said to Peter before them all, " If thou, for all
thou art a Jew, livest like a gentile and not like a Jew, by
what right dost thou constrain the gentiles to live like
Jews ? " [1]

There can, of course, be no question that it is St. Peter who
is here spoken of under his Aramaic name of Cephas, neither will
anyone seriously pretend that the fault imputed to him involved
the forfeiture of sanctifying grace, but, chosen apostle and Head
of the Church as he was, he is set before us as still subject to
human infirmity.   In this minor matter of Jewish observance
he sacrificed principle to expediency, fearing to give offence.
On the other hand, his censor and fellow-apostle St. Paul does
not seem always to have shown himself superior to those little
antipathies and resentments which are apt to cause so much
trouble among good people ; for in the 15th chapter of the
Acts of the Apostles, we read :

And Paul and Barnabas continued at Antioch, teaching
and preaching with many others the word of the Lord.
And after some days Paul said to Barnabas : Let us return
and visit our brethren in all the cities wherein we have
preached the word of the Lord, to see how they do.   And

[1] Galatians ii, 9–14 (Westminster Version).

Barnabas would have taken with them John also that was surnamed Mark. But Paul desired that he (as having departed from them out of Pamphylia and not gone with them to the work) might not be received. And there arose a dissension, so that they departed one from another, and Barnabas indeed taking Mark, sailed to Cyprus. But Paul choosing Silas departed, being delivered by the brethren to the grace of God.[2]

There is no reason to doubt that Barnabas and John Mark were zealous ministers of the word, but a coolness seems to have arisen between St. Paul and the other two, and they went in future their separate ways.

Even more striking is the contrast under the old dispensation between the commendations lavished upon King David and the unworthy conduct for which he was more than once rebuked and visited with God's chastisements. There is no need to repeat the story of David's terrible sin, nor to condemn him for his numbering of his people or his weak indulgence to his son Absolom, but even on his death-bed, in his last charge to Solomon, we find a vindictiveness which it is hard to reconcile with our conception of God as the Father of Mercies.[3] Nevertheless in the New Testament, as in the Old, David is presented for our veneration as one officially identified with the divine purposes. St. Paul, preaching in the synagogue at Antioch, makes the language of the Old Testament his own when he says : " And when He had removed him (Saul), He raised them up David to be King, to whom giving testimony He said, ' I have found David, the son of Jesse, a man according to my own heart, who shall do all My wills.' And of this man's seed God, according to His promise, hath raised up to Israel a Saviour, Jesus."[4] King David, in spite of many noble qualities, was human, quite terribly human, in his subjection to those strong passions by which men are swayed. But, for all that, God did not disavow him as His representative. Even after the record of the royal prophet's infidelities and crimes was set out in

[2] Acts xv, 35-40.   [3] I Kings ii, 5-6, 8-9.   [4] Acts xiii, 22-23.

Holy Writ for every man to read, his name was held in veneration by the people of Israel, and the Christian Church for all time to come will give glory to God in those glowing words of repentance, thanksgiving and praise which King David was inspired to leave to posterity in the Book of Psalms.

It cannot, then, be any great matter of surprise that the Church has always recognised the human infirmity of her Pontiffs regarded as individuals. In their official capacity as teachers and pastors of the sheep of Christ, they are invested with the prerogative of infallibility, that is, they are divinely protected from error in their *ex cathedra* pronouncements regarding faith and morals. But as men, they may be narrow in their outlook, mistaken in their judgments, and sinful, or even criminal, in their actions. It cannot be too strongly insisted on that there is no thought in the pages which follow of setting aside any verdict of history, however unfavourable to the popes, which has been fairly and patiently arrived at by a study of reliable evidence. There have undoubtedly been periods when terrible scandals prevailed at the court of Rome, but I do not think that any serious attempt has been made on the Catholic side to suppress the facts or to make light of them. No one could use more uncompromising language than the saintly Oratorian, Cardinal Baronius, honoured among Catholics as the second " Father of Ecclesiastical History," in condemning the terrible abuses which prevailed in the tenth and part of the eleventh century. He does not hesitate to use plain language. He tells us that the most abandoned harlots governed at Rome, that it was they who transferred sees, appointed bishops and procured the promotion of their own paramours to occupy the chair of St. Peter. He is reluctant to call those so intruded legitimate pontiffs, though there were no others, for he declares that all the formalities of election and rites of consecration were disregarded. Christ had fallen asleep in Peter's bark, and, what was worst of all, the disciples themselves remained stertorous and supine, so that there was no one to awaken Him. Nevertheless, he adds, the Master was surely there, otherwise nothing could have saved the ship from foundering.[5] In another place, Baronius, still speaking vaguely of the century as a whole, explains how this deplorable condition of things had arisen. It was, he says, due to the brute force of despotic princes in that age of iron who imposed their own nominees upon a clergy and people already demoralised by incessant feuds, tumults and deeds of violence. The men who arrogated to themselves during that period the election of the Roman Pontiffs were fiendish in their cruelty and injustice.

And, oh shame ! oh, the pity of it ! What monsters did they not impose upon that apostolic throne which angels regard with reverence ! What woes originated from this source ! What dark and bloody tragedies ! Alas ! alas ! for the age in which it was reserved for the spouse purchased by the Redeemer at the price of His own blood, the spouse without stain or blemish, to be so defiled with the filth cast upon her as to be made, like her divine founder, the object of scorn and the laughing-stock of her enemies.[6]

Naturally this language has often been quoted by the assailants of the Catholic Church, quoted for the most part without any attention being paid to the historic background, the universal lawlessness, ferocity and lust which, as Baronius points out, were mainly responsible for the terrible degradation into which the papacy had fallen. So far from extenuating the evil conditions which he deplores, it is now the general opinion of scholars, who have at their disposal a wider range of historical sources than were then open to him, that the learned Oratorian was pessimistic and that the scandals were not so uninterrupted or quite so grievous as his language would suggest. He accepted at their face value and without qualification the sweeping diatribes of Liutprand, Raoul Glaber, Bonizo, St. Peter Damian, and other emotional writers of the tenth and eleventh centuries, some at least of whom were unscrupulous partisans. As we shall have occasion to notice more than once in the course of the pages which follow, extravagance of statement is above all

[5] Baronius, *Annales*, A.D. 912, §8.   [6] Baronius, *Annales*, A.D. 900, §3.

characteristic of an age of blood and iron. The exaggerations used by pious people in condemning vice were often hardly less misleading than the calumnies of malicious time-servers who sought only to please their secular patrons. It is at any rate clear that Baronius, the friend of St. Philip Neri, writing in Rome as the apologist of Catholic orthodoxy, made no attempt to suppress discreditable facts which, rightly or wrongly, he believed to be the truth ; and the same, speaking generally, may be affirmed of the scholarly historians, from Mabillon and Muratori to Hergenröther and Duchesne, who have followed in his footsteps. The latest biographer of the mediæval Popes, Mgr. Horace Mann, has adhered loyally to this tradition of candour, but he has found it necessary to make some protest against the indiscriminating censure passed upon a long succession of Pontiffs who do not all deserve to fall under the same condemnation. He speaks with just severity of a very loose statement of the late Dr. Adrian Fortescue, who wrote that during a century and a half (884–1046) " there is hardly one, perhaps not one Pope, who was an ordinarily good bishop. It is a long story of simoniacal elections, murder and violence of every kind, together with shameless lust."[7] This is certainly going far beyond the facts which can be proved with any reasonable show of evidence. Even in the worst cases there is much that remains doubtful, and Mgr. Mann's long and painstaking investigation has brought him to the following general conclusions :

> Excluding the acknowledged intruders (*invasores*), i.e. the antipopes Christopher and Boniface VII, as also " Donus II," for the simple reason that there was no such Pope, thirty-seven Pontiffs filled the chair of Peter from the death of Stephen (891) to the accession of St. Leo IX (1049). Of these, considering them strictly as *Popes* and not taking into account what they may have been before they became such, the impartial verdict of history cannot condemn as really a disgrace to their sacred calling more than four

---

[7] Fortescue, *The Orthodox Eastern Church*, p. 172.

at most. These four would include the *two* youths, John XII and Benedict IX, whose very youth is some excuse for their evil deeds, Stephen VII, the probable tool of a vengeful queen, and the very doubtful case of Sergius III. But John X and Benedict VIII are not to be set down as bad Popes or bishops, because they fought the Saracens ; on the contrary, under the circumstances, it was much to their credit. If we allow that Gregory V tolerated or encouraged the unnecessarily degrading punishment of a most worthless man who thoroughly deserved punishment, is that enough to brand him as wicked ? And if it is conceded that one bishop was made Pope by the influence of a woman with whom he had had unlawful connections before he became Pope, does it follow absolutely that as Head of the Church he continued his evil life ? Authentic evidence goes to show that, even if the confused stories of the libellous Liutprand are accepted as sober history, John X, of whom the above is said, was a worthy Pontiff. Supposing, further, it is granted that the son of a bad woman mounted the apostolic throne, must we perforce see the advent of a ruffian ? As a matter of fact, John XI (of whom this is alleged by one, who, on his own showing, was a prurient-minded, conceited, spiteful flatterer, viz., Liutprand) showed himself the possessor of an unblemished character.[8]

It is possible, of course, that Mgr. Mann may have been unduly biassed in favour of the accused pontiffs, but the evidence against them which he rejects is certainly not convincing, and the prevalence of much slander at a later date suggests the need of caution in arriving at unfavourable conclusions. On the other hand, we have every reason to bear in mind the barbarity of the times in which they lived and of which they were in some sense the product. Even Gibbon does not hesitate to admit that " the most powerful senators, the marquises of Tuscany and the counts of Tusculum, held the apostolic see in a long

[8] Mann, *History of the Popes in the Early Middle Ages*, Vol. V, pp. 295-296.

and disgraceful servitude. The Roman pontiffs of the ninth
and tenth centuries were insulted, imprisoned and murdered
by their tyrants ; and such was their indigence, after the loss
and usurpation of the ecclesiastical patrimonies, that they could
neither support the state of a prince, nor exercise the charity of
a priest."[9]   Quite in accord with this is the recent judgment
of Professor Whitney.   Speaking of one of the least defensible of
the " bad Popes," Benedict IX, he notes the significant fact
that " the description of his depravity becomes more highly
coloured as years go by and the controversies of Pope and
Emperor distort the past " ; but to this, a little further on, he
adds the observation :

> Attention has been too often concentrated on the profli-
> gacy of Benedict IX, which in its more lurid colours shines
> so prominently in later accounts. What is remarkable,
> however, is the corruption, not of a single man, even of
> a single Pope, but of the whole Roman society. Powerful
> family interests maintained it ; the imperial power might
> counterbalance them, and, as we have seen, the Papacy
> had been lately treated much as a German bishopric.[10]

It was the practice touched upon in this last remark which
lay at the root of the evil.   The principle for which St. Leo IX
and St. Gregory VII were later to contend with a vigour and
tenacity which, humanly speaking, saved the Church of God
from utter collapse, was the freedom of ecclesiastical appoint-
ments from the control of the great secular potentates.   The
abuse had arisen innocently enough.   Its first germs were
probably to be found in the early developments of the parochial
system.   In many places, and especially in rural districts, it
was the private chapel of the local magnate which became the
parish church, and it was his chaplain who was transformed into
the parish priest.   Thus the landowner grew to be looked upon
as the *patronus ecclesiæ*, the patron of the living, claiming the right
to present for ordination any cleric of his own selection.   It was

[9] Gibbon, *Decline and Fall of the Roman Empire*, ch. 49.
[10] *The Cambridge Medieval History*, Vol. V (1926), p. 19.

an easy transition to extend this idea to a whole diocese when the larger part, or even the whole, of that diocese lay within the domain of some great feudal prince or earl. From the ancient principle of " no land without a lord " it seemed natural to deduce the conclusion " no church without a lord." We can hardly be surprised, then, that the more important feudatories, who were virtually masters of a tract of country as big as a province, were prone to regard each episcopal see as a mere fief which the lord was free to bestow upon whom he would. No doubt these claims were not allowed to pass unchallenged while the papacy was unfettered and some measure of independence was recognised and sustained by the Carolingian emperors. But intermittently the emperors themselves sought to exercise influence in such matters. So long as they promoted the appointment of good and worthy subjects, no great harm was done ; but as the times grew more corrupt, as authority was weakened and western Europe was broken up into endless discordant factions, the appointment of bishops was regarded more and more as a source of revenue, and flagrant simony became almost universal. If the monarch was irreligious and unprincipled, he either kept the see vacant in order to enjoy the revenues, or else sold the office to the highest bidder. On the other hand the type of bishop who secured the possession of any see by such methods was bound to have the worst influence upon his clergy and upon the Church at large. When the shepherds of the flock were themselves licentious and corrupt, it would have been a moral miracle if the rank and file of the priests and clerics had not degenerated in an equal or greater degree. Upon the bishop depends the admission of candidates to ordination, and he is also ultimately responsible for their education and for the maintenance of ecclesiastical discipline. The climax was reached when, amid the tumults and dissensions which ravaged Italy in the tenth century, the Kings of Germany and the Counts of Tusculum turn by turn set up Popes almost at will. The papacy became for a period a sort of appanage to the ruling house of Theophylact or else was virtually put up for sale. The simple fact that in the space of less than a century and a half (900–1048) the names of 33 Popes, many of whom died violent deaths, figure in our records, is itself a sufficient commentary upon the evils of the time. No greater moral wonder is recorded in history than the preservation of the bark of Peter when overwhelmed by such a tempest. It righted at last, but only as the consequence of the resolute stand taken up by St. Gregory VII and his successors on the question of investitures, as well as in the legislation adopted to repress simony and to enforce the celibacy of the clergy.

Outrageous as are the excesses with which such pontiffs as Sergius III, John XII, and Benedict IX stand charged, the Popes of the tenth century, as Mgr. Mann has remarked, were not so disedifying as those of the Renaissance period. " The temporal position of the former," he says, " was weak, while that of the latter was strong." There can be little palliation for the moral depravity and the shameless nepotism of Rodrigo Borgia, who, in spite of a simoniacal election, ruled the Church for eleven years (1492–1503) as Alexander VI, without any serious opposition being raised against his authority. Attempts have been made—notably of late years by Mgr. Peter de Roo in a work which runs to no less than five volumes[11]—to exculpate the Pontiff from the gross misconduct with which he stands charged. But the whole contention, like that of previous apologists, completely breaks down in the face of documentary evidence leaving no loophole for escape. Burchard's Diary would alone suffice to prove that the dissolute life of Alexander continued after he became Head of the Church, and in the face of the critical edition of the Diary by Celani, it cannot any longer be pretended that the passages reflecting on the Pope's scandalous libertinage are malicious interpolations. Moreover, in the latest edition of von Pastor's *Geschichte der Päpste* fresh evi-

---

[11] *Materials for a History of Pope Alexander VI*, 1924, New York Universal Knowledge Foundation. On this work see *The Month*, April, 1925, pp. 289–303.

dence of irregularities is adduced confirming his previous judgment. The only excuse that can be offered—and it is a poor excuse enough—is that under the neo-paganism of the Renaissance public opinion condoned every kind of moral laxity. Alexander, says Señor Sanchis y Sivera, " lived in a state of society in which illegitimate children were not held in less consideration than legitimate offspring," and he goes on to quote the saying of Æneas Silvius (Pope Pius II), " Italy is governed by people born out of wedlock." It would be easy to multiply testimonies to the same effect from many other sources.

As a ruler Alexander showed himself to be far from contemptible, and there is a good deal of evidence which proves that during his pontificate the administrative functions of the papal office were not neglected. He was in a measure popular, and, in spite of the violence and rapine of his son, Cæsar Borgia, the impression generally formed of Alexander may be gathered from a little summary printed at Venice in 1507, four years after his death.

He was a pontiff whose splendid qualities were matched by equally great vices. There was nothing mean about him. He was intelligent, eloquent, tactful in adapting himself to the character of everyone he met, most energetic in matters of business, and, though he had never given much time to literary pursuits, it was clear that he set no small store upon learning. He was always so punctual in paying his soldiers that, whatever happened, he was able to count upon a willing and most loyal army. All these virtues, nevertheless, were marred by vices which need not be mentioned here and by his overmastering desire to secure a great position for his bastard children.[12]

Alexander VI was not the only Pope of the Renaissance period against whom grave charges were made, but there is hardly any other who, upon reliable evidence, stands convicted of shameless concubinage during his actual tenure of the papacy.

[12] *Chronica delle Vite de Pontefici et Imperatori romani*, by Petrarch and others (Venice, 1507, fol. 88, verso).

Neither is there any occasion in the present connection to review all the accusations which, either maliciously or in good faith, have been levelled by controversial assailants against other pontiffs. It is sufficient to point out that no pretence is made that the papacy from the point of view of the moral conduct of its representatives offers a stainless record. Just as Baronius goes even beyond the demonstrated facts in denouncing the scandals of the tenth century, so his continuators, Raynaldus and Mansi, are unmeasured in their condemnation of the deplorable example set by Alexander. It is noteworthy also that this plain speaking is not limited to works likely to find their way only into the hands of scholars. The " History of the Popes " (*Storia de' sommi Pontefici*), by Giuseppe de Novaes, a work written, as the title-page proclaims, " for the use of studious youth," is in no way more reserved. Though it was dedicated to Pope Pius VII, printed at Rome with the formal licence of ecclesiastical authority, and circulated in several editions, the author does not hesitate to charge Alexander with " unbridled depravity " (*sfrenata dissolutezza*)[13] as well as with such other vices as avarice and cruelty, while his open recognition of his four sons and his daughter, Lucrezia, is stigmatised with equal vigour.

The important point is that in all this matter we must distinguish between the man and his office. Popes are infallible in the exercise of their prerogative as teachers of the Universal Church, but as individuals they are by no means impeccable. Fifteen hundred years ago the great St. Leo wrote : " Even in an unworthy successor the dignity of Peter is not extinguished," and it is certainly deserving of remark that in those few cases— and they are not numerous—in which a notably bad example was given by the moral lapses of the representatives of Christ on earth, no false doctrine has been taught, no principles have been laid down which would lead men to believe that wrong was right and that there was no distinction between good and evil. Our Lord never said to His apostles " he that doth as you

13 Novaes, *Storia*, etc. (3rd Edition, Rome, 1822), Vol. VI, p. 117.

do, doth as I do and pleases Me," but only, " he that heareth you, heareth Me, and he that despiseth you despiseth Me." The historian, von Pastor, while speaking in the severest terms of the evil life of Rodrigo Borgia, calls attention at the same time to the fact that " in matters purely concerning the Church, Alexander never did anything which justly deserves blame ; even his bitterest enemies are unable to formulate any accusation against him in this respect."[14] Similarly Mgr. Mann, in reference to the scandals of those earlier centuries of which we have spoken, remarks very truly :

> Fortunately, among the troubles of this weary period heresy was not one. Neither heresy nor schism added to the difficulties of the Roman pontiffs. They were not called upon to give any important guidance to the Church in what it had to believe or practise. No doubt the spiritual influence of the Papacy decreased during the century and a half of which we are speaking, but its spiritual prerogatives, unlike its temporal, did not fail ; and at the close of this disastrous period it was to give abundant evidence of its undying life by suddenly manifesting the most astounding vigour in both the spiritual and the temporal spheres.[15]

Certainly, then, there have been " bad Popes," for the Popes are human, and human nature is both weak and inconstant. We all know from daily experience how even good men and strong characters will at times grow weary of the effort to live up to a higher standard than that observed by the world around them. We, most of us, require to be protected against our own infirmity of purpose, and when the tone of public opinion sees no harm in immorality and is ready to condone all lapses, the power of temptation is multiplied a hundredfold. It was only amid the anarchy of the tenth century and the neo-paganism of the fifteenth that grave papal scandals occurred which are strictly susceptible of proof. Moreover, at both

---

[14] Pastor, *History of the Popes*, (English trans.), Vol. VI, p. 140.
[15] Mann, *The Lives of the Popes in the Early Middle Ages*, Vol. IV, pp. 37-38.

periods there were not a few notably good Pontiffs who led worthy lives and upon whom no suspicion rested. For the rest, we have little better than legend, idle gossip and calumny, the worthlessness and the prevalence of which it will be the object of the chapters which follow to demonstrate.

CHAPTER II

THE CAMPAIGN AGAINST PIUS IX

To illustrate the nature of the prejudice against which the Holy See at almost all periods of history has had to contend, we cannot perhaps do better than take in the first place a particularly flagrant example from recent times. There are many people yet living who remember the pontificate of Pius IX and the almost universal tribute of respect evoked by his death in 1878. In the notice devoted to him by Father C. Kempf when writing on *The Holiness of the Church in the Nineteenth Century*, it is stated that his successor next but one (Pius X) ordered a preliminary enquiry to be set on foot with a view to his canonisation. This does not, of course, amount to a formal *introductio causæ*, and apparently the matter has not advanced further, but there can be no question that the pontiff who convened the Vatican Council, and who afterwards showed so much fortitude in the face of adversity, was considered by his Catholic contemporaries to be a man of great personal holiness.

When Pius IX died on February 17th, 1878 [writes Father Kempf] even his bitterest enemies bestowed unreserved praise upon his private life. No one dared to call in doubt the spotless integrity of his conduct or the sincerity of his piety. Others who are great as scholars, poets, politicians, military leaders and the like are often miserably small if we measure their lives by the standard of Christian morality. The only thing they found to blame in Pius IX was that he was "too Catholic." Those who knew him more intimately considered him a saint.[1]

---

[1] *The Holiness of the Church in the Nineteenth Century;* I quote from the English translation published by Benziger at New York in 1916; pp. 33-34.

No reason exists for supposing that this estimate is in any way exaggerated, but it can hardly be maintained that the Pope's detractors were so few as Father Kempf would here seem to suggest.

Undoubtedly Pius from early youth was extremely devout, of irreproachable conduct and much venerated by all who came in contact with him. At the same time a very little inquiry shows that neither during his long pontificate nor after his death was his private life free from the attacks of a rabble of vile calumniators, who figured among the honoured associates of such revolutionaries as Garibaldi and Mazzini, men whom it is now the fashion to acclaim as heroes. Few who have not themselves investigated the matter have any idea of the lengths to which the assailants referred to were capable of going. The intensity of hatred displayed in the case of so blameless and kindly a pontiff is highly significant, and conveys a useful lesson, to which we must return later on. Meanwhile this may serve as an excuse for reviving the memory of abominable slanders which now for many years past have happily fallen into oblivion.

So far as printed testimony is concerned, I have not been able to trace any of the scandalous stories which were eventually circulated concerning Giovanni Mastai's early life further back than 1859, when he had already been thirteen years Pope. Of course it is likely enough that in revolutionary circles and among the swarm of political refugees who congregated in such centres as Paris, Geneva, Brussels and London, all kinds of vile anecdotes were current long before this. No sensible man who knows the tone of—say—Gavazzi's lectures can doubt that any imputation of immorality against an ecclesiastic, were he priest, friar or pope, would have been received with acclamation by fanatics of this stamp. It may also be that these evil stories were published by the more disreputable newspapers of liberal and anarchist tendencies before they found their way into books which had some little pretension to be treated as serious literature. But the fact remains that the earliest procurable work which plainly charges Pius IX with having led a life of debauchery as a young man is that entitled *La Rome des Papes*, printed in three volumes in 1859.[2] The book appeared anonymously, but no secret was afterwards made of the fact that the author was a certain Luigi Pianciani, who was then a political refugee. After the occupation of Rome by Victor Emmanuel he returned to Italy and there he was more than once elected Syndic of the City, a dignity roughly equivalent to that of Lord Mayor. The Preface of the *Rome des Papes* lets us know plainly enough what we are to expect. " We shall specially devote ourselves," the author tells us, " to the task of making the life of Pius IX thoroughly known so that the reader coming to understand this may be able to form an appreciation of the Papacy in general."[3] " We shall narrate the story of his childhood," he says again, " we shall expose the excesses and the passions of his youth, we shall strip him of the prestige that envelops him, in order to show him as he really is." And once more, a little later, the writer pretends to repudiate indignantly the idea that he ought to be deterred from these promised revelations by the thought of the scandal they may cause. " What ! " he cries. " Is a pope to be guilty of imposture . . . . is a cardinal to yield to every human frailty, is a bishop to become a common swindler, is a prelate to make a shameless living by procuration and adultery, and will you venture to tell me that these things are merely the secrets of private life ? "[4]

The *Athenaeum*, then and for many years later the leading English weekly devoted exclusively to literary criticism, was not a journal swayed by any undue sympathy for the papal system, but in noticing very briefly the first volume of this precious compilation it gave its impressions frankly enough.

---

[2] The title page runs *La Rome des Papes, son origine, ses phases successives, ses mœurs intimes, son gouvernement, son système administratif.* Par un ancien membre de la Constituante romaine. Traduction de l'ouvrage italien inédit. Bâle, Librairie Schweighauser ; London, John Chapman, 8, King William Street, Strand, 1859.

[3] Op. cit. Preface, p. xv.   [4] Ibid., Preface xviii.

The anonymous writer of this volume [says the reviewer] is at war with the Popedom and eats the bread of exile. But his bias might have been forgiven, had he confined himself to stating what he knows from personal observation or through the medium of history concerning the system he so fiercely and laboriously condemns. Instead of this he retails a monstrous variety of scandalous anecdotes, numbers of which may be authentic, but which nevertheless could not be established by evidence, and, therefore, may on the other hand be impeached as wholly false.[5]

Now, as anyone will discern who takes the trouble to make minute comparisons, this book *La Rome des Papes* has been for a number of later calumniators of the papacy a sort of mine from which they have quarried their materials. They have added to them and embellished them with still more realistic details. They have put into grosser words things which Pianciani has sometimes only insinuated. But the legend of Pius IX's dissolute youth has been drawn mainly from the writings of this violent revolutionary, a man whose extravagant fanaticism betrays itself in every page of the volume. It is difficult to believe that these stories can have been told in good faith, and yet such is the blind and unreasoning passion conspicuous in Pianciani and some other writers of the same party, that we hesitate to assume that he was consciously lying. There are always scoundrels in every group of resentful and proscribed men who find their interest in playing upon the furious hatreds which the situation evokes. The fungus grows with incredible rapidity in such surroundings. The tiniest grain of fact, a mere name, a single chance encounter, is sufficient nucleus to build up a whole mountain of scandal, and that which a man has heard half a dozen of his intimates repeat, he soon declares to be an unalterable conviction and a matter of common knowledge among all the thinking men of his country. How utterly wild and unverified was Pianciani's information regarding the domestic life of the Mastais of

5 *The Athenaeum*, 11 February, 1860, p. 204.

Sinigaglia may be judged from one slight but not unimportant detail. In *La Rome des Papes* (II, 358) he states categorically that Giovanni Mastai (Pius IX) had four sisters, Theresa, Delia, Virginia and Thecla, with three brothers, Joseph, Gaetano and Gabriel. But when the Léo Taxil case[6] came on before the French courts in the suit brought against Taxil by the Pope's nephew, Maître Delattre, Taxil's counsel, stated that the father of Pius IX had six children—Gabriel, Giuseppe, Gaetano, Ercole, Thérèse-Isabelle and Gian-Maria (Pius IX),[7] i.e. one girl and five boys, instead of four girls and four boys. Seeing that Maître Delattre constantly quoted from Pianciani in the course of his address, it is plain that this rectification was made advisedly and with the knowledge that in such a matter as the number and names of his own uncles and aunts the Pope's nephew could not be bluffed. Whether Pianciani had invented these names just for the sake of seeming well-informed or whether he copied them from some unreliable authority no one can tell ; in any case his data must surely be wrong.

To pain the reader with the details of the half a score of amours which Pianciani lays to the charge of Pius IX, beginning with hateful insinuations made against the Pope's home life is surely unnecessary. Let it be sufficient to say that every kind of criminal indulgence is laid to his charge. The young Mastai is represented as being consumed by a hopeless passion for the Princess Helen Albani, but Pianciani tells his readers that when she rejected his addresses the disappointed suitor " turned from the Princess to the lowest classes of society . . . love was succeeded by debauchery." But licentious conduct is not the only fault of which he stands accused. In the same pages he is represented as utterly heartless (p. 358), as making an uncertain income by cheating at cards (ibid. and p. 369), as committing simony in order to secure for himself one of the canonries of St. Peter's (p. 373), as detested for his arrogance and cruelty at the hospital of San Michele (p. 385), as a monster of treachery to those who trusted to his

[6] For this see further in ch. III.   [7] Plaidoyer de Mre. Delattre, p. 27.

honour (p. 390), as incurring universal odium when Archbishop of Spoleto (p. 394), as secretly devouring the romances of Sue, Dumas, and Georges Sand when Bishop of Imola (p. 396), etc., etc. We say nothing here of the incredible barbarities, the acts of oppression, the blunders, the follies, the hypocrisies, the contemptible meannesses laid to his charge in his capacity of Sovereign of the States of the Church. That many of these accusations are utterly in conflict with notorious facts a very little reading soon discovers. For example a monograph was printed in 1877 regarding the five years spent by Mastai as Archbishop of Spoleto (1827–1832). However one-sided may be the documents contained in this, they at least show that the Archbishop was not universally unpopular, for the Gonfaloniere and Anziani of Spoleto memorialised the Pope as soon as they heard the rumour of his translation, begging that their beloved Archbishop might not be taken from them.[8] But it would be absurd to attempt to deal seriously with these wild outbursts of political hatred by any refutation in form.

Let us turn to the two other calumnious biographies of Pius IX which contributed most to blacken the good name of the Pontiff in the eyes of those who were eager to believe ill of him. The first of these in order of time was the libellous work of Pierre Vésinier which was printed in French at Berlin in 1861 and translated into German the same year. Anyone who will take the trouble to look up the account given of Vésinier in such impartial sources as Larousse[9] or the *Grande Encyclopédie*, will easily learn what kind of man he was. Throughout his life he was identified with revolutionary principles. After the Coup d'État of 1851 he hastily quitted France and took refuge first in Belgium and then in Switzerland, where he met Eugène Sue and became his literary assistant. Expelled

8 *Memoire storiche della Vita episcopale in Spoleto del Santo Padre Pio IX*, Rome, 1877. See especially pp. 80–86, where the official documents are given *in extenso*.

9 I call Larousse impartial in these matters because, as every one knows who has consulted it, the first edition has a marked anti-clerical bias.

from Switzerland, he returned to Belgium. There in 1860 he was charged before the Cour d'Assises of Brabant with the publication of " two obscene pamphlets," *Le mariage d'une Espagnole* and *La femme de César*, and was sentenced to eighteen months' imprisonment and 2,000 francs fine. Shortly afterwards he was expelled from Belgium and came to England. After the Franco-German war he became one of the leaders of the Commune. He edited the *Journal Officiel* during the period that the Commune was in the ascendant at Paris, and on May 24th he signed the decree which ordered portions of the city to be set on fire in order to prolong the resistance. After the suppression of the Commune he returned to England and founded in London a Journal, *La Fédération*, to propagate Communist principles. It is plain from his published writings that Vésinier's mind was deeply embittered against all representatives of authority and religion,[10] while the taint of indecency is never far removed and constantly comes to the surface when opportunity offers.[11] What sort of biography of Pius IX such a writer would be likely to produce can easily be imagined. With *La Rome des Papes* before him, Vésinier simply recounts in greater detail the scandalous stories of the Pontiff's early life in which that work abounds, but he not infrequently embellishes them, and the tone which he contrives to impart to the whole is peculiarly revolting. For example, speaking in general terms of the supposed love adventures of Mastai's youth, he remarks :

If he had yielded to the promptings of his heart and allowed himself to be carried away by the seductions of an ardent passion, we should be the last to dream of blaming him. On the contrary, we should have congratulated him and we should have said with Christ that many things would be forgiven him because he had loved much. But of

[10] Even with his fellow revolutionaries he seems to have been constantly at loggerheads, Larousse says : " Ce fut vers 1869 que Henri Rochefort, faisant allusion à l'extrême difformité physique de Vésinier, malingre, laid et bossu, lui donna le surnom de *racine de buis*, qui lui est resté."

[11] The *Grande Encyclopédie* says of Vésinier : " Romancier lui même, mais fort peu lu, il écrivit des pamphlets, plus obscènes que politiques, contre Napoléon, contre l'Impératrice Eugénie et contre le Pape."

generous self-abandonment there was unfortunately not a trace in his composition. Cold egotism and boundless vanity formed the key-note of his character. In unguarded moments he frequently confessed, to quote his very words, as repeated by one of his friends : " I have no sort of fondness for anyone. I could see father, mother, brothers and sisters perish without a tear. Why then should I allow my peace of mind to be disturbed ? "

This last utterance is taken textually from *La Rome des Papes*, but Vésinier italicises it and adds a footnote to say that all the passages so printed by him are indisputably authentic and that in fact his whole account of the youthful excesses of Pius IX is of the most scrupulous exactitude,[12] being derived from the testimony of eye witnesses or that of the Pope's intimate friends. After wearing himself out by a dissolute life, Mastai, according to the same authority, was reduced to despair by the recurrence of the epileptic seizures which blocked every avenue to advancement. He accordingly turned pious and " invented a new dogma," that of the Immaculate Conception, which he afterward defined as Pope. But even after his conversion Vésinier does not allow him the credit of sincerity. This unscrupulous slanderer represents Mastai as a fashionable young Abbé, using his popularity for the most vile purposes.

> Prédicateur aimé, confesseur adoré, amant fortuné, toutes les joies lui furent prodiguées par ses jolies pénitentes.[13]

The third biographer of Pius IX who claims some special notice is M. Petruccelli della Gattina. He also was a revolutionary who had come to Paris in 1848 as a political refugee from Naples, where he had been elected deputy and had fiercely attacked the Ministry. In July 1871 Petruccelli della Gattina

---

[12] Vésinier's words are " Tout ce qui concerne la jeunesse de J. B. Mastai est de la plus scrupuleuse exactitude. C'est un de ses anciens camarades d'enfance, qui a été témoin de tous les faits que nous racontons ou confident des détails que nous citons, qui nous les a fournis " (p. 5). Yet anyone who compares the two books will find that the passages which Vésinier so distinguishes are taken bodily from *La Rome des Papes* of Pianciani.

[13] Ibid., p. 12. All these things are repeated and further developed in some of Vésinier's later works of fiction, e.g. *Mœurs Impériales*.

was expelled from France upon the restoration of orderly government after the war and the Commune. Since his expulsion, observes Larousse, writing in 1874, he has shown himself " the deadly foe of our country " (l'adversaire acharné de notre pays). In some respects the biography written by Petruccelli della Gattina, entitled *Pie IX, Sa Vie, Son Règne, l'Homme, le Prince, le Pape*[14] is the vilest of all. Not only is the legend of the Pope's dissolute youth repeated and extended, but the writer in the plainest language declares that these irregularities continued after he had become Head of the Church. Mastai is represented as so utterly devoid of all moral sense as to believe that he was making a great reformation in his life when upon his ordination " he gave up all his old acquaintances in the world of fashion and devoted himself to a little Jewess of the shop-keeping class stowed away somewhere in the quarter of the Ghetto." As Pope he carried on intrigues, so Petruccelli della Gattina assures us, with three ladies whom he names. One of them was the Abbess of Fognano, another the Countess Spaur, widow of the English antiquarian Dodwell, and the third was an old friend of Mastai's, Donna Chiara Colonna, the object of the most violent passion of his life. " All Rome," says this veracious biographer, " still talks of the follies he committed for this charming personage." When Pius IX fled from Rome to Gaeta in 1849, the real reason why he quitted the city, so we are told, was because the Countess Spaur, who happened then to be in the ascendant, was afraid to remain there any longer, and the Pope, on the other hand, could not endure to be separated from her for even a few days.

Probably many readers will be disposed to consider that calumny so gross and so obviously malicious should only be treated with contempt. But the unfortunate part of it is that people do not distinguish between these cases of political and religious hatred and those that occur in ordinary life. In ordinary life it is a fairly trustworthy principle that " where there is smoke there is fire." If there is much talk about the

[14] Published at Brussels 1866.

loose morals of a private citizen there is likely to be some
foundation in fact. Stories may be enormously exaggerated,
quite harmless acts may be most cruelly misinterpreted, but
one is pretty safe in drawing the conclusion that even an
unprincipled calumniator will select a point for attack which he
knows to be a weak one. He does not want his lie to be discredited by its being in conflict with facts notorious to all. But
in the case of religious and political animosities, feeling is often
so deeply roused that men will believe any and every kind of
evil of their opponents. The unscrupulous calumniator passes
undetected. His story is swallowed so greedily that crowds
at once make it their own in a sort of good faith and they are
even up in arms at any rectification as if it were a personal
affront. Thus a tradition is rapidly formed, to doubt which
in their eyes would be impious.

These are the circumstances in which that other most vener-
able adage, " Only throw enough mud and some of it is sure
to stick," unfortunately comes into play. For Catholics, no
doubt, and for a fair proportion of reflecting and unprejudiced
Protestants, the matter is plain enough. Pius IX in this relation
was simply the victim of unscrupulous calumny. Not one
shred of evidence worthy of the name has ever been adduced
which would cast a doubt upon the probity and integrity of his
private life at any stage of his career. But for the careless
tourist who spent a few weeks or months in Italy, or for the
journalist or the purveyor of popular literature whose only
thought was to amuse his public, the simplest course was to
assume that Pius IX was like other men in his youth, neither
a paragon of virtue nor a monster of vice. His friends said
that his morals were snow-white, his enemies declared that
they were sooty-black ; it would save a good deal of trouble to
take it for granted that they were neither one nor the other,
but simply grey. There would be no difficulty in quoting
endless examples of this attitude of mind. I hope I may be
pardoned for calling attention to one or two that are especially
characteristic. One of the earliest of these is the book of a

tourist, a Mr. C. R. Weld, published in 1865 and entitled *Last Winter in Rome*. It is a gossipy volume of considerable bulk and generally inoffensive in tone. At that period, of course, Pius IX was still ruler of the papal states, and very naturally Mr. Weld contributes a short sketch of the life and character of the actual sovereign of Rome. His account, though decorously toned down, is plainly derived from the same sources as Pianciani and the rest, possibly from the pages of one or the other of them. We are told " that in youth Pius was noted for his dandy dress, appearing always in a semi-military uniform,[15] wearing boots and spurs, and seldom seen without a cigar in his mouth."[16] This, no doubt, even if it were true, would be innocent enough, but combined as it is with the suggestion of entanglements that were not so innocent, it serves only to give them a verisimilitude which they would otherwise lack. Weld goes on to say that when disappointed in love Mastai " plunged into dissipation, drank deeply and gambled largely " and he insinuates that as bishop and cardinal he was so under the influence of women, notably the Abbess of Fognano and Countess Spaur, that his minister, Cardinal Antonelli, found it necessary to banish the latter lady from Rome.[17]

Not less remarkable is the treatment of the Pope's early history in the two volumes of Mr. Legge, *Pius IX, the Story of his Life*, published in London in 1875,[18] that is to say when Pius was already an old man of 83. The biographer has clearly laid the books referred to above under contribution, but he suppresses the more unsavoury details and tells his story as if he had made personal inquiry into local traditions.

There are yet living in Rome a few who, in their youth, were familiar with the handsome and much-admired dandy,

[15] Pius IX himself denied in the most positive terms that he had ever had any connection with military life or had had any thought of entering the papal Noble Guard.

[16] C. R. Weld, *Last Winter in Rome*, p. 70.

[17] Weld, *Last Winter in Rome*, pp. 75-76.

[18] See especially I, pp. 21–33 ; Mr. Legge seems to have made much use of a venomous *Vita di Pio IX* by " Italo Fiorentino," Milan, 1874.

John Mastai-Ferretti, who by successful gambling was
enabled, in spite of the miserable pittance of three pounds
a month . . . to maintain a fashionable appearance,
always wearing a semi-military uniform, boots and spurs,
and seldom seen without a cigar in his mouth.

Mr. Legge further states that the young man fell desperately
in love with a daughter of the Prince Albani. She rejected
him for a more wealthy suitor, whereupon we are told that :

Mastai, whose devotion had been extreme, was now mad
with jealousy and rage, and sought to alleviate his misery
in a life of dissipation. He gambled heavily ; and his
noble birth, fascinating manners and handsome person
secured him hosts of admirers.

Even T. Augustus Trollope in his widely-read *Life of Pius
IX* (London, 1877, 2 vols.), though he refers to Petruccelli by
name and explicitly condemns his scandalous stories of Mastai's
youth, nevertheless accepts the description of the future pope's
costume, " half civil, half military, with a touch of the barber's-
apprentice in it " as probable enough. " The young provincial
dandy," he declares, " was very far at that time from dreaming
of the Church as a profession ; and it is certain that he was
looking forward to a military career." Further he states that
he fell in love with his foster sister, one Signorina Morandi,
who married another man, and who later as the poor widow
Ambrogi, appealed to the Pope for help ; but Pius would do
nothing for her.[19]

Although English Protestants have thus compromised for a
milder form of scandal, still among Continental Freemasons
these charges in their most abominable form have continually
been repeated. One would have thought that even vindictive
hatred would hesitate to pursue the kindly old man beyond the
grave, the more so that for seven years he had been stripped
of the temporal power and was virtually a prisoner in the
Vatican. The fact is, however, that the very year of Pio
Nono's death produced a flood of such literature, meant no

[19] Trollope, I, pp. 11–14.

doubt as a counterblast to the veneration displayed for his memory by many who were by no means clerical or even Catholics. It would be useless to give a catalogue, but I may mention as particularly infamous the work, *Vita intima e publica di Pio IX Papa* (Milan, 1878), of a well-known literary hack, Oscar Pio. This writer reproduces all the vile slanders of Petruccelli, while with extraordinary effrontery he dedicates the compilation to his own mother. At any rate a fly-leaf at the beginning of the volume bears the formal inscription : " To my Mother, Clato Fattiboni Pio, who by her example first inspired me with the love of study and labour." One can only hope that Oscar Pio's lack of any sense of the value of historical truth was not derived from the same source.[20]

While fully recognising the contemptible character of the slanders of a man like Taxil, of whom we shall have to speak further, it must not be forgotten that Pio Nono's other accusers had a certain standing in the eyes of quite a considerable section of their countrymen. They were, as already said, the friends of Garibaldi and Mazzini, and they had the support of even such a literary genius as Victor Hugo. Count Luigi Pianciani, as he was styled later in life, was not only twice over Syndic of Rome, but he was also at one period Vice-President of the Italian Chamber. The literary abilities of Petruccelli della Gattina, even as a writer of French, which was not his own language, were generally recognised. He was the collaborator of Jules Claretie in a play which was printed under their joint names.[21] Further, Petruccelli's *Histoire des Conclaves*, a bulky work in four volumes, will be found constantly cited in bibliographies

[20] Another specimen of the same type of literature is a brochure entitled *Giovanni Maria Mastai, Papa Pio IX*, by F. D. (Milan, 1878). It is embellished with a number of wretched woodcuts illustrating among other things the Pope's love adventures as a young man. Another similar pamphlet, attributed to one Don Luigi de Potosi, professes to cite a document in the archives of the papal police describing the arrest of Mastai with some women of bad character in a drunken brawl. But there are many similar brochures, both of this and of earlier date.

[21] This was the *Famille des Gueux*, first represented and published in 1869, that is to say three years after the appearance of Petruccelli's infamous *Vie de Pie IX*.

as if it were a serious contribution to papal history. But even more noteworthy was the influence which the calumnies of Pianciani and Petruccelli exercised upon such writers as Weld, Legge and Adolphus Trollope—the last-named a brother of the famous novelist Anthony Trollope. These were normal English tourists, with no special antipathy to popery, but nevertheless, as stated above, it is quite clear that their judgment had been more or less warped by the vile aspersions which the anti-clerical faction had scattered broadcast. Even in responsible works of reference the influence of this campaign of calumny can be traced. Thus in McClintock and Strong, *Cyclopaedia of Biblical and Ecclesiastical Literature*, New York, 1879, Vol. VIII, p. 249, the authors tell us, when speaking of the alleged miraculous cure of Pius IX's epileptic attacks : " Secular writers less anxious to paint the miraculous manifestations in Pio's youthful days declare that he was a libertine and that stretched upon a bed of sickness he repented of his sins and by a life of abstinence and purity gradually recovered." They also state positively, upon the authority of T. A. Trollope, that before becoming a priest, the Pope had been a member of a lodge of Carbonari, and mention without disapproval the report that " he even visited a body of Freemasons in Philadelphia," regardless of the fact that Pius never in his life set foot in the United States.

Although every Catholic writer without exception speaks of the early life of Pius IX as absolutely free from reproach, still such slanders as those referred to are apt to leave an uncomfortable feeling behind them that there may be some skeleton in the cupboard, some dark page which the partiality of ardent eulogists has pasted down and studiously refrained from investigating. So abundant were the tributes paid to the high character of Pius IX in his later years even by those who were not Catholics[22] that any discussion of the evidence seems almost superfluous, but by a piece of good fortune we possess, regarding

[22] As a single illustration one may mention F. Hitchman's *Pius IX, a Biography*, London, 1878. The book is dedicated to Mr. Alfred Austin, who later became Poet Laureate.

that same period of his career which has been most foully calumniated, the testimony of a hostile witness whose opportunities of obtaining accurate information were exceptionally great. John Baptist Nicolini, who describes himself as " Deputy to the Tuscan Constituent Assembly and Officer of the General Staff of the Roman Army," was a revolutionary of the most extreme type. He was the friend of such men as Mazzini, Saffi, Garibaldi and Father Gavazzi. Like them, he was a political refugee both before and after the Roman Revolution of 1849. On both occasions he sought refuge in the British Isles and there he produced in English two or three books, notably a *History of the Jesuits*, which to this day remains one of the most venomous attacks upon the Order ever written. But what especially concerns us here is a life of Pius IX which Nicolini published in Edinburgh in 1851. As we shall see, the author informs us that he was himself brought up in Sinigaglia and was intimately acquainted with all the family of the Mastai, more especially with Count Joseph, the Pope's brother.[23] The importance of this becomes manifest when the fact is recalled that eight or ten years later the calumnious pens of Pianciani, Vésinier and others were proclaiming to the world that Sinigaglia had rung with the excesses and debauchery of Pius IX (Giovanni Mastai) in his youth. At the risk of a long quotation it will be best to leave Nicolini, writing, be it remembered, in the year 1850 or 1851, to speak for himself. What follows is taken from the first chapter of his short biography of Pius IX.

The life of a man who, within the brief compass of a few months, has been adored almost as a god and execrated as the worst of tyrants, cannot fail to excite the deepest interest. By the people of England, more especially, must this interest be strongly felt since it is this same man whose wanton imprudence has but lately disturbed their

---

[23] This assertion is confirmed by other statements made by Nicolini in his *Life of Father Gavazzi*. In this latter work (p. 5), speaking of the year 1846, he says, " After having been 18 years in exile, I returned before the middle of Nov. to Sinigaglia, where my family resided." And then he goes on to speak of his talks with Count Joseph Mastai.

tranquillity,[24] and who even now tries to raise rebellion and civil war in Ireland.

Brought up in the Pope's native town, intimately acquainted with all his family, personally connected with many of the principal events of his pontificate, I have thought myself qualified to relate his history, if not as an accomplished writer, at least as a well-informed biographer.

In narrating the history of Pius IX, it shall be my endeavour to forget nothing, to omit nothing, however good or bad it may be. He shall be praised and blamed, whenever in my humble opinion he deserves it. Although in these times of excitement impartiality may be but a poor recommendation, yet I intend not to libel the man but to write his history. . . .

I shall confine to a page or two the early life of Giovanni Mastai. He was born at Sinigaglia on the 13th June, 1792. He was the seventh child of Count Mastai, one of those of our noblemen, who possess a splendid palace, an ancient name, a magnificent genealogical tree, and a revenue of from two to four hundred pounds. Giovanni, the youngest of the family, perceiving that, like all others similarly situated, he must either maintain himself or be contented with a scanty pittance at the board of his eldest brother, determined to become either a soldier or a priest. After some hesitation he betook himself to the trade of the latter, as the less dangerous and more lucrative. He became, then, a priest, and, setting aside his superstitious strictness in the observance of the external forms of religion, *a very exemplary one*. Being a patrician and a bigot, he quickly advanced in the career of honour and dignity. He became a Prelate, a Bishop, and, at the death of Gregory XVI, he was Cardinal Archbishop of Imola. In each of these capacities few would have acted more praiseworthily than did Mastai. A stranger to political intrigue—assiduous in

24 The reference of course is to the so-called " Papal Aggression " of 1850, when Pius IX restored the hierarchy in England.

performing his pastoral duties—charitable to the poor—
the friend and consoler of the afflicted—strictly moral in
his private life—he was most dearly beloved by his flock.
The meekness of his character—his perfect freedom from
political bias—the hope entertained by all the other cardinals of domineering over a Pope entirely uninterested in
temporal affairs—all contributed to his being elevated to
the Chair of St. Peter. After only two days' conclave, on
the 16th June, 1846, he was elected Pope and assumed
the name of Pius IX.[25]

A little further on Nicolini continues thus :

When the new Pope was elected, the Romans, who were
ready to revolt, determined to try their last experiment.
If a man like Giovanni Mastai, whose pure and uncontamin-
ated life—whose piety, meekness and charity everyone ad-
mired–should prove no better than the former Popes–then all
was over and Popery would have ceased to reign over Italy.

All minds were in great suspense and anxiety, but Pius IX
soon relieved them. Urged by his friends, who were
liberals, and prompted also by his own compassionate
heart, on July 16th, a month after his accession to the papal
throne, he proclaimed a large and generous amnesty. . . .
The Roman States never witnessed such exultation. . . .
On my return from exile, I was told by my parents, and by
the Pope's own brothers, that many of the unfortunate
inhabitants of the Romagna, whose chains Pius had broken,
came to his palace at Sinigaglia and after having exhausted
all other expressions of gratitude, contrived to detach from
the walls of the house a portion of the cement, which they
carried home to their families as a sacred relic.[26]

Nicolini goes on to urge that the flattery turned the Pope's
head, and also that he was weak and easily wrought upon by
the advocates of a repressive policy. But he never disputes

[25] *The History of the Pontificate of Pius the Ninth*, by G. B. Nicolini of Rome,
Deputy to the Tuscan Constituent Assembly and Officer of the General
Staff of the Roman Army. Edinburgh, 1851, pp. 2–3.
[26] Nicolini, p. 8.

his integrity of life. For example, he says : " Assuredly the
renown of the Pope's virtues has brought many Protestants to
the Romish Church."[27]   " The conduct of the Pope was irreproachable,"[28] but he adds that " Count Joseph, the Pope's own
brother who had been an exile and was a patriot, conversing
upon our hopes and fears with the author of this work, said
' I am afraid that they will work upon his feeble and timorous
conscience. If they persuade him that it is a sin to concede
any reform we are lost.' He was right."[29]

When Nicolini used this language he was writing of what he
had learnt at first hand. His own frequent references to this
or the other member of the Mastai family,[30] show that, as
he declares, he was intimately acquainted with them all. He
had been brought up in the same spot and they were the principal people of the district. Neither could he have any possible
motive for bearing witness to Mastai's innocent youth. As a
rule he depicts the priests to whom he refers as steeped in
debauchery. He carries his anti-clerical fanaticism so far as
to declare that a vast correspondence found upon the premises
of the Dominicans in Rome proved that " in almost every one
of these letters the writer had VIOLATED THE SECRETS OF THE
CONFESSIONAL "—the small capitals are Nicolini's own. Again
he paints a quite atrocious picture of the immorality of Pope
Gregory XVI[31] and of Cardinal Antonelli—though, be it
noticed, he pretends here to no personal knowledge. He is
clearly only echoing the vile gossip of the revolutionaries
among whom he lived. Of his readiness to speak in the most
denunciatory terms, even of Pius IX himself, after the liberal
policy of the first years of his pontificate had been reversed,
it is hardly necessary to multiply proofs. On page 26 he tells
us that " after the bombardment of Rome Pius was execrated
by every honest Italian heart " ; on page 30 he speaks of " his
deceitful and hypocritical policy " ; on page 40 he calls him
" the heartless and hypocritical Pius," on page 41 he apostro-

[27] p. 10.
[28] p. 11.
[29] Nicolini, ibid., p. 11.

[30] See, e.g., p. 60 n. and p. 63.
[31] Of this something will be said in
      the next chapter.

phises the Pope thus : " O worthy friend of Ferdinand of
Naples ! profane no longer the name of the Almighty, cease to
call thyself His representative ! but take at once the only name
that posterity will accord thee, that of TYRANT," and this
tone is maintained throughout the rest of the book. For
example, p. 56 : " The conduct of the Pope henceforth became
nothing but a series of schemes to deceive his subjects. His
position was critical, but he trusted in the Jesuitical art and the
notoriously barefaced impudence of Priestcraft to bring him
safely out of it." On page 87 he says : " It was Mastai, who
once a mild charitable man, had become a cruel and vindictive
despot." Further, we have to remember that at the time this
volume was penned Nicolini was in perfect safety, living under
the British flag and writing in English for a public who just
after the famous " papal aggression " of 1850 would have been
ready enough to receive any highly-coloured narrative of the
scandalous excesses of Mastai's youth.[32] None the less in the
Preface of the volume, written, as the contents show, after
the little work was completed, he again refers to the subject in
the same self-laudatory tone !

> I have rendered to all [he says], including the greatest
> enemies of my own party, that justice which is their due.
> I have respected every conviction and opinion which,
> although contrary to my own, I have believed to be con-
> scientiously held and to spring from pure sources. I rejoiced
> to relate the noble qualities and the kind disposition of
> Giovanni Mastai, and I would have been glad to have
> shown, through every page of my book, my gratitude to
> the giver of the amnesty. But the truth must be told.
> The wrongs inflicted upon an entire nation cannot pass
> unavenged ; and if adverse circumstances prevent us from
> effectually subduing the cruel oppressor, we must at least
> consign his name to the maledictions of posterity.[33]

[32] The lectures of Gavazzi and Achilli were the sensations of the hour.

[33] Preface, pp. xiii-xiv. Nicolini seems never to have receded from this
presentment of the early life of Pius IX. In his *History of the Jesuits*, the

Nicolini's volume, insignificant in size and appearance—it
ran to no more than about 150 pages—seems to have attracted
little attention. I cannot find that a second edition was ever
published or that it was translated into any foreign language.
It was not of course a book that would have been read by
Catholics, while for Protestants of the extreme No-Popery type—
the only people of English speech who were particularly interested
in the Vatican—such tributes as those we have just quoted,
vouching as they do for the personal integrity of Mastai, would
have rendered the history very tame reading indeed.

It is to a large extent characteristic of the vile stories which
this testimony of Nicolini so conclusively contradicts that they
are protected from discussion, and consequently from refutation, by their very nastiness. Even if the law of libel in any
particular country[34] had permitted an appeal to the courts of
justice, the question would always arise whether the advantages
of a favourable verdict would outweigh the risks and drawbacks
inevitably entailed by a prosecution. Not least among them
must be reckoned—first, the increased publicity given to the
charge by legal proceedings ; secondly, the expense necessarily
incurred ; thirdly, the loss of dignity involved in the appeal to
an outside tribunal—an appeal which might seem to imply that
the appellant could not afford to treat such aspersions with
silent contempt—and lastly the danger that failure upon some
technical point of law might be interpreted as failure to prove
the baselessness of the accusation itself. On the other hand,
the charges were in their own nature such that the only

---

preface to which is dated 1859, he still speaks of " the meekness of his character
and the purity of his life," pp. 470–471 (Edn. 1893). Gavazzi also has nothing
evil to say of the early years of Pius IX. See his *Lectures in New York* (1853),
p. 229.

34 Nothing could be more significant than the fact that the libels published
against Pius IX during his lifetime were issued under circumstances which
would have made any legal remedy practically impossible. *La Rome des Papes*
of Pianciani appeared without the author's name and was printed in Switzerland in 1859–1861. Vésinier's *Life of Pius IX* both in the French and the
German edition was produced in Berlin in 1862. Petruccelli della Gattina's
book saw the light in Brussels in 1866. Vésinier's scandalous novel *Mœurs
Impériales*, 1868, was brought out in London.

adequate disproof lay in the accuser's inability to substantiate them by evidence when challenged to do so. Need it be said that to force a refugee living in a foreign country either to produce such evidence or to admit that he was lying would be an almost hopeless undertaking whatever the means employed ?

With such an example before our eyes as the calumnies directed against Pius IX, it is not difficult to realise how slow we should be to credit either in whole or in part the equally vile accusations with which the Pontiffs of the Middle Ages were assailed by their detractors.   Men were not less malicious in those days, and their malice was not restrained by the checks which publicity through the press and rapid communications . now offer to the circulation of unfounded slanders. Neither can it be said that the world was then less credulous, or that political passions did not run so high.   Anyone who recalls the fierce vendettas of the Italian communes and the awful retributions exacted by the faction which for the moment was uppermost, will be able to judge of the likelihood that reports damaging to an opponent would ever be weighed impartially. Mr. H. O. Taylor in his valuable work, *The Mediæval Mind*, deplores the violence of the invectives which, like the corruptions denounced by them, was common to all these centuries.   " From the testimony of more definite accounts," he says, " one perceives the rudeness and cruelty of mediæval life, in which the Church likewise was involved.   In order to rise, it had to lift the social fabric.   To this end many of its children struggled nobly, devoting themselves and sometimes yielding up their lives for the betterment of the society in which their lots were cast."[35]

The same high authority in another part of his work cites in illustration the writings of the German Imperialist, Walther von der Vogelweide, describing how " in excess of wrath Walther inveighs against the Pope," and adding : " The sweeping nature of his denunciation raises the question whether he merely attacked the supposed treachery of the reigning Pope, or was opposed to the papacy as an institution hostile to the

[35] H. O. Taylor, *The Mediæval Mind* (Edn. 1925) Vol. I, p. 492.

German nation." " The answer," he declares, " is not clear.
Mediæval denunciations of the Church range from indictments
of particular abuses, on through more general invectives, to the
clear protests of heretics impugning the ecclesiastical system.
It is not always easy to ascertain the speaker's meaning.   Usually
the abuse and not the system is attacked.   Hostility to the latter,
however sweeping the language of satirist or preacher, is not
lightly to be inferred."   But the strange thing is that people
like Walther, though they were apparently ready to believe
any evil whatever that was rumoured concerning the Holy See,
were not necessarily scoffers.   " In matters of religion," says
Mr. Taylor again, " Walther apparently was entirely orthodox,
and a pious Christian."[36]   It must, therefore, be borne in mind,
that though scandalous tales concerning the Popes were often
recounted in pre-Reformation days by writers who passed for
decent-living men, we have no sort of guarantee that their
judgment was not warped by political or class prejudice.   Members of a religious Order were particularly prone to believe that
a Pontiff hostile to their privileges or to the spirit of their particular rule must be a man capable of almost any atrocity.

---

[36] L.c. Vol. II, pp. 61-63.

Chapter III

SOME OTHER MODERN SLANDERS AND SLANDERERS

Although the unprecedented duration of the pontificate of Pius IX and the fierce political passions engendered by the " Young Italy " movement caused him perhaps to be more shamefully vilified than any of his predecessors, still there have been few occupants of the papal chair whose moral character has not at some time or other been assailed by calumny. What is exceptional in the case of Pio Nono is the completeness of the vindication afforded by such testimony as that of Nicolini, politically his declared antagonist, but at the same time his fellow townsman and the intimate friend of members of his family. As already pointed out, Nicolini was sufficiently honest not to bear false witness about facts of which his own eyes and ears had made him cognizant. But as soon as we pass beyond the range of his personal experience, we find him as ready as any of the other revolutionaries to propagate the vilest gossip current among the agitators whose society he frequented.

Speaking of Pope Gregory XVI (Cappellari), Pio Nono's immediate predecessor, Nicolini gives his readers to understand that the reports circulated concerning his private life " had alienated from him as Pontiff all the honest and conscientious men among the religious Catholics,"[1] and he adds offensive details concerning these same reports. The statement quoted on the face of it is ridiculous, as anyone may learn who will consult the diaries or the correspondence of the period. But the violent political animosities engendered by the then papal policy of repressing free speech had encouraged the disaffected to take

---

[1] See Nicolini, *Pius IX*, pp. 6-7.

advantage of every unconventionality in the conduct of Gregory which could conceivably be misrepresented to his discredit. In particular it was known that he was on familiar terms with the family of his secretary, Gaetano Moroni, and the very worst construction was put upon the intimacy. No good purpose could be served by retailing the extravagant stories circulated in this connection. Not a shadow of proof was ever forthcoming for any of them. They were coined in the same mint as those fabrications regarding Pius IX which have already been dealt with, but whereas in the case of Pio Nono the whole rested upon thin air, the well-known but perfectly innocent friendship between the aged Pontiff[2] and the family of his Cameriere gave the detractors a peg on which their vile insinuations could be hung. The fact seems to have been that the Pope, a former Camaldolese monk, was a simple and genial scholar who disliked formality. While still an abbot he had made the acquaintance of young Moroni, who was at that time apprenticed to a barber, and had discovered in him a very genuine capacity for secretarial work. He, therefore, when Cardinal, took him into his service and encouraged him in his project of compiling a vast ecclesiastical encyclopaedia (*Dizionario di Erudizione storico-ecclesiastica*) which in course of time was published under that title in 103 volumes. That Gaetano Moroni, as *ajutante di camera* to the Pope, was a thoroughly capable official, who conducted an incredibly vast correspondence, and possessed an immense fund of out-of-the-way, if rather uncritical, learning, cannot be disputed. There is not a shadow of truth in the suggestions of his detractors that he did not write his *Dizionario* himself, or that he owed his advancement to anything but his own industry and ability.

None the less the ex-Barnabite Gavazzi, the friend of Garibaldi, in his book, *My Recollections of the Last Four Popes*, written of course as a counterblast to Cardinal Wiseman's memoirs bearing a similar title, refers to the matter thus :

One instance of the cunning trickery of Gaetano was the

---

[2] Pope Gregory XVI was 65 when he was elected Pope, and he died at the age of 79 in 1846.

desire to pass as one of the first scholars of his day by claiming the authorship of " the Dictionary of the Regular Orders, the most remarkable ecclesiastics and ecclesiastical events." This dictionary in fact belonged to him no more than the peacock's feather to the crow, or the lion's skin to the ass of the fable. . . . By distributing his favours Signor Gaetano increased the gratuitous articles of his dictionary, and the dictionary filled his purse, for Gregory obliged all the communes to buy it. Here we see a thief who steals even the reputation of authors. . . .[3]

Thereupon follows in Gavazzi's book a scurrilous attack upon the Pope himself, recounting for the edification of his readers all the odious gossip in which the Roman revolutionaries coupled Gregory's name with that of " la bella Gaetanina," for it was so, we are told, that they were pleased to refer to the wife of " Moroni the barber."[4]

It is fair comment upon this statement to observe that the demonstrable untruth of the first portion—even the name and character of the dictionary are travestied—altogether discredits the second. The many manuscripts of Gaetano Moroni which are still preserved bear witness to his laborious industry. When his patron Gregory XVI died, Gaetano, far from having amassed a million francs, was a poor man with a large family who had to depend upon his earnings. Only 38 volumes of the *Dizionario* had appeared and his calumniators freely prophesied that the undertaking would now collapse ; but the compiler lived on for another 37 years and produced 65 more volumes as well as indexes, working, we are told, as much as fourteen hours a day. At the time of Moroni's death in 1883, a long article under the title of " Il Confidente di Gregorio XVI " was devoted to him in the *Nuova Antologia*,[5] an Italian

---

[3] Gavazzi, *My Recollections of the Last Four Popes* (1858), p. 276.

[4] *Cf.* the unpleasant tone of T. A. Trollope, *Life of Pius IX*, Vol. I, p. 159.

[5] Vol. 42, Nov.–Dec. 1883, pp. 263–281, by D. Silvagni. The writer's sympathies were by no means papal or clerical, as his book *La Corte di Roma* plainly shows, but he finds nothing to blame in the relations of Gregory with the Moroni household.

periodical of high standing, which does justice to the remarkable range of his erudition and entirely acquits him of taking undue advantage of the favour he enjoyed with his patron.

As stated above, it is unquestionable that Pope Gregory was a man of very simple and kindly nature. Even as supreme Pontiff, he observed an order of the day which was monastic in its regularity. As an illustration of his unceremonious affability, which his traducers no doubt found it convenient to misinterpret with sinister intent, it may be sufficient to cite the description given by the Comte de Falloux of one of his interviews with the Holy Father.

> He maintained upon the throne [writes de Falloux], the customs and austere simplicity of a Camaldolese cloister. His features were commonplace, but intelligent and benevolent. Etiquette was maintained in his ante-chamber, but dispensed with in his presence, where one knelt as to a father rather than to a sovereign. . . . At our last audience we brought so large a basket of rosaries for him to bless that he laughingly asked us how we had got them there. We replied that our servants had carried them up to his very door. " Are they," he asked, " also from your good province of La Vendée ? " " Then make them come in, I will give my blessing to them at the same time as to you." He had them sent for, and with great affability, asked various questions of both the man and his wife, without any apparent consciousness that he was setting an example of that sort of equality which Christianity introduced, and of which it is still the only model.[6]

It would be easy to quote many similar examples of Pope Gregory's readiness to lay aside formality and to make his visitors thoroughly at home in his presence. Serious students of the history of the Papal States in the mid-nineteenth century dismiss the stories circulated by Gavazzi, Nicolini and the rest as worthless calumnies. The Danish Lutheran bishop, F. Nielsen, though he speaks in the severest terms of Gregory's

---

[6] de Falloux, *Mémoires d'un royaliste*, 1888.

political administration, makes only brief reference to his moral character. " Malicious tongues," he writes, " were busy —as it seems without cause—in interpreting the kindness of Gregory XVI to Gaetano and his wife in a way very derogatory to the Pope's morality."[7] Still more valuable is the testimony, even though it be mainly negative, of the Italian statesman, L. C. Farini, in his work *The Roman State from 1815 to 1850*. Farini, as we learn from Mr. Gladstone's preface, was a politician who had twice been banished from Rome during the pontificate of Gregory XVI, and who had consequently little reason to say complimentary things of a ruler whom he regarded as an incompetent despot. Nevertheless he remarks :

I have now arrived with my succinct narrative nearly at the close of the reign of Gregory XVI, and have used, in regard to his temporal government, that serious language which truth and my conscience have dictated. I am therefore especially glad to bear an honourable and respectful testimony to his conduct as pontiff, to his constant zeal for the growth of the Catholic religion, and to the prudence and conciliatory spirit, of which he gave proof in managing the affairs of the Jesuits of France, as also to the courage and noble-mindedness with which he defended the Catholics trodden down by Russian tyranny.[8]

One other citation must suffice in vindication of Pope Gregory's good name. It is taken from an article in the *Quarterly Review* (1858) dealing with Cardinal Wiseman's *Recollections of the Last Four Popes*. The writer evinces little sympathy for the Cardinal or for the Catholicism which he represented, but in speaking of Cappellari's election to the pontificate, he says :

[7] F. Nielsen, *History of the Papacy in the Nineteenth Century* (English trans.), Vol. II, p. 82. It is a curious illustration of the permanent mischief worked by calumny that though Nielsen rejects the charges of debauchery brought against the early life of Pius IX, he does not entirely acquit him, and gives references to Vésinier and Petruccelli della Gattina as if they were serious authorities. See Vol. II, p. 111 note.

[8] L. C. Farini, *The Roman State from 1815 to 1850*, translated by the Rt. Hon. W. E. Gladstone, M.P. for the University of Oxford, London, 1851, Vol. I, p. 138.

He was not a man of extensive views, nor of a high order
of intellect, but he was not deficient in sound sense nor in
good intentions. He was sincerely devout, steady in his
attachments, a warm friend and not a bitter enemy. . . .
In all his difficulties he showed constancy and moral
courage. His love of justice was strong. . . .

He was self-indulgent in trifles. He loved good cheer ;
the state of his health probably made the fasts of the Church
extremely painful to him ; and the resource of the scrupulous Catholic in such cases is wine. The stories of his
intemperance we believe to be utterly unfounded. They
were invented by malice and they gained strength from an
affection of the nature of a polypus (subsequently cured)
which disfigured his nose.[9]

There can be no object in giving further illustrations of the
flood of calumny which has been poured out at all periods upon
the successors of St. Peter and from which so very few have
entirely escaped. What is one to expect, for example, from a
book which bears the following title—I translate the French
original quite literally :—" History of the Popes, Mysteries and
Iniquities of the Court of Rome, Crimes, Murders, Poison-
ings, Parricides, Adulteries, Incests, Debaucheries, and Turpitudes of the Roman Pontiffs from St. Peter down to our own
days." Neither must the reader suppose that this book of
Lachâtre is a contemptible little brochure, the ignoble character
of which is patent to all even from its external form. On the
contrary, the third edition, in four volumes, which I have before
me, is a work in imperial 8vo, lavishly illustrated with a pro-
fusion of by no means ill-executed engravings. It appeared
during the years 1883–1884 in penny numbers, and it certainly
could never have been brought to completion, in view of the
outlay entailed, unless it had been purchased by several
thousands of subscribers.

Passing over, then, the crimes and immoralities which have
been attributed to such Popes as Pius VI and Pius VII and

[9] *The Quarterly Review*, October 1858, Vol. 104, pp. 111 and 134.

even to a Pontiff so near our own days as Leo XIII,[10] I venture to draft in summary form,, a few conclusions suggested by what we have already seen. It is plain, I submit—

(1) That, in the case of public men, and notably of the Popes, a blameless life and a conscientious discharge of duty afford no security from calumny, even of the foulest kind.

(2) That the danger of this is enormously increased when political passions and material interests come into play.

(3) That when a slander is widely circulated, the truth of the charge is apt to become a real conviction with many of those who live amid the surroundings in which it is taken for granted.

(4) That the possibility of opposing a conclusive disproof to such insinuations of gross depravity is largely a matter of chance. It happens, for example, that Nicolini, a fellow townsman, wrote a biography of Pius IX in England before any breath of calumny had assailed his early life, but the existence of such testimony is a pure accident which normally could not be counted on.

(5) That the tendency of the biassed critic, writing years after the event, even when honest in intention, is to treat such slanders as exaggerations rather than as inventions, and to assume that truth is best attained by steering a middle course between panegyric and denunciation.

(6) That in such political, religious, and, in general, revolutionary campaigns no more scruple is felt by the leaders as to the type of men with whom they associate themselves than is felt concerning the weapons they employ.

On this last head it will not be out of place to offer some further comment by calling attention to the case of the notorious Léo Taxil. Casual reference has already been made to the suit in which he was prosecuted by Count Girolamo Mastai,

[10] *L'Empoisonneur Léon XIII, compte-rendu complet de l'affaire du Chanoine Bernard ; vols et empoisonnements commis avec la complicité du Pape actuel* is the title of a book by Léo Taxil, printed about 1884.

the Pope's nephew, for the libels contained in the book *Les Amours Secrètes de Pie IX*. Taxil was sentenced by the Court to pay 60,000 francs damages, though by dint of appeals and legal chicanery he wore out the patience of the prosecutor and evaded the penalty. The point of special interest in the present connection is that this peculiarly vile personage, who had been engaged for some years in an anti-clerical propaganda which carried shamelessness to the very verge of obscenity, was not only treated as a friend by General Garibaldi, but encouraged by him to continue the campaign. Taxil declares that it was Garibaldi, then (1881) honorary Grand Master of the Italian Freemasons, who suggested the idea of the Ligue Anti-Cléricale of which Taxil was the organiser in France.[11] Taxil, it may be admitted, is an unreliable witness, but there can be no question that he was on intimate terms with the " Hero of Caprera." In the Italian edition of Garibaldi's letters published in 1885, after his death, two letters are included addressed to Taxil. No doubt we should never have seen these if Taxil's quarrel with the Freemasons and his " conversion " to Catholicity had taken place earlier, but in the first part of 1885 he was still regarded as a sound anti-clerical. Accordingly, on March 9, 1882, we find Garibaldi writing a letter from Naples beginning, " *Mio carissimo Leone Taxil*," and commenting with the General's usual violence upon the progress of the French war in Tunis. " My very dear Léo Taxil," he writes, " it is all over. Your priest-ridden Republic will never deceive anybody again. The love and veneration I formerly bore it have turned into contempt,"[12] etc. What is also certain is that when Taxil was prosecuted by Count Mastai, counsel for the former produced certain letters of Garibaldi in court, by way of evidence that his client could not be regarded as a disreputable person. Moreover, a foul and scurrilous novel, written by Taxil in 1879 and entitled *Le Fils du Jésuite*, bears the dedication : "À celui que j'affectionne comme un père, à Garibaldi, je dédie ce livre ; Léo Taxil " ;

---

[11] See Taxil, *Confessions d'un Ex-Libre-Penseur*, pp. 320–321.
[12] *Epistolario di Giuseppe Garibaldi*, Milano, 1885 ; Vol. II, p. 329.

while there is prefixed to the book a sort of introduction, headed *Pensées Anti-Cléricales*, which is signed by Garibaldi himself. The tone of this document may be judged from its first sentences :

> The Scriptures, which idiots and rogues are wont to call holy or sacred, place beside the first human couple, the serpent, who takes advantage of the weakness of the first woman to effect her ruin. This precious fable would have been greatly improved if the reptile had been exchanged for a priest. For it is the priest who is the real personification of malice and mendacity.

And further on :

> Liberty, in my opinion, ought not to exist for mosquitoes, for reptiles, for assassins, for thieves, for tyrants—neither ought it to exist for priests, who are just as dangerous as these.

As an example of the language of Taxil's periodical, the *Anti-Clérical*, at the time when Garibaldi was lending it his full encouragement, the following may serve. The British Museum chances to possess a copy of the *Procès des Congrégations contre Léo Taxil*, and I have taken the trouble to cast my eye through it. It would be impossible to reproduce here the more disgusting portions of the article in the *Anti-Clérical* for which M. Taxil was prosecuted, and it was only one among scores of such. It must be sufficient to state that the title was *Pourritures Congréganistes*, and to quote such a passage as the following. " Ces misérables " (*i.e.*, the teachers of Marseilles belonging to the male religious orders) " ont toutes les passions bestiales." . . . " Du premier jusqu'au dernier, les instituteurs congréganistes sont tous des monstres ; les découvertes qui se font chaque jour sur leurs mœurs épouvantables, autorisent à penser et à dire qu'il n'y a pas une seule exception dans ces associations d'êtres vicieux." In this case Taxil was fined 12,000 francs.

But the part played by the founder of the *Anti-Clérical* in the campaign of calumny against the Popes seems to call for

somewhat fuller treatment.   While it is true that for more than
thirty years past he has been utterly dicredited and that no one
would now dream of putting trust in anything he has written,
still the work of the foul literature which he composed or edited,
but in any case spread broadcast in thousands and thousands
of copies, is not easily undone.   The kind of people influenced
were not those who verify statements by insisting on exact
references.   An impression is produced by mere reiteration,
and who shall say whether it can ever be eradicated.   Thanks to
the fact that M. Taxil, from 1885 to 1897, went through a phase
of real or pretended conversion during which he professed to
make revelations of a most startling character regarding Continental Freemasonry, the history of his earlier career has been
written with remarkable frankness by those who can in no way
be suspected of clerical sympathies.   It may consequently be
worth while to set before the reader a full translation of the
account given in the supplementary volume of Larousse's *Grand
Dictionnaire*.

TAXIL, LÉO (GABRIEL ANTOINE JOGAND-PAGÈS), a French
writer, born at Marseilles, 20 March, 1854.   A pupil of the
Jesuits, he became a violent anticlerical, and during a
period of ten years he attacked the Church, the clergy,
and the Pope in a long series of publications, the titles of
which are given below.   Most of them created a scandal,
but this was much more due to their violence than to
literary talent, which was conspicuous by its absence.   In
his boyhood Taxil had been sent to the reformatory of
Mettray, and there had had ground of complaint against
the chaplain ; at any rate this was the reason he assigned
for becoming a freethinker.   One of his earliest pamphlets,
À bas la Calotte (8vo, 1879), brought down upon him a
prosecution for insulting the form of worship legally recog-
nized in France,. but the jury acquitted him.   He was less
fortunate in 1881, and found himself compelled to pay
4,000 francs damages for having unscrupulously appro-
priated a work, *Les Sermons de mon Curé*, written by M.

Auguste Roussel, which had been published some time before, but which Taxil reprinted under his own name (1880) as soon as he heard of the author's death. Certain religious Congregations also obtained a verdict against him on a charge of libel in 1883, resulting from his publication of *Calotte et Calotins, histoire illustrée du Clergé et des Congrégations* (3 vols. 8vo, 1880–1882). The following year he was again prosecuted and sentenced to 3,000 francs fine and fifteen days' imprisonment on account of the obscene engravings inserted in one of his dreary compilations, *La Prostitution Contemporaine* (8vo, 1883). Finally, his *Amours de Pie IX*. (8vo, 1884), published under the pseudonym of A. Volpi, a work as ridiculous as it was contemptible, led, at the suit of Count Mastai, the heir of the late Pope, to a verdict of 60,000 francs damages and the compulsory insertion of the sentence in sixty newspapers. Taxil, to evade responsibility, had pretended that the pseudonym A. Volpi concealed the identity of one of the staff of the *Figaro*, M. G. Moynet, but the latter, not content with a formal denial, took the next opportunity of thrashing his traducer with the cane he was carrying. Taxil took out a summons against his assailant, but thought it wiser not to carry the matter further. His other works, though they did not result in legal proceedings, are all of the same character. The following are their titles : *Debrayas*, a comedy in one act (1873) ; *Almanachs anticléricaux et républicains* for 1879 and 1880 ; *Les Soutanes grotesques* (1879) ; *La Chasse aux corbeaux* (1878) ; *Le Fils du Jésuite* (1879) ; *Les Bêtises sacrées, revue critique des superstitions* (1881) ; *Les Borgia, histoire d'une famille de monstres* (1881) ; *Les Pornographes Sacrés, la Confession et les confesseurs* (1882) ; *La Bible amusante, pour les grands et les petits* (1882), a work which first of all came out in parts with the title of *La Bible Farce ; Un pape femelle, aventures extraordinaires et crimes épouvantables de la papesse Jeanne* (1882) ; *Par la grâce du Saint Esprit*, roman (1882); *L'Empoisonneur Léon XIII. et les cinq millions du Chanoine*

(1883) ; *Marat et les héros de la Révolution* (1883) ; *Pie IX. devant l'Histoire, sa vie politique et pontificale, ses débauches, ses folies, ses crimes* (3 vols. 1883), this was a different work from that called *Amours de Pie IX.* ; *Les Maîtresses du Pape*, roman (1884) ; *Les Livres secrets des Confesseurs dévoilés aux Pères de Famille* (1884), *La Plume de l'Ange* (1884) ; *Les Trois Cocus* (1884) ; *Le Sacrement du Curé* (1884) ; *La Vie de Jésus* (1884) ; *Vie de Veuillot immaculé* (1884). All these works, which are hardly more than clumsy compilations and in which M. Taxil had a certain number of collaborators, when he did not for some small sum buy the volume ready made, were published by the " Librairie Anti-Cléricale," which he had founded in Paris in the Rue des Écoles and which soon assumed considerable developments. He also became proprietor and editor of sundry newspapers, notably the *Midi républicain* of Montpellier, the *République Anti-Cléricale* and the *Anti-Clérical* started by him in Paris. He was also the founder of the " Ligue Anti-Cléricale," which in 1885 had 15,000 members. Although he was expelled from the Masonic brotherhood in 1882, after his conviction for literary piracy (the appropriation, already mentioned, of the *Sermons de mon curé*), he nevertheless occupied the presidential chair at the " Congress of Free-thinkers " in 1885. But already he was suspected of wishing to make a change of front, and a short time afterwards the report obtained currency that he had humbly returned within the fold of the Church. The statement has been made that the figure agreed upon by the Vatican as the price of M. Taxil's abjuration was a million francs. We can only say that this was a very large sum to pay for a very inconsiderable personage. Certain it is, in any case, that this tempestuous pamphleteer, after having abjured his errors before the papal nuncio himself, Mgr. di Rende, made a pilgrimage to Rome and received the absolution of Leo XIII. It was also said that to give proof of his repentance he became a Carthusian. Since that date he has published a number of other books as dull as those already mentioned, but aggressively religious and anti-republican in tone.[13]

A list of these last publications is then given, beginning with the *Révelations complètes sur la franc-maconnerie, Les Frères Trois-Points* (1885), but no purpose would be served by copying it here.

This account was printed in 1890, and it was not until seven years later that Taxil, who had meanwhile invented " Diana Vaughan " and had grown more and more wildly extravagant in his pretended revelations of Freemasonry, Satanism, and " Palladism," at last reached a point when credulity could bear no more and the exposure of the " mystification " followed. Then he went back to the republication of the old filthy and blasphemous literature of the Librairie Anti-Cléricale. How far this shameless calumniator, who deserves a place, if ever a man did, in the Malebolge of any modern Inferno, was sincere in his conversion must always be matter of doubt. There is some reason to believe that his submission to Rome and his breach with his old associates were for the time being entirely genuine, but perseverance was lacking, and Taxil must have found, possibly within a few weeks of his reconciliation to the Church, that his resolution was unequal to the sacrifices demanded of him. Still, having irretrievably incurred the contempt of his anticlerical friends, he could not go back to them. Hence he determined, it seems, to play out his part of convert and to embark upon a series of bogus revelations of Masonic horrors which for a long time proved as remunerative a source of income as his attacks on religion had been. Now amongst the other volumes which Taxil gave to the world at this period was one[14] of the nature of an autobiography and entitled *Confessions d'un Ex-Libre-Penseur*. That all the statements of fact made in this narrative deserve implicit confidence can by no means be taken for granted. It seems

[13] Larousse, *Grand Dictionnaire Universel du XIX\u1d49 Siècle*.   Deuxième Supplément, 1890, p. 1903.

[14] The epilogue is dated by the author December 25, 1886.

certain, in view of subsequent criticisms and disclosures, that in
many matters Taxil, while accusing himself with an affectation
of candour and compunction, has presented his own conduct
in a less revolting light than would have been imposed upon
him had he been moved by a strict regard for truth.   None
the less, a book of " Confessions," after a public career which
had scandalised the world as profoundly as Taxil's, was bound
to contain many humiliating avowals.   When the writer is
admitting his own culpability there is no sufficient reason to
distrust him, and in connection with our present subject the
account which he gives of the origin of the scandalous romance
which he wrote under the title of *Les Amours secrètes de Pie IX*
is of some little interest.   M. Taxil explains how certain
anticlerical deputies in the Italian Parliament had, as far back
as 1860, allowed themselves to give currency to a mass of
discreditable insinuations regarding Pius IX in his early life.
This vile gossip had been amplified and circulated in print in
Switzerland and Belgium, and Taxil, meeting with some of
these brochures, decided to utilise them in a romance which he
proposed to publish in a newspaper, the *Midi Républicain,*
committed to his editorship in 1881.   The paper was a languish-
ing affair, and the new editor conceived the idea of advertising
it by making it the vehicle of a sensational scandal.   The publication as a feuilleton of some story which would excite an uproar
among all good Catholics seemed the very thing for the
purpose.

It was thus [says Taxil] that the idea came to me of
utilizing the wretched pamphlets attacking the private life
of Pius IX. which I had collected in Switzerland.   It was
I, then, who furnished the suggestion if not the plan of that
abominable story, the title of which I now blush to write.

Integrity of life being the crowning virtue of a Pope, it
was needful to represent the deceased Pontiff as a man
given over to debauchery.   For this reason, the romance
which was to blacken his reputation was entitled *The Secret
Love Affairs of Pius IX.*

But this was not all. In order to make the story more racy, we had to invent an Abbé Meslier of some sort.[15] Accordingly we created an imaginary secret chamberlain of the Pope, whom we christened Carlo Sebastiano Volpi, and the story appeared with this fictitious signature. I even composed a letter for the pretended chamberlain, and this was printed as a Preface, and helped further to impose upon the public. This, however, constituted my whole personal share in the work. Still, if I am not the author of the story, I fully recognize that I, more than any one else, am responsible to the public who have been so shamefully tricked. I offer no excuse. The original conception was mine, the mud, in other words, the raw material of lies, which the author watered down by adding new characters and incidents, was collected by me and supplied to him for the purpose.[16]

Taxil goes on to declare that in a fortnight the circulation of the newspaper had enormously increased, while the indignation of the Catholic party knew no bounds. A protest of the ladies of the diocese of Montpellier received more than two thousand signatures in a very brief period, and public opinion spoke so strongly, that the proprietors insisted upon the suppression of the feuilleton. Taxil had to submit, but he at once recommenced the publication of *Les Amours de Pie IX* in the *Anti-Clérical*, and shortly afterwards it appeared in book form. It would be useless to detail the history of the subsequent prosecution of Taxil by Count Mastai Feretti, nephew of the deceased Pope. A verdict with 60,000 francs damages, as already stated, was given against the libeller by the courts, but after endless delays the Count departed in disgust, leaving Taxil free to go on printing and advertising his abominable

[15] This was a fictitious character of Voltaire's. Voltaire pretended that he was a real personage, that the curé had lost his faith while acting as a priest, and that he had left a compendium of atheist teaching to the world in his will.

[16] *Les Confessions*, pp. 237, 238.

story as impudently as ever.[17] Moreover as the list of publications, quoted above, sufficiently shows, Taxil persistently added to his offences.   A pretended biography, *Pie IX., devant l'Histoire*, with a sub-title which included the words " his debaucheries, his follies, and his crimes," was issued by him not long afterwards in three volumes.   Further, in 1884, a new edition of the *Les Amours de Pie IX.* was issued, and the publication was advertised all over Paris by means of a pictorial poster, in which the well-known features of the late Pope were shown, surrounded by the vignettes of a bevy of women representing his supposed mistresses.   The French Republic at that time still, of course, maintained diplomatic relations with the Vatican.   The Papal Nuncio protested to the French Government against this outrage, and the posters were torn down by the police.   The Government talked of prosecuting the author, but the Republican journals raised such a storm over this intervention, that the threatened proceedings were dropped.

For the most part the publications of the *Librairie Anti-Cléricale*, however atrocious, were printed and advertised without interference of any sort.   One of Taxil's books was entitled *The Poisoner, Leo XIII.*, and in a passage of a volume belonging to the same collection and written by a certain Alfred Paulon, the Pontiff named is charged with unmentionable vices, a libel which, as in many similar cases, is protected from any really effective exposure by the fact that it does not lend itself to quotation.[18]   Neither can this brazen audacity be altogether a matter of surprise· when one finds among the most persistently advertised publications of the *Librairie Anti-Cléricale*, a parody of the Bible with grotesque illustrations and a comic Life of Jesus Christ, also illustrated, in which the purpose of casting ridicule upon the person of our Saviour stands open and undisguised.[19]

[17] See *Les Confessions d'un Ex-Libre-Penseur*, p. 203.

[18] A. Paulon, *Dictionnaire Rigolo-Clérical*, Paris, 1883, p. 108, cf. p. 143.

[19] Though we have not had the opportunity of examining either of these works, their blasphemous profanity is abundantly made evident in the detailed summary of contents published in the advertisement sheets of many volumes of the *Librairie Anti-Cléricale*.   It would be easy to quote, but such illustrations would simply outrage the reader's sense of decorum without any good result.

As we have already mentioned, Taxil, when at last compelled to drop his assumed part, and to avow his career of deception, returned to the publication of the same class of literature which had occupied him before his conversion. Nearly all the more atrocious volumes of his collection were promptly reprinted, if indeed, they had ever been out of print, *Les Amours de Pie IX.* among the number. Perhaps the most effective illustration we can give of the kind of anti-religious works which are still unblushingly sold by certain Paris booksellers, is to reproduce in facsimile the advertisement which adorns the back cover of a volume purchased only a few years since. It is only when one realises all the anti-religious venom which underlies the mere publication of such a list, that one comes to understand something of the gall and bitterness which distresses us at times in the writings of Catholic champions of the temper of the late Louis Veuillot. If the Catholic party in France often seem *intransigeant* and extravagant in their hatred of republican governments, Jews, Freemasons, and *id genus omne*, they have been through experiences during these last forty or fifty years of which not one Englishman in a hundred is capable of forming any idea. It would be difficult to imagine anything more likely to provoke the indignation of a decent-minded Christian than the advertisement reproduced photographically on the back of this page. And the covers of every book published in the Librairie Anti-Cléricale are crowded with announcements of the same character.

A LA MÊME LIBRAIRIE

La Bible Amusante, par Léo Taxil, *avec quatre cents dessins comiques de* Frid'Rick . . . . . . **5 »**
Célèbre édition, format in-8º écu, beau volume de 824 pages. En dehors de 400 spirituels dessins, qui sont, à eux seuls, une critique aussi joyeuse que complète des divers épisodes bibliques, cette édition contient un texte très développé *[vingt-mille lignes]* comprenant les citations *textuelles* de l'Écriture sainte (avec indication des versets), et reproduisant toutes les réfutations opposées par Voltaire Fréjet, lord Bollinbroke, Toland et autres savants philosophes

La Vie de Jésus, par Léo Taxil. Un fort volume, illustré de 50 dessins comiques, du célèbre caricaturiste Pépin. Même format que la *Bible amusante*, et son pendant, pour toute bibliothèque philosophique. . . . . . **4. »**

Le Capucin enflammé, roman comique, par le R. P. Alleluia, de l'Ordre de la Sainte-Rigolade. Un volume illustré. **3.50**

Le Couvent de Gomorrhe, par Jacques Souffrance, roman historiqne. Mœurs abominables et mystères horribles des communautés religieuses. Illustré. . **3.50**

Le Moine incestueux, orgies des couvents, par Edmond Ploert. Un volume illustré **3.50**

Les Amours d'un Supérieur de Séminaire, par Achille Le Roy. Un volume illustré. **3.50**

La Belle Dévote, par Jean Vindex, roman passionnel, couverture illustrée, par Jack Abeillé **3.50**

L'Alcove du Cardinal, par Jean Vindex. Un fort volume illustré de nombreux dessins, dans lequel l'auteur dévoile toutes les turpitudes et les mensonges du clergé. couverture illustrée en couleurs. **3.50**

Les Débauches d'un Confesseur, par Jean Pauper, suivies des **Galanteries de la Bible**, par Evariste Parny. Un fort volume illustré par Lacarière, couverture en couleur. **3.50**

FACSIMILE OF THE COVER OF A WORK OF LÉO TAXIL, PUBLISHED SINCE 1900; SEE PRECEDING PAGE.

CHAPTER IV

THE POPE WHO WAS A FREEMASON

ALTHOUGH the Freemasons rightly claim that Léo Taxil was expelled from their fraternity in 1881, three or four years before he made his submission to Rome, still he was undoubtedly a Mason, and fully recognised as such at the time when he founded the *Anti-Clérical* and began the publication of *Les Amours secrètes de Pie IX.*, with a crowd of equally abominable lampoons culminating in *La Bible farce* and its comic illustrations. Despite the fact that he had on several occasions, between 1872 and 1880 been prosecuted, mulcted in damages, and once at least been sent to prison, either for libellous attacks on the clergy or for his profanity in caricaturing Catholic worship,[1] the committee of the Grand Orient apparently saw nothing in this which called for animadversion. It was only when he contested an election against one of their own candidates that they took action and found it necessary to get rid of this insubordinate member whose indiscretions were compromising them. There can be no reason to question the authenticity of the congratulatory letters addressed to him in 1880[2] by various French Lodges after the publication of *Le Fils du Jésuite*, already referred to, under the aegis of Garibaldi. The leaders of the Grand Orient were thoroughly in sympathy with such attacks on the Church. *Écrasons l'infâme* was undisguisedly their motto, and *l'infâme* of course meant Catholicism.

The condemnation of Freemasonry by the Holy See is of ancient

[1] In ch. VI of his *Confessions d'un Ex-Libre Penseur* other prosecutions are mentioned which are not noticed in Larousse.

[2] See *Les Frères Trois-Points*, ch. I, where the text of some of these is printed.

date. Twenty-one years after the foundation of the London
Grand Lodge in 1717, Pope Clement XII by his Bull *In eminenti*
forbade the Catholic faithful to join any such Masonic fraternities
or to retain membership with them, under pain of excommunication.[3] How far the reasons assigned for this prohibition
were justified will be seen later. Let it only be noted here that
the condemnation was renewed by several subsequent Popes,
and in particular by Pius IX in his Allocution *Multiplices inter*,
delivered on 25th September, 1865. The Freemasons are an
influential body, and it is not surprising that both in the English
and the Continental Press many violent articles were published
expressing surprise or indignation at the renewal of papal
hostilities. " Whatever can the Pope be thinking of," wrote
The Times in a leading article, " to select this innocent and
convivial association for these tremendous denunciations ? . . .
It reminds us of Jupiter thundering in a clear sky, to witness
these rattling thunderbolts let loose upon so unobtrusive a
society as the Freemasons. . . . We can only explain such an
uncalled-for burst of pontifical wrath on the supposition that
the Pope is profoundly ignorant of the circumstances of modern
life and society."

Such language, one might retort, is equally inexplicable
except on the supposition that the leader-writer was himself
not less profoundly ignorant of the character of Continental
Masonry. His appreciation of the aims and practice of the
English Lodges was no doubt just enough, but the Grand Orients
of France, Italy and Belgium were always and everywhere
actively militant, and anyone who will take the trouble to look
up the terms of their own pronouncements, as recorded in the
early volumes of the *Revue Maçonnique*, the *Monde Maçonnique*, or
the *Rivista della Massoneria Italiana*, will find that they identify
themselves without disguise with the principles of the French
Revolution, that they claim for Freemasonry the credit of having

---

[3] It is a little difficult to see why Protestants should feel so aggrieved at this
papal ordinance. The penalties inflicted by an excommunication do not
affect *them*. The Pope does not address himself to them or attempt to lay
any burden on their conscience.

brought about that great cataclysm, and that they are openly pledged to the overthrow of the Catholic Church, and, indeed, of all forms of revealed religion. The Masonic periodical last named, commenting on this very allocution of Pius IX, proclaimed that the Pope was perfectly right. " To Masonry is due, if not as an organising, at any rate as an inspiring force, all, absolutely all, that has been effected from 1859 to our own days towards shaking off the moral yoke of the Vatican."[4] Mazzini, Garibaldi, Lemmi and Pike, the dominating influences in the Craft during the third quarter of the nineteenth century, never made the least secret of the determined war they were waging against Catholicism and the Papacy. In these circumstances many of the fraternity found a peculiar interest in circulating the report that the author of the denunciations of the *Multiplices inter* had himself been initiated as a Mason, and indeed some, not content with this, went further and professed to furnish proof that he had been formally expelled from the Order for perjury after a regular trial.

The earliest reference which I have been able to trace in print to the supposed initiation of J. M. Mastai as a Mason is again to be found in *La Rome des Papes* by Pianciani published in 1859. It is characteristic of this writer that he practically contradicts himself in the statements he makes about it. On the one hand he declares that Mastai was pressed to become a Mason at Sinigaglia but was probably deterred by fear of excommunication, on the other he asserts that Crétineau-Joly later on discovered some Masonic documents implicating Pius and endeavoured to blackmail the Pontiff by threats of publishing them.[5] However it may be with Pianciani, Vésinier and Petruccelli della Gattina at any rate state unhesitatingly that Mastai joined a Masonic lodge. What is of more importance, T. Adolphus Trollope, who, as we have seen, rejects in emphatic language the charges of early debauchery brought against the Pope, believes that in this matter he has probably not been maligned.

[4] *Rivista della Massoneria Italiana*, Vol. XVIII, p. 114.
[5] Pianciani, *La Rome des Papes*, II, pp. 365–367.

It has constantly been asserted [he says] and as constantly denied, that the young Mastai was a Mason. It is exceedingly probable, considering the complexion of the times and the liberalising tendencies of his then surroundings, that he did become a member of the order. Nor is there the slightest reason for deeming it any ground of censure that he should have done so ; or for thinking that it is *on that ground* impossible that he should subsequently have looked at the matter from a papal point of view.[6]

The point, of course, is that if Mastai, whether as lay Catholic or cleric, became a Freemason he acted in defiance of a most grave and perfectly well understood prohibition of the Church. If Pius IX as a young man had been the debauchee and the hypocrite that his enemies pretend, then his initiation as a Mason would be quite probable, but otherwise the reverse would be the case. Those who made this allegation were perfectly aware that such a lapse from the obligations of a Catholic would be fatal to the popular conception of Pius as an innocent lad who had consecrated his heart to God from early youth. As a result of this state of feeling, the assertion that Pius IX had been a Mason was indignantly contradicted by Catholics, while on the other hand many anticlericals were eager to discover documentary evidence which would place the allegation beyond dispute. As usual, the Pope's assailants were not wanting in audacity. The mere absence of anything that could be called evidence, did not deter them from circulating the most precise statements on the subject. It would be useless to multiply illustrations. Let the following sentence from a work published as late as 1880 serve as a specimen of the rest : " In 1805," says Lachâtre in his account of Pius IX, " Mastai had himself affiliated to a *Vendita*[7] of the Carbonari at Macerata, and earlier still he had been enrolled among the Freemasons of Sinigaglia, where his name is entered upon the register of

---

[6] Trollope, *Pius IX*, I, p. 10 note.

[7] Literally " sale " ; this was the name given to reunions of the Carbonari.

the lodge."[8] None the less if we accepted all the statements thus boldly put forward we should have to believe that Mastai had been initiated a Freemason half a dozen times over and in as many different places ; which is not in itself likely. All the more keen then the desire among Masons themselves in their Masonic journals to produce unequivocal proof that the Head of the Church despite all his anathemas had been inconsistent enough to enrol himself at one time in their ranks.

Seemingly the earliest attempt to place the fact of Mastai's initiation beyond dispute was made in 1868. The *Monde Maçonnique* of Paris announced in February of that year that satisfactory evidence was forthcoming from Sicily which would be placed before their readers without delay. The promise was not redeemed until August, when it appeared that the evidence, such as it was, though sent from Messina, referred not to Sicily but to Philadelphia in the United States. The account stated that Mastai " in the time of Gregory XVI " (sic), returning from a mission to Chile, passed through Philadelphia and being there initiated as a Mason was most diligent in attending the lodges. On one occasion in particular he delivered a speech containing the following sentences : " In truth it is from you, my illustrious brothers, that I receive to-day the true light. I have been up to this in the most dense fog. I am entirely convinced that Freemasonry is one of the noblest associations known to the world and I am proud to have been admitted a member." The extravagance of all this was too glaring even for the readers of the *Monde Maçonnique*. The simple fact was that Mastai on returning from his mission to Chile in 1825, seven years before Gregory XVI was elected Pope, came straight back from South America without ever setting foot in the northern continent at all. In the end inquiries were made in Philadelphia itself with the result that the *Monde Maçonnique* in February 1869 published the official replies received and declared itself satisfied that Pius IX had

[8] Lachâtre, *Histoire des Papes* (Edn. 1880), Vol. III, p. 351. The life of Pius IX is only found in this, the third edition.

never been initiated as a Mason in Philadelphia. Other attempts to supply evidence followed, but all collapsed upon investigation. It would be futile to go into details, but one case perhaps merits special notice on account of the quite marvellous play of the imagination for which some individual must have been responsible.

Shortly after the death of Pius IX another Masonic journal of Paris, the *Chaîne d'Union*, in its number for April 1878, printed a long letter from M. Lebrun, an architect and a Freemason, whom the editor declared to be a man whose veracity was above suspicion.[9] M. Lebrun described how in the year 1865 he had been in intimate business relations with a certain M. Déforges, who declared that he had been "godfather" to Pius IX on the occasion of his Masonic initiation. Pius IX was then, as he alleged, in a cavalry regiment serving under Napoleon and in garrison at Thionville. M. Déforges supplied many details about the gay, not to say dissipated, life then led by Mastai. He further declared that after Mastai became Pope he (Déforges) paid him a visit at the Vatican and was well received. The Pope talked over old times with him and called him jocosely "mon petit lieutenant."

Needless to dwell upon the chronological and other difficulties which at once raised vehement suspicions as to the trustworthiness of this narrative. Search was made in the military archives and it was found that J. M. Mastai had never served in Napoleon's army. Ultimately in the number for October 1878 (p. 371) the editor of the *Chaîne d'Union* admitted in express terms that Mastai had never served in a French regiment and, to use his own words : "Consequently Count Mastai Feretti never formed part of the garrison at Thionville. This is the best proof that he was never admitted as Mason in the lodge of this town."

We may pass over the photographs (sold in thousands) which by a process of more or less ingenious faking professed to be

[9] He introduced him as "bon Franc-maçon et citoyen d'une honorabilité incontestable et incapable d'avancer un fait quelconque à la légère."

likenesses taken of Pius IX as a young Abbé dressed in soutane and rabbat, but wearing at the same time a Masonic scarf with all its distinctive emblems. The contrivers of this unscrupulous fraud had evidently forgotten that long before photography came into use for taking portraits Mastai had been consecrated Archbishop and consequently would never have worn the particular form of ecclesiastical costume in which he was represented, even if he had been so crazy as to have his portrait taken in such a guise. It is, however, only right to mention that the Masonic journal *Chaîne d'Union* in 1885 (p. 367) strongly protested against the sale of these bogus photographs, fully admitting at the same time that they had beyond all question been produced by fraudulent means.

With regard to Sinigaglia it may briefly be said that when Pius IX was a young man, there was no Masonic lodge at Sinigaglia. Finally we may note that shortly after the publication of Leo XIII's antimasonic Encyclical *Humanum genus* another attempt was made to produce documentary evidence which would prove that Pius IX had himself been a Freemason. In an article in the *Monde Maçonnique* of Paris in 1885 a M. Léon Bigot professed to print the text of the diploma given to John Mastai Feretti by a Masonic lodge of the Scotch rite at Palermo in the first fortnight of August 1839. The moment the document was printed, its spuriousness was made manifest by a crowd of blunders and anachronisms which many of the Masonic fraternity were not slow to point out. Most glaring of all, in 1839 Mastai was Bishop of Imola (he was made Cardinal at the end of that same year), and his signatures in the registers and other official documents of the see showed that he had never quitted the town during the first fortnight of August when he was supposed to have been at Palermo. The forgery was completely and finally exposed in the rival Masonic journal the *Chaîne d'Union*, already mentioned, in a long article of 1st October, 1885.

But the most remarkable and significant of all the happenings connected with the alleged Freemasonry of Pius IX was the " *incident* Floquet," as it may conveniently be called, which occurred when M. Floquet was President of the French Chamber of Deputies, on 11th December, 1891. A member of the Government, M. Fallières, then Minister of Justice and of Worship, was delivering a speech upon the pretended aggressiveness of the French episcopate. There was a question of a certain admonitory circular calling the attention of the Bishops to this and that, when one of the deputies interpolated a taunting remark asking whether the circular had been previously submitted for approval to the heads of the French Freemasons. M. Fallières retorted that the question had nothing to do with Freemasonry, and a tremendous scene ensued of which the first phases are thus recorded in the *Journal Officiel*.

The President (*M. Floquet*) *addressing the Right.*

Surely you cannot be unaware that Freemasonry has been fully authorised for years past. What is more, it has numbered amongst its dignitaries many individuals who have belonged to your own party. (*Protests from the Right.* Hear, Hear, *from the Left.*)

M. Fallières. With your permission, gentlemen, I should like to say that this is a question upon which I can express no opinion, seeing that I myself am not a Freemason. (Uproar.)

The President. Very well, I who am a Freemason—

M. le Comte de Bernis. I can't congratulate you—

The President.—am able to tell you that Freemasonry has long ago been authorised. You know it perfectly well, you gentlemen who are making all this disturbance. (*Applause from the Left.*)

M. le Comte de Bernis. Authorised by whom ? By you I suppose.

The President. It has in particular been authorised by Pius IX, who belonged to that body (*Loud applause from all the benches on the Left and Centre. Protests from the Right.*)

Monseigneur Freppel. That is untrue (*C'est faux*).

M. le Comte de Bernis. This is atrocious. It is an imposture. I defy you to prove it. (*Loud exclamation from the Left.*)

M. de Baudry d'Asson. It is abominable.

M. le Comte de Bernis. An unparalleled piece of insolence.

M. de Baudry d'Asson. It is an abominable lie.

M. le Comte de Bernis. Prove it. I defy you to prove what you have stated.

Mgr. Freppel. It is a calumny.

(Meanwhile round after round of applause is addressed to the President from the same benches.)

It is impossible to quote further ; the scene was long protracted. The Right refused to allow the debate to proceed until the President explained his words. The President threatened penalties for obstruction and it seems characteristic of the methods of the Republican French Government that the first person to be " named," as we should say in English parliamentary procedure, was the Bishop of Angers, Mgr. Freppel, though to judge from the report, his attitude throughout had been perfectly correct and dignified. Member after member on the Right—M. le Comte de Mun, M. Paul de Cassagnac, M. Provost de Launay, etc.—rose to his feet, called upon the President to substantiate his words and declared himself ready to be called to order. " It is you, M. le Président, who ought to be called to order," ejaculated the Baron de Mackau indignantly. Eventually some sort of hearing was accorded to M. Fernand de Ramel, who evidently spoke as an authority on procedure and who, addressing himself to the President, urged very forcibly :

> You have laid aside your character as President, you have taken part in the discussion and in accordance with the Standing Orders of the House you ought to leave the presidential chair and come down to the tribune to make your explanation.

These protests were not without effect. The President seems to have murmured something about being exasperated beyond endurance, and also named the *Grand Dictionnaire* of Larousse as his authority for the statement made concerning Pius IX. That he could not have meant to insult the memory of Pius IX was, he declared, evident from the fact that he only attributed to him a quality which he was proud to claim for himself. This particular explanation was received with thunders of applause from the Left, but the futility of the logic is apparent when one reflects that by parity of reasoning it would be no libel for a married citizen to proclaim that the Pope had a wife and as many children as he had in his own family.

The inevitable result of such an incident was to revive the whole discussion. The old familiar stories were repeated, to be met with the same refutations. We are only concerned here to notice a challenge which in January 1892 was copied into several Italian newspapers and which had the effect of eliciting the following telegram addressed to the *Secolo* of Milan by Adriano Lemmi, Grand Master of the Italian Freemasons.

In consequence of the article which I read in No. 9252 of your Journal (7th Jan. 1892), and to put an end to further wild talk, I ask you to publish the following statement.

On the 12th of December last, the Chancery of the Grand Orient of France telegraphed to me to ask if I possessed any documents showing that Pius IX had been a Mason. The Chancellor of the Grand Orient of Italy, by my direction, replied in the following terms :

It has constantly been rumoured that Pius IX had belonged either to the Carbonari or to the Freemasons, but no serious documentary evidence has yet been produced to show that he had been initiated in any of the Reunions (*Vendite*) [10] or Lodges of Italy.

[10] *Vendite* (sales) as previously explained was the technical name of the meetings of the Carbonari. Such pretended "sales" were the natural occasions when charcoal burners would come together to discuss their secret purposes.

In this way it will be seen that all the insinuations of clericals and renegades fall to the ground.

Adriano Lemmi, Grand Master of the Italian Freemasons. By the "insinuations of clericals" Lemmi presumably means the suggestion that the Freemasons wished to claim Pius IX as a member of their body, although they were well aware that no evidence existed of his ever having joined them. Finally, to our thinking, the most satisfactory proof of all, if further evidence is needed, is the fact that three times over, the question of the Freemasonry of Pius IX has been raised in the *Intermédiaire*, the French equivalent of the English weekly, *Notes and Queries*. The French journal, like the English, is read by a large number of literary people, interested in out-of-the-way scraps of information, and is rather anti-clerical in tone. On each occasion no serious attempt has been made to furnish evidence of the initiation of John Mastai. On the contrary, Freemasons of standing have written to declare that the discussions in Masonic journals had made the fact plain that no such evidence existed.

"It is now ten years," said a contributor, who described himself as a former member of the Council of the Grand Orient of France, "that this story has been in circulation, and surely it is a surprising thing that not a single one of the Pope's contemporaries [this was written in 1874 when Pius IX was still living], has come forward to say that he remembered meeting him in a Masonic lodge"; and then the writer goes on to describe in detail the utter collapse of every attempt to supply definite information.[11] To letters written to the *Intermédiaire* in this tone, practically no answer was attempted either on this or any subsequent occasion.[12] It does not seem too much to infer that this may be taken as a final decision of the question so much debated.

But even now this ridiculous calumny is still circulated. In 1922, there was published in London a pretentious work[13] by

---

[11] See *L'Intermédiaire*, Vol. III, p. 702. 10 Dec. 1874.
[12] See Vol. XVIII (1885), pp. 322, 461, 492 and Vol. XXIV (1891), p. 999.
[13] *Roman Catholicism and Freemasonry*, London, W. Rider, 1922.

F

Mr. Dudley Wright, who is now the editor of an English Masonic journal and who on the title page proclaims himself the author of several books dealing with Masonry. The numerous misprints and blunders which occur in the volume do not give a very favourable idea of the writer's level of education, but that does not prevent him from making many categorical statements as to matters of fact, which in almost every case are unsupported by any verifiable reference. After devoting some forty pages, almost entirely made up of extracts from contemporary newspaper attacks, to Pius IX's Allocution *Multiplices inter* (1865) against secret societies, Mr. Wright remarks :

> But strange to say, there is no doubt that Pius IX was himself a Freemason. His signature still exists in the books of one of the Italian Lodges of Montevideo. Shortly after his ordination Mastai Ferretti was sent as Auditor to the Vicar-General of Chile, and at one time it was believed that he was initiated into Freemasonry in that country. When in later years he was appointed Apostolic Delegate in Uruguay, he appeared in the Lodges as a fully qualified Freemason, and a writer in the *Libertad del Pensamiento*, a Madrid journal, in 1870, said that there was in existence in the possession of one whose name he gave (Soussingeas) a portrait of the Pope in Masonic regalia. Quite recently [! !],[14] however, any doubt that may have existed on the question was put on one side by the discovery of the initiation of Pope Pius IX into Freemasonry in the Lodge Eterna Catena of Palermo on 15 August 1839."[15]

One might have thought that Mr. Dudley Wright would have seen some slight improbability in the story of Mastai's initiation as a Mason at Palermo on the feast of the Assumption in 1839, seeing that at that date he had already been an Arch-

[14] This " quite recently " gives an idea of Mr. Dudley Wright's trustworthiness. The Palermo story, as stated above, was exposed by the Masonic journal *Chaîne d'Union* in 1885.

[15] *Roman Catholicism and Freemasonry*, p. 172.

bishop for more than twelve years.[16]   Even prudential motives
ought to have restrained him from such an indiscretion—for
his handsome face was as well known as any in Italy—on the very
eve of his promotion to the Cardinalate. But Mr. Wright
knows more than this, and it will again be best to let him tell
the rest of the story himself.

In 1874 [says Mr. Wright] the *Voice of Masonry* published
the following item of news :

" At the semi-annual meeting of the Grand Lodge of
Masons, Scottish Rite, of the Orient of Palermo, Italy [sic], on
27th March last, Pope Pius IX. was excommunicated from
the Order.   The decree of expulsion was published in the
official Masonic paper at Cologne, Germany [it seems a
little curious that the Italian, or rather Sicilian, Masons
should go so far afield to publish their decrees], and is
preceded by the minute of the Lodge in which he was
initiated, and is as follows :

" ' A man named Mastai Ferretti, who received the
baptism of Freemasonry, and solemnly pledged his love and
fellowship, and who afterwards was crowned Pope and
King, under the title of Pio Nono, has now cursed his former
Brethren and excommunicated all members of the Order
of Freemasons.   Therefore, said Mastai Ferretti is herewith,
by decree of the Grand Lodge of the Orient, Palermo,
expelled from the Order for perjury.'

" The charges against him were first prepared in his
Lodge at Palermo in 1865, and notification and copy thereof
sent to him, with a request to attend the Lodge for the
purpose of answering the same.   To this he made no reply,
and for divers reasons the charges were not pressed until he
urged the Bishops of Brazil to act aggressively towards the
Freemasons.   Then they were pressed, and, after a regular

[16] Imola, though a suffragan see, was regarded as a diocese of great importance, and its bishops were at that time almost invariably raised to the
Cardinalate. Mastai had been made Archbishop of Spoleto in 1827, but
was translated to Imola in 1832. He was named Cardinal (*in petto*) five
months after the supposed date of his initiation as a Freemason.

trial, a decree of expulsion was entered and published, the same being signed by Victor Emmanuel, King of Italy, and Grand Master of the Orient of Italy."

The King thus returned his compliments for the " major excommunication " which the Pope had sent him a few years previously " with the Pope's kind regards." " It is difficult," said the *Pall Mall Gazette* in October 1874, " to see what retort Pius IX can make to this decree, unless indeed he has in reserve some still more formidable maledictory missile to launch at the Grand Lodge of the Orient. But in these days, unfortunately, a papal anathema is hardly as terrible as a Masonic decree."[17]

This is the sort of rubbish which, as a legacy from such shameless calumniators as Count Pianciani and Léo Taxil, is still served up, even in England, to the readers of *The Freemason* and *The Masonic News*, to which journals Mr. Dudley Wright has successively acted as editor. In Italy the campaign of slander conducted against Pius IX for more than thirty years found its climax in a peculiarly disgraceful outrage which marked the passage of the remains of that Pontiff to their final resting-place. It may be explained that it is the traditional custom on the death of a Pope that the body should be deposited temporarily for the space of some two years in the walls of St. Peter's and then conveyed to the tomb prepared for it elsewhere, in this case the basilica of San Lorenzo *fuori le mura*. I quote the account of the incident sent to the *Times* by its Roman correspondent and copied in *The Tablet* for July 16th, 1881.

Rome, July 13. The hope, and indeed the general expectation, that the removal of the remains of Pius IX would be effected in perfect order has been woefully disappointed. Upon whom rests the responsibility for the grave scandal that has occurred, I must, for the present, leave you to gather from a simple narration of the facts. A mere rumour on Monday afternoon that the body of the late Pope was to be removed completely absorbed public attention during

[17] Wright, *Roman Catholicism and Freemasonry* (1922), pp. 174–175.

the whole of yesterday. By 11 o'clock in the evening the streets from one side of the city to the other along which the *cortège* would pass were lined with people. All the most respectable part of the population, with their wives and families, were outdoors, and the Piazza of St. Peter's was crowded. In the corner close to the archway to the sacristy and the door called Santa Marta, a great number of persons with torches were assembled, but beyond that point no one was permitted to pass. A few minutes after midnight a funeral car, covered with a splendid crimson velvet pall surmounted by a cushion, and drawn by six horses, came through the archway, preceded by a plain, closed carriage, and followed by four others, in which were seated those members of the Chapter of St. Peter's, and others whose official duty it was to consign the body to those waiting to receive it at San Lorenzo. As this simple *cortège* passed into the piazza the torchbearers I have mentioned, among whom were many ladies and even children, formed themselves in a line behind—a line which extended completely across the piazza. The number of torches was estimated at 2,000. As the procession moved, those taking part in it chanted prayers for the dead, but it had scarcely proceeded half the distance to the Bridge of St. Angelo when the existence of a disturbing element became manifest. Some men began singing popular songs in parody of the chanting and cries of an antagonistic and insulting character were raised. This, however, was but the beginning. As the *cortège* passed along the streets forming what is called the Strada Papale these excesses increased in violence, and I may state at once that they were perpetrated all along the route by a distinct group of persons who, as fast as they were dispersed by the police at one point, darted down the side streets and reappeared with increasing audacity further on. Their number has been variously estimated at from 40 to 100. Near the Piazza Venezia they made an attempt to extinguish some of the torches, and a momentary conflict took place. To prevent greater disorders, some troops were drawn across the ascent to the Magnapoli, but, proving insufficient, the cordon was broken and the assailants tore along the Via Nazionale, heading the procession and singing " Garibaldi's Hymn." At the Piazza di Termini stones were thrown at the carriages. Here again the police endeavoured to form a cordon, but they were unable to stand their ground, but two companies of soldiers coming up, the Italian Riot Act, in the form of a peremptory legal intimation and three trumpet calls, was read, and the rioters dispersed, to reappear again in full force in front of the Basilica San Lorenzo as the funeral car came up. Here the scene beggars all description. The rioters, the torchbearers, and the people already assembled in the piazza there, were in a moment mixed up in a tumultuous mass surging round the car and between the carriages, the rioters howling and yelling, the women screaming, and the police striving with might and main to restore order. The legal intimation and the three loud trumpet calls were made, and the mob fell back for a moment to regain its ground as quickly. A second and a third time were the three trumpet calls blown before any clearance could be effected, and finally, after a determined struggle, the car was backed up to the iron gateway of the portico. The coffin was got out as quickly as its enormous weight permitted, and it was immediately rolled into the church, the doors were closed, and the funeral rites, which, with various official acts to be performed, were not concluded when I left the Basilica at four o'clock this morning, commenced in peace.

As might be expected, the occurrence of such an incident was the signal for the outbreak of a flood of newspaper polemics. The anti-clerical journals sought to throw the whole blame for the disturbance on the ecclesiastical authorities, though some of them, unrebuked by the Government, wrote in such terms as these : " The carrion (*carogna*) of Pius IX . . . but for the bayonets of the soldiers and the revolvers of the police, would have been flung out of the hearse. . . . The clericals were hissed and we applaud the hisses. We should have applauded even more loudly if the remains of the old booby (*sciocco*) had been thrown from the Bridge of St. Angelo into the Tiber." A few of the rioters were arrested and light sentences passed upon them. But every legal expedient was resorted to to impede the execution of even this modicum of justice. It was not until two months later that the final court of appeal was reached. In a long and reasoned judgment the Court exonerated the participants in the procession from all blame and confirmed the sentences. A full account of the disturbance was included in this statement which corroborates in all essentials the description of the *Times* correspondent quoted above.[18]

---

[18] The more important passages of the judgment are printed in *The Tablet* for September 10, 1881, p. 414.

CHAPTER V

WHY POPE CLEMENT XII CONDEMNED
FREEMASONRY

So much of the calumny with which the Papacy has been
assailed in modern times has come from the workshops of the
Continental Grand Orients, and the plea has so often been put
forward by their Anglo-Saxon associates that the Popes themselves have been the assailants and have provoked such reprisals,
that I cannot think it alien to the purpose of the present work to
discuss the origin of these hostilities in some little detail. It is
perhaps not unnatural that those non-Catholics who have
become members of Masonic lodges for social, political or even
professional reasons, should feel a certain resentment at the severe
terms in which the organisation has for many years past been
denounced by the Church in a long series of pontifical enactments. In English-speaking countries the majority of Masons,
as we may gladly recognise, are law-abiding citizens who have
no thought of attacking religion or plotting against the existing
social order, while many are conspicuously charitable, responding
to almost any appeal made in behalf of education, philanthropy
and mutual good will. Nevertheless in the year 1738 when
the " Speculative " Masonry with which we are now familiar
was still only in its infancy, Pope Clement XII published the
Bull *In eminenti* condemning the whole institution as fundamentally deistic and immoral. Moreover the Roman Pontiffs
his successors have never receded from that position, but have
continued to stigmatise the Craft and its aims, holding it
responsible in very large measure for the anti-Christian principles which produced the French Revolution, and for the

legacy of communism, sedition and intrigue which forms so grave a menace to the peace of modern states.

It is not, however, the purpose of the present chapter to discuss the abstract problem of the unlawfulness of secret societies, or to enlarge upon the fierce anti-clericalism of that militant continental Masonry with which the Papacy is most nearly in contact.   Much might be written on both these heads, but I am anxious here to lay stress upon the historical background of the first condemnation of the movement, for there are aspects in the case which have been little noticed and which seem to constitute a full justification of the strong measures then adopted. Apart from certain denunciatory epithets which may be described as the " common form " of such pronouncements, there is nothing exaggerated in the language of the Bull, no statement of fact which cannot be substantiated by contemporary evidence.   Few Masons, I am convinced, have any sort of idea of the solid grounds which the Holy See then had for regarding their mysterious society with mistrust ; and, as I have elsewhere had occasion to argue, Voltaire, the Encyclopedists, the leaders of the French Revolution, Garibaldi, Mazzini, Margiotta, Lemmi, Nathan, Pike and other prominent members of the Craft, have surely done their best not only to justify the very worst forebodings outlined by Pope Clement in 1738, but also to exclude the possibility of any mitigation of the anathemas which he was the first to promulgate.

But before we go further it will be well to have before us the terms of the Papal decree.   The portion relevant to the purpose of this chapter is of no great length, but it contains the grounds upon which the prohibition of such secret organisations was based.   The rest of the document only enforces the warning by enacting the penalties of excommunication against those Catholics who refuse to obey its mandate.   The Pope says :

It has come to our knowledge and indeed it is a matter of public notoriety, that there has been a great development, spreading far and wide and growing in strength from day to day, of certain Societies, Meetings, Clubs, Reunions,

Conventicles or Lodges, commonly known by the name of
" Liberi Muratori," " Francs Maçons," or otherwise
variously designated according to the local idiom, in which
men of no matter what religion and sect, content with a
certain affectation of natural virtue, are mutually banded
together in a close and exclusive league, in accordance with
laws and statutes which they have framed for themselves.
Further they concert measures in secrecy and are bound
under extravagant penalties by an oath taken on the Bible
to shroud their activities in impenetrable silence. Since,
however, it is of the very nature of wrong-doing to betray
itself and to give itself away by the outcry which it raises,
hence the aforesaid associations or assemblies have excited
such vehement suspicion in the minds of the Faithful that
to enroll oneself in these Lodges is in the judgment of men
of sense and high principle tantamount to incurring the
stigma of a libertine and a miscreant ; for assuredly if such
people were not doing evil they would never have so much
hatred of the light. Moreover their ill-repute has spread
to such a degree that in very many countries the associations
aforesaid have some time ago been proscribed by secular
rulers and have been wisely suppressed as dangerous to
the safety of the realm.

To economise space it will be convenient to sum up the allegations contained in this indictment of primitive Freemasonry
under the following five heads : (i) rapid extension ; (ii)
naturalistic, i.e., deistic principles ; (iii) extravagant oath of
secrecy ; (iv) evil repute of the members and (v) hostility on
the part of the civil authorities. I propose to say a few words
about each, but to take these points in the reverse order,
beginning with the last.

While there is no dispute at all about the fact that organised
" speculative " Masonry began with the foundation of the
Grand Lodge of England in 1717, there is considerable obscurity,
as the best authorities admit, regarding the early propagation
of the Craft in foreign countries. It is quite unnecessary to

attempt to discuss the matter here.   The one point which stands
out beyond the possibility of question is that the Roman Pontiff
was not the first to take alarm at the rapid extension of the new
organisation and to decide that the occasion called for effective
measures of repression.   It was apparently the Dutch Republic,
which certainly was not swayed by any papistical sympathies,
that opened the campaign in November 1735, two and a half
years before Pope Clement published his Bull.   In the English
periodical called the *Political State* for January 1736 we may
read :

> Some private societies of gentlemen, who call themselves
> Freemasons, having been set up in Holland, the mob began
> first to show their dislike to such meetings by threatening
> to pull the Lodge about their ears, but soon after the States
> of Holland thought fit, it seems, to pass a resolution against
> such private assemblies.

After quoting the terms of the " Plakkaat " by which these
meetings were prohibited at Amsterdam, the account goes on :

> Such another " Plakkaat " has been published against
> them at the Hague and 'tis said their Lodges or assemblies
> are to be suppressed throughout the whole province of
> Holland ; for the Dutch, it seems, look upon them as
> academies, not only of libertinism and debauchery, but of
> faction and rebellion, and therefore those who keep or
> frequent such assemblies, are to be punished as disturbers
> of the public tranquillity.

May I be pardoned for emphasising the statement that the
Dutch looked upon the Lodges " as academies of libertinism
and debauchery " as well as of sedition, for this deserves to be
remembered in connection with one of the other counts made
prominent in the Papal indictment.

Passing to France, which at that time still exercised a pre-
dominant influence in the counsels of Europe, we find that before
the beginning of April 1737 active measures were being taken
against the Masonic fraternity.   The English news-journals
make frequent reference to the subject.   There was evidently

at first a good deal of talk in Paris about the sensation which this mysterious society was producing and the rapidity with which it had spread. The " Mémoires " of the Duc de Luynes under date March 9 and March 18, 1737, have long paragraphs on the subject, and the Parisian gossip finds its echo in such a newspaper as the London *Evening Post*, which on March 17 reports from that city :

> The Order of Free-Masons lately established here meets with great success ; everyone is desirous of being admitted a member, and numbers are daily *taken in* at the expense of ten louis-d'ors each. Among them are the Prince of Conti, all the young dukes, M. de Maurepas, M. Saint-Florentin, etc. There are nineteen lodges already constituted. The Ladies are about to establish a counter-Order in imitation of this, to which none will be admitted but such as know how to keep a secret.

The note of persiflage in this and some similar references is patent enough, but there were other journals which took the matter seriously and an article which appeared in the *Craftsman* for April 16, 1737, was very widely reproduced. A single sentence is to our purpose here :

> I know that these men [the Freemasons] are generally looked upon in England as a parcel of idle people who meet together only to make merry and play some ridiculous pranks, but it is very plain that the wise Governments of France and Holland look upon them in a very different light ; and I humbly hope to see my own country follow the example of the latter by suppressing such dangerous assemblies.

There can be no question that the French authorities at that date were thoroughly in earnest in their determination to nip the movement in the bud. A brief report of one of the raids which then took place may be cited from the *London Evening Post*.[1]

> The 2 of August N. S., the Lieut. General of the Police

[1] See the issues for July 28 and August 2, 1737.

of Paris, went to the French Freemasons Lodge, attended with his posse, where he broke open the door and brought away all the ensigns of their order, such as trowels, leather aprons, hammers, registers of reception etc. with a severe prohibition to all taverns, ordinaries, eating-houses etc. to harbour them.

If the Duc de Luynes may be trusted, the authorities had been considerably influenced in this matter by the report of the French Ambassador in Holland.   He informed them that the Dutch Police had not only obtained possession of a copy of the Masonic oath but that they had discovered the existence of a political cabal to get the Prince of Nassau elected Stadtholder, the majority of the persons implicated being Freemasons.[2]

While France might conceivably be supposed to have been swayed by Catholic prejudices, the reverse at any rate would have been the case at Geneva.   Nevertheless we learn that when a lodge, known by the name of " Le parfait Contentement," was founded there by certain Englishmen in 1736, the Genevan clergy protested vigorously, and after full discussion the Council decided that the Master of the Lodge, one George Hamilton, should be forbidden to enrol any of the citizens in his Society.[3] The fact of this hostile action of the Protestant Cantons is not denied by the most scholarly Masonic writers of our own day, and Dr. W. Chetwode Crawley regretfully informs his readers[4] that though " the name of Switzerland has ever been associated with freedom, yet the Cantons of Geneva and Berne were among the first to suppress the Lodges and to proscribe the Fraternity."

Much the same suspicion of the new organisation seems to have been manifested in Germany, for we find the London *Evening Post* of October 22nd, 1737, reproducing part of a letter from Heidelberg to the following effect :

As a Lodge of Free-Masons, who pretend to derive their

[2] *Mémoires du Duc de Luynes*, Vol. I, p. 240.

[3] A. Singer, *Der Kampf Roms gegen die Freimaurerei* (1925), p. 12.

[4] In the learned Masonic periodical *Ars Quatuor Coronatorum*, Vol. XXIV (1911), p. 107.

origin from the building of the tower of Babel, has been lately established at Mannheim, our Elector in order to extirpate that Society, has published an edict forbidding all officers and soldiers of his troops, and generally everyone of his subjects, of what rank or condition soever, to enter into it upon pain of being broke and incurring the indignation of his Electoral Highness.

In Hamburg again, though it was a free town and by no means likely to be influenced by Papal anathemas, the burghers in 1738 took the alarm and warned all public officials under threat of severe penalties not to allow themselves to be associated in any way with the Masonic lodges.[5] Moreover the same well-informed work which supplies this information states that a proclamation against Freemasonry was said to have been published in Stockholm, also in 1738, though the writer declares that he had not sufficient information to be able to affirm the fact for a certainty.[6]

In the light of these few quotations, which might be added to, it is abundantly clear that Pope Clement was justified in saying that before he issued his decree the Masonic lodges in very many countries had already been proscribed by secular rulers.

But to come now to heading iv. Was Clement misrepresenting the popular feeling of his contemporaries when he stated that by the mere fact of becoming a Mason, a man wrote himself down as a libertine and a miscreant (*pravitatis et perversionis notam incurrere*) ?

I can only answer that there is a quite curious amount of evidence that in using such language the Pope was echoing a wide-spread belief which existed among Protestants as well as among Catholics and was very general even in far-off England. But in order to deal with this point more thoroughly it will be necessary to touch upon another heading (No. i), i.e., the question of the spread of secret societies and the confused ideas regarding

[5] I take this from a German work, *Der neu-aufgestreckte Brennende Leuchter des Freymaurer-Ordens*, published at Leipzig in 1746, p. 80. It is written altogether from the Masonic standpoint and the author was evidently in close touch with Dr. Anderson, the editor of the English Constitutions. [6] Ibid., p. 88.

them which must inevitably have resulted in the popular mind. When the Bull *In eminenti* used an array of synonyms, *societates, coetus, conventus*, etc., to designate the parties aimed at in the decree, we may fairly assume that there was no idea of limiting the ban to one particular form of secret organisation. The " Liberi Muratori " were most talked about, but Clement could not undertake to define what associations might be comprehended under that term. His edict was directed against the whole class. In Book IV of the *Dunciad*[7] the poet Alexander Pope jeers at the Freemasons, coupling them with two other societies known as Gregorians and Gormogons, and W. J. Courthope in his note on the passage very truly remarks that " throughout the eighteenth century there was a mania both in England and on the Continent for joining secret societies, some of which were formed merely for convivial, but others for political purposes."[8]   Similarly the late Professor Troeltsch, a Lutheran, notes that " the eighteenth century was crowded with secret societies and free-thought unions, the secrecy being resorted to partly as a protection against the power of the State Church and partly as a means of attracting the masses or, as it might be, of outrivalling the attractions of Church life."[9]   An interesting example of the resulting vagueness in the use of terms may be cited from the *Political State* for April 1736, two years before the publication of Clement's Bull.   The bantering tone is, of course, only to be expected in an English journal commenting on matters of Papal administration.

A society was some time since erected at Rome under the name of " La Cuchiara," after the model of the society of Freemasons here in England,[10] but the priests at Rome

---

[7] Lines 571–576.

[8] Pope's Works, edited by Elwin and Courthope, iv, p. 376.

[9] See *The Encyclopedia of Religion and Ethics*, VI, p. 122.

[10] Whether this was strictly speaking a lodge of Freemasons I am unable to say.   But another lodge, unquestionably Masonic, and different from the first, existed in Rome in 1735–1737, the Minute Book of which is still preserved. It seems to have been a political organisation of Jacobites, supporting the Pretender.   See the monograph of W. J. Hughan, *The Jacobite Lodge in*

being of opinion that no society but their own has a title to any mysteries, they looked upon this as an encroachment upon their privileges and therefore several persons, who were members of this new sort of mysterious society, were seized and imprisoned, and the Inquisition are busy in diving into their mysteries, but as yet they are as much in the dark about them as they are about their own, for the persons imprisoned will make no discoveries . . . Particularly the name their society assumed perplexes all the *literati* and all the dealers in mystery about Rome ; for as the word *cuchiara* in its literal sense signifies no more than a spoon, it is thought there must be some great mystery concealed under the metaphorical use of that word. But others who are apt to take things in their most natural meaning, imagine that the members of this society were great lovers of good eating, especially of good soups, for which reason they assumed the name of " La Cuchiara " and that for the same reason the Freemasons in England ought to give their society the name of " La Bichiera."

All this raillery plays round the widely-spread popular idea that carousals and deep potations formed one of the main purposes of Masonic reunions. The writer of the above seems to have shut his eyes deliberately to the fact that *cuchiara* meant not only a ladle but a mason's trowel—Florio is explicit upon the point—and consequently provided a natural title for any lodge of the initiated. *Bichiere* is a drinking cup, and the final suggestion, of course, amounts to this that the Masonic fraternity in England might appropriately be known as the Order of the Tankard.[11]

Thoroughly in accord with this idea are certain features in

Rome, 1910. The Grand Master of the Roman Lodge was George Seton, fifth Earl of Winton. Of him we read in the published Diary of Mary, Countess Cowper (p. 98) that " his natural character is that of a stubborn, illiterate, ill-bred Brute. He has eight wives."

[11] It is highly significant that, as early as 1723, R. Samber in his *Ebrietatis Encomium*, ch. XV, observes that the Freemasons are " very great friends of the vintners."

the pictures and prints of William Hogarth, the great English satirist of eighteenth century manners and morals. Hogarth was himself a Mason and consequently knew the Lodges from inside, but when in 1737–1738 he painted his series entitled "The Four Times of the Day," he deliberately chose, as the central figure of his picture "Night," a drunken Freemason, wearing the apron and all the insignia of the Order, who is reeling along supported by a boon companion. Further it is averred that in this intoxicated Worshipful Master we have a portrait of the best known police-magistrate of that day, Sir Thomas de Veil, who was also a Mason and a fellow-member with Hogarth of a lodge held at the Vine, Holborn. Some scandalised brethren have pleaded of late that Hogarth could not possibly have meant this, but Mr. Calvert, in an important work published in 1917 to commemorate the bicentenary of Freemasonry, shows little patience for such scruples. "If the figure," he says, "is intended to represent Sir Thomas de Veil, it is notorious that he was a debauchee, it is a fact that he was a member of the Fraternity, and it is obvious that he is drunk, and there's an end of it."[12]

But there is besides this much evidence in contemporary journalism—though I must confine myself here to one or two brief specimens—which indicates very clearly that in the popular mind at that period Freemasonry and dissipation were quite closely associated.

A paragraph in the *London Magazine* for March 1737[13] refers as follows to the first steps then recently taken in Paris for the suppression of the French lodges :

> The Society called Freemasons so famous and so much encouraged in this kingdom, having lately set up a lodge at Paris, the French nobility and gentry began to be as

---

[12] *The Grand Lodge of England*, 1717–1917, by Albert F. Calvert, P.M. (London, 1917), pp. 108–109.

[13] It is to be noted that at this period it was the regular custom for monthly journals to appear *after* the termination of the month of which they bore the imprint. The *London Magazine* for March was probably not printed before the beginning or middle of April.

fond of being admitted into it as even the British were, but as the French ministry are careful not to allow of any customs being introduced that might tend to debauch the morals of the people, and as this society seems greatly to promote drinking and tippling at taverns and ale-houses, an edict of the King's Council was immediately issued for suppressing it.

Three or four months later in the same year the *Gentleman's Magazine* for July communicated to its readers a piece of gossip recently forwarded from Rome.

The Society of Freemasons lately detected at Florence makes a great noise. They pass there for Quietists, but here 'tis said they are of the Epicurean sect and that there's no law too severe to deal with them. The Pope sent thither the Father Inquisitor of that [sic, ? the Holy] Office, post to Florence in order to prosecute them, at the request of the Grand Duke of Tuscany, who was absolutely resolved to extirpate the whole sect.

To this is appended the comment : " As His Highness is since dead, and the Duke of Lorraine who was made a Freemason in England[14] is to succeed, this persecution may not go far."

Probably the unsavoury reputation for dissolute habits which attached to the early initiates was also fostered in some measure by the malicious criticisms of such rival societies as that of the Gormogons. For example in the pamphlet entitled *The Grand Mystery of the Freemasons Discovered*, which was in effect a Gormogon manifesto, the Masons are described as drunkards who were " the standing jest of the vulgar and the derision of men of sense."[15] But perhaps more than anything else the connection with Masonry of some of the most notorious libertines who were the leading spirits of the Hell-Fire Clubs in George I's reign[16]

[14] Francis Stephen, Duke of Lorraine, is said to have been made a Master-mason at Houghton Hall, Norfolk, the residence of Sir Robert Walpole, in 1731, between November the fourth and the eleventh. He afterwards became Grand Duke of Tuscany and in 1745 Emperor, as Francis I.

[15] See the *Ars Quatuor Coronatorum*, Vol. VIII, p. 125.

[16] These clubs are not to be confounded with the Medmenham Hell-Fire Club of Wilkes and Francis Dashwood much later in the same century.

must have served to discredit the former in the popular estimation. The Duke of Wharton, whom Lord Mahon describes as a man of splendid talents, but who " had early plunged into the wildest excesses and professed the most godless doctrines "[17] had previously been President of one of the London Hell-Fire Clubs, but nevertheless in 1722 he was elected Grand Master of the Freemasons. It was not a squeamish age but even the Government of George I had felt constrained to make an effort to suppress the blasphemous orgies of which the Hell-Fire Clubs made little secret. On April 28th, 1721, an Order in Council, bringing the matter to the notice of the executive, was issued with the following preamble :

> His Majesty having received information which gave him great reason to suspect that there have been lately and still are, in and about the cities of London and Westminster, certain scandalous clubs and societies of young persons who meet together and in the most impious and blasphemous manner insult the most sacred principles of our holy religion, affront Almighty God Himself, and corrupt the minds and morals of one another ; and being resolved to make use of all the authority committed to him by Almighty God to punish such enormous offenders and to crush such shocking impieties, etc., etc.

The Lord Chamberlain is thereupon bidden to call together His Majesty's Justices of the Peace of Middlesex and Westminster and strictly to enjoin them to take effectual measures " for the utter suppression of all such detestable practices."

It has been suggested that this edict was aimed at the Freemasons, but there is certainly no ground for such an assumption. On the other hand there is every reason to connect this injunction with a satirical print belonging to the same period, which represents a debauch and bears the title " The Diabolical Masquerade, or the Dragon's Feast, as acted by the Hell-Fire

---

[17] Lord Mahon, *History of England from the Peace of Utrecht*, Vol. II, p. 27. Pope's portrait of " Wharton, the scorn and wonder of our days," a man " from no one vice exempt," is well known.

Club of Somerset House in the Strand." A poem is appended
in four stanzas, of which the first runs :

> Thus impious wretches, without fear or shame,
> Feast and sing praises in the Devil's name ;
> Deride those Sacred Powers they ought to dread
> And live, as if in Hell, before they're dead.[18]

It is easy, however, to understand that the vague rumours of
such excesses circulating among the people will have contributed
to lend a sinister reputation to all secret associations of which
the exact purpose and aim were not known. Moreover, as
already noticed, some of the leaders in the Hell-Fire scandals
developed into prominent Freemasons. One of the most
scholarly historians of the Craft, in their leading periodical,
has written of the Marquess, afterwards Duke, of Wharton as
follows :[19]

> During his sojourn in Ireland (1717–1719) Wharton
> seems to have come into contact with an even more con-
> summate profligate, the first Earl of Rosse. This nobleman
> was no whit Wharton's inferior in reckless debauchery or
> intellectual ability, and far his superior in personal courage
> and honour. The two boon companions sat on the same
> benches and spoke and voted on the same side in the Irish
> House of Lords. The elder peer, the Earl of Rosse, was just
> the man to dominate the younger and the weaker, and in
> the comparatively limited social circles of Dublin must
> have been in constant contact with him. Just as the one
> was credited in the gossip of the day with being the guiding
> spirit of the Hellfire Club in Dublin, so the other emulated
> that sorry distinction in London. Now the extraordinary
> thing about this pair of peers is that each of them became
> Grand Master of Freemasons.

[18] See G. W. Reid, *Political and Personal Satires*, Vol. II, p. 588, No. 1719.

[19] See the *Ars Quatuor Coronatorum*, Vol. VIII (1895), p. 145, Lord Rosse
was Grand Master in Dublin in 1726 ; the Duke of Wharton in London in
1722. It was under the auspices of the Duke of Wharton that " the Constitutions of the Freemasons " were drafted by Dr. Anderson and printed in
1723.

Dr. Chetwode Crawley, the author of this statement, was himself an ardent Mason and by no means friendly to Catholicism. In some of his articles he has protested, not without bitterness, against the violence of the Papal anathemas. But has he not here supplied considerable justification for the harsh judgment which Clement felt called upon to pronounce in 1738 upon the moral principles of the early members of the Craft? A mysterious association of recent growth, veiling all their purposes and activities in the profoundest secrecy, but of which such men as Wharton and Rosse were the elected chiefs —and there were others of the same kidney—could hardly fail to inspire distrust in any well-ordered community.

It is not possible, without unduly protracting this excursus, to say more than a few words of the remaining counts in the Papal indictment. That the Pontiff was right in condemning the extravagant terms and blood-curdling penalties of the oath hardly anyone will dispute. It is now frankly admitted by Masonic writers that the various betrayals and exposures of the secrets of the Craft, beginning with " The Mason's Examination " published in the *Post Boy* as early as 1723, were made by people who were perfectly well-informed. The brethren did their utmost to suppress this issue of the paper, tearing the pages out of the copies in the Coffee Houses and buying up all they could find at half-a-crown or five shillings a copy, but naturally they failed. Indeed it is to these very exposures that the Masons themselves now turn for information as to the earliest procedure of the lodges.[20] Moreover the information obtained in Paris by M. Hérault, the Lieutenant-General of the police, through the intermediary of a courtesan, seems to have been quite reliable. Freemasons like Bertrin du Rocheret were in a frenzy of panic because their grips and passwords were becoming matter of common gossip[21] and it is practically certain that all this information was passed on to the Papal court. The apology

[20] See the article of Mr. Herbert Poole in the *Ars Quatuor Coronatorum*, Vol. XXXVII (1924), pp. 4-43.

[21] See A. Cherel, *Un Aventurier religieux au XVIIIème siècle—André Michel Ramsay* (Paris, 1926), p. 56.

for Masonry delivered at Paris by the Chevalier Ramsay was
publicly burnt in Rome early in 1739 by order of the Holy
Office.[22]

Finally, the Deistic tendencies of this secret organisation are
plainly indicated even in the text of the " Old Charges," and it
may be noted that Professor Cherel has quite recently made it
clear that the Chevalier Ramsay, the principal agent of Masonic
propaganda in France, like his friend and spiritual mother,
Madame Guyon, always retained a deep sympathy for a
mitigated form of naturalistic religion in spite of his outward
acceptance of the teachings of Catholicism.

It would seem, then, that Pope Clement XII in 1738 had
ample grounds for his attitude of suspicion, and that he was
only doing his duty as a vigilant pastor in seeking to protect his
flock from the contamination which he apprehended. Deism,
that form of religion, or irreligion, which consists in the rejection
of all revealed doctrine, was the great danger of the age, and it
was being insidiously propagated by such men as Bolingbroke,
Matthew Tindal, Toland and their sympathisers on the Continent. The teachings of Freemasonry, as many of its own
supporters frankly admit, were beyond all question Deistic from
the first, and the trend of its further developments, more particularly outside England, has always been in the direction of
a complete repudiation of creeds and of any sort of ecclesiastical
authority.

---

[22] *The Gentlemen's Magazine*, April (1739), p. 219.

Chapter VI

ON SOME MEDIEVAL FABLES

THE bitter hostility of which the Popes have often been the object has arisen in many different ways and manifests itself in many different fashions. In Latin countries the causes of this hatred have been largely political, as we have seen, but even though all positive ground of complaint on that score has ceased since the occupation of Rome in 1870, the tradition of fierce malevolence is still kept alive by Masonic and other anti-clerical organisations and the campaign is carried on with a fanaticism which is unscrupulous as to the methods it employs.

In England the attitude even of the extremely bigoted Evangelical is much more negative. He dislikes the Papacy because he resents the idea of any foreigner claiming spiritual dominion over Englishmen and because he has been told all sorts of things about the horrible greed and corrupt morals of the Roman Court. But prejudice in this matter has long been dying down in this country. The more violent attacks upon the Holy See are now for the most part confined to cheap and nasty books, pamphlets and newspapers, which are discredited by their illiteracy and their very get up. For this reason one cannot speak in terms too severe of an attempt made some few years ago to push in this country a substantial volume which, after the manner of the Continental anti-clericals, revived the most preposterous fables to the discredit of the Papacy, gilding the pill for light-minded readers with the promise of a salacious setting. For several months together in the years 1911–1912 an advertise-

ment was inserted in various highly respectable journals[1] which
has an intimate bearing upon our present subject, and which,
in spite of its length, it seems desirable to reproduce entire.
The headlines of the original were conspicuous from afar in
characters too large to be conveniently imitated, but the text
of the announcement ran as follows :

At all Libraries and Booksellers throughout the United Kingdom.

THE LOVE AFFAIRS OF THE VATICAN

By Dr. ANGELO S. RAPPOPORT. Illustrated, 16s. net.

The history of Rome and the Popes has often been
treated in an exhaustive manner, but there is scarcely
any authoritative work dealing with the more intimate side
of the affairs of the Vatican. Dr. A. S. Rappoport, who
has made a special study of the lighter side of history, and
especially of the influence exercised by the favourites of
kings and queens upon the politics of nations, endeavours
to show the important part played by the favourites of
the Popes in the history of the Vatican and Christianity.
As an impartial historian this author draws attention to
the discrepancy existing between the noble and sublime
teaching of Christ and the practice of His followers.

Beginning with the earliest history of the Bishops of
Rome, who soon became the spiritual rulers of Christendom,
he deals with the morality of the priests and the various
love affairs of the Popes. The word of the Prophet, " And
the women rule over us," may literally be applied to the
history of the Papacy during the Middle Ages and the
Renaissance. For not only were such famous courtesans
as Theodora and Marozia the actual rulers of the Vatican,
and in possession of the Keys of Heaven, but a woman
one day ascended the throne of St. Peter and became Pope.

[1] The advertisement spoken of may be found, for example, in *The Times
Literary Supplement* for February 29, 1912. The publishers were Stanley Paul
and Co. The book afterwards disappeared from their lists, and was issued
in an abridged form with the imprint, " London, Barter's Handbooks, 12
York Buildings, Adelphi, W.C." But Messrs. Stanley Paul have since
published other volumes by Dr. Rappoport, notably *Splendid Sons of Sin*, 1928.

The author further relates the story of Pope Alexander VI. and Signora Venozza, of Pope Leo X. and a French Court beauty, of Sixtus V. and the beautiful English heretic Anna Osten, of Innocent X. and his sister-in-law Olympia, and of many other Popes. Dr. Rappoport is a philosopher as well as a master of light biographical literature, and unobtrusively he teaches a lesson and draws a moral ! Whilst exposing the intrigues of the Papal Court, he does justice to such Popes as were worthy Vicars of Christ.

The significance of this manifesto is enhanced in the sheet actually before us, by its being printed immediately below a companion description, in equally conspicuous type, of *The Life of Cesare Borgia*, by Rafael Sabatini. Indeed it is impossible to say to which of the two books an announcement belongs, which shrieks at the reader midway between the two prospectuses:

FIRST EDITION SOLD IN A FEW DAYS

*₊*SECOND EDITION BEING RAPIDLY EXHAUSTED

THIRD EDITION IN PREPARATION

Of the Borgia book, we are told among other things,

It is a record of certain very human, strenuous men in a very human, strenuous age ; a lustful, flamboyant age ; an age red with blood and pale with passion at white heat ; an age of steel and velvet, of vivid colour, dazzling light and impenetrable shadow ; an age of swift movement, pitiless violence and high endeavour, of sharp antithesis and amazing contrasts, and one which had become unable to discriminate between the merits of the Saints of the Church and the Harlots of the Town. Therefore, it honoured both alike, extolled the carnal merits of the one in much the same terms as were employed to extol the spiritual merits of the other.

The volumes were issued at an uniform price of 16s. net, and at the top of the column an arresting hand points to the confident challenge

☞ THE TWO MOST SUCCESSFUL BOOKS OF 1912

To return to Dr. Rappoport's volume, with which alone we are here concerned, it is plain that unless we attribute to the publishers a deliberate intention of misleading the public, the description above quoted committed them to a good deal. In the first place it is clearly implied that the book is a serious contribution to our knowledge of the past. In speaking of the author as an " impartial historian," as " a philosopher as well as a master of light biographical literature," and in declaring that " scarcely any authoritative work " dealing with the influence of women at the Vatican has yet appeared, the publishers must certainly have intended to convey that this *was* an authoritative work and the result of special study.

Secondly, the claim is made that the book is written with a high moral purpose and that it is impartial, so that the worthy Popes have had justice done to them.

Thirdly, certain definite items in the contents are specified. We are told, what would materially enhance the interest of English readers, that Dr. Rappoport relates the story of Sixtus V. and the beautiful English heretic, Anna Osten. Scandals are promised concerning Leo X and a French Court beauty, and as a climax, likely to arouse attention in those feminist days, we are assured that " a woman one day ascended the throne of St. Peter and became Pope."

It may be noted that in point of fact not one word was said in the book, as actually published, either about " the beautiful English heretic Anna Osten " or about " Pope Leo X and a French Court beauty." Nevertheless this prospectus was bound up within the covers of the book itself, and the advertisement was repeatedly reprinted unchanged for more than a month after the book was in circulation.

If one could by any means persuade oneself that the above professions were made in good faith, merely as the result of honest and invincible prejudice against the Catholic Church, we should be inclined to leave this unsavoury topic severely alone. But it is just the affectation of an exalted purpose which shows itself here and in Dr. Rappoport's address to his readers, which calls irresistibly for comment. At the risk of repeating something of what has already been given in the publishers' advertisement, this protestation must be quoted entire :

To the Reader.

This book has not been written out of malice or love of scandal. It has been conceived in a spirit of impartiality, animated by the wish to draw attention to the discrepancy existing between the noble and sublime teaching of Christ and the practice of His disciples. I have endeavoured also to show the important part played by the favourites of the Popes—those Popes who preached abstinence and contempt for women—upon the history of the Vatican and Christianity. Whilst exposing the intrigues of the Papal Court, I have not hesitated to do justice to the Popes who were worthy Vicars of Christ. In the result, I hope that readers animated by a sense of justice, will find no cause of offence in my book—for I have meant none.

As for the principal sources upon which this study has been based, I have enumerated them in the appended bibliographical list.

A. S. R.

Rome, the Eternal City,
    January, 1912.

Fresh from this declaration of impartiality and high moral purpose, we open the book and are confronted, before travelling very far, by a chapter of thirty pages devoted to the story of Pope Joan. This is not treated as a quaint legend or as a digression from the serious aim which the writer has in view.

The story [says Dr. Rappoport] of the woman who attained to the headship of the Church is unique in the annals of history. Catholic historians have done their best to prove the absurdity and impossibility of the story of Pope Joan. But without wearying the reader with a long discussion of the pros and cons, I shall relate it according to the evidence transmitted by trustworthy authorities.[2]

It is the amours of Joan upon which he insists :

She felt the necessity of finding a confidant and a lover among the young prelates who surrounded her, in whose embraces she could find consolation, &c., &c. . . . Young Baldello became the lover of the Pope whom people adored (sic) under the name of John VIII.

As a slander on the papacy no one could attach any particular importance to this resuscitation of the fable of Pope Joan. It is chiefly noteworthy as a proof of the bad faith of the author. It is as inconceivable that Dr. Rappoport was unaware that the story is rejected by responsible writers of all creeds, as it is certain that he did not even pretend to justify the slander by the production of new evidence. And yet the advertisement above cited would persuade us that the author, a Jew, who spends his time in writing on salacious themes and sordid scandals,[3] was anxious to vindicate by this book, " the noble and sublime teaching of Christ," to enforce a lesson and to draw a moral. Happily it is not often that we are brought face to face with cant of this unpleasant type. What is manifest is the appeal made to pruriency on the one hand and to anti-papal prejudice on the other.

[2] Rappoport, p. 84, cf. p. 96 : " Why should the Church of Rome take so much trouble to prove the story a fable when Cardinal Baronius does not hesitate to declare that ' many monsters have occupied the Papal throne ' ? " The same argument is repeated in almost the same terms on p. 102. To which we may reply that it is the non-Catholic historians who have been foremost in refuting the legend, and this not because the fact was intrinsically impossible, but because there is not a scrap of serious evidence to support it. There is ample testimony that Pope John VIII was not a woman, that he did not come from England or Germany, or die in the manner which the fable attributes to Pope Joan. See Mann, *Lives of the Popes*, Vol. III, pp. 231–352.

[3] In 1912 an advertisement announced another new work of Dr. Rappoport on *Famous Artists and their Models*, stating that he " has made a special study of the history and psychology of the model," and assuring purchasers that " the romantic nature of the subject and the beauty of the illustrations make it a volume of special charm." He is also the author of *Royal Lovers and Mistresses ; The Curse of the Romanovs ; Mad Majesties ; Leopold II, King of the Belgians ; The Fair Ladies of the Winter Palace ;* and *Splendid Sons of Sin* (1928), etc.

To argue at length the question whether Pope Joan ever existed would be ridiculous in the present state of knowledge. Probably the most effective way of illustrating the unscrupulousness of those, who without even the pretence of any fresh argument, dish up this ancient fable anew, will be to quote in the briefest terms the verdict of the various popular encyclopædias to be found on the shelves of a reference-library, like that of the British Museum Reading Room. Here are the results of a few minutes spent in such an experiment. In the *Encyclopædia Britannica* (1929, Vol. XIII, p. 71), Joan is declared to be " a mythical female Pope." In the *New International Encyclopædia* (New York, 1919, Vol. XIII, p. 123), we are told that " the unhistorical character of this story is now universally admitted." *Chambers' Encyclopædia* (Edinburgh, 1925, Vol. VI, p. 343), in a relatively long article, describes Joan as " a fabulous personage, long said to have filled the papal chair as John VIII." As far back as 1839, the *Penny Encyclopædia* (Vol. XIII, p. 123), spoke of Pope Joan as " a supposed individual of the female sex," and while admitting the whole story to be apochryphal, was anxious to show that " Protestants did not invent the tale, as they have been accused of having done." The best-known German encyclopædias, *Meyers Konversations-Lexikon* (1897, Vol. IX, p. 590), and *Brockhaus' Konversations-Lexikon* (1902, Vol. IX, p. 965), both designate the story as *Sage* and *Fabel*, and are both eager to assure us that " the Protestant Blondel in 1657 first demonstrated its unhistorical character." So far as regards France, *La Grande Encyclopédie* (Paris, 1895, Vol. XXI, p. 100), declares that " the baselessness of the legend is no longer disputed by anyone." Further, it may be noted that the only book of reference which expresses even the shadow of a doubt on the subject is the notoriously anti-clerical Larousse, *Grand Dictionnaire Universel*, which in its older edition (1873, Vol. IX, p. 938), professes to state the arguments on both sides, and to leave the reader to decide the question for himself. But the *Nouveau Larousse Illustré* (Paris, 1902, Vol. V, p. 396) remarks : " Already rejected in the eighteenth century by Bayle and even by Voltaire, the legend of Pope Joan is now no longer supported by anyone."[4]

It would be absurd to try to amplify this consensus of opinion, but it may be worth while to remark that the more important histories, when they do not disdainfully pass the legend by, as unworthy of notice, content themselves with trying to explain how this preposterous fable ever came to be believed : Döllinger's *Papst-fabeln* is universally appealed to as having said the last word on the subject, and it is referred to by such different writers as Professor Bury in his edition of *Gibbon* (1898, Vol. V, p. 298)—Gibbon himself rejected the story a century and a half ago—and by Gregorovius in his *Geschichte der Stadt Rom* (5th Ed., 1906, Vol. III, pp. 108 seq.). The same is true of *The Historians' History of the World*[5] (1907, Vol. VIII, p. 567), published by the *Times*.

This last work is referred to, not because any special importance attaches to it, but because it bears on the title-page of each volume the name of Dr. Angelo Rappoport as one of its contributors, and because *Who's Who* declared, no doubt upon information supplied by Dr. Rappoport himself, that he was " Revising Editor " of this work. It is distressing to think of the violence this conscientious moralist must have done to his convictions when he allowed the *Historians' History* to inform the world that the story of Pope Joan was a baseless fable, unless indeed we suppose that his point of view has changed since it occurred to him that there was money to be made by putting together a *chronique scandaleuse* of papal irregularities.

Moreover we find that even the notorious anti-Roman historian, Dr. Theodore Griesinger, from whom Dr. Rappoport, in this very book, has borrowed many pages without acknowledgment, rejects the legend completely.

The first doubts of the story [says Griesinger] arose with

4 " Dejà rejetée, au XVIIIᵉ siècle, par Bayle et même par Voltaire, la légende de la Papesse Jeanne n'est plus aujourd'hui soutenue par personne."

5 This section is headed " The Myth of the Woman Pope," and in the course of it we read, " the story of the pontificate of Joan was received as fact from the 13th to the 15th century, but it has been discredited by later researches."

the Renaissance and to the credit of Protestant writers it must be admitted, they have done most to dispel the fable. Their investigations proved that not a single author of the ninth century refers to the story.[6]

There will be occasion in future chapters to speak further of *The Love Affairs of the Vatican* which its publishers felt justified in advertising as one of the " two most successful books of 1912 " ; but before we turn to the more general question of medieval legends of the Popes, it may be interesting to show that if this shameless volume found many purchasers, it was solely the scandals promised by its title and not any charm of style which attracted readers. Mr. Rafael Sabatini's *Life of Cesare Borgia*, with which it was coupled, might at least claim consideration for its literary form, but Dr. Rappoport, in the incredible banality of his dialogues and descriptions, never rises above the level of the dullest penny dreadful. Take the most dramatic of his efforts, the scene heralding the downfall of Joan, the Popess.

Another legend related that at that time strange happenings occurred and that the minds of men were troubled by wonderful phenomena, clearly announcing the wrath of Heaven to the superstitious crowds of early mediævalism. The Tiber overflowed its banks, inundated the country, carried away churches and houses, and drowned men and beasts. The locust devastated the harvest and ruined the vine. The people, maddened by such calamities, clamoured for the intervention of the Pope. Cannot the Holy Father, who commands the celestial powers, can he not excommunicate the evil forces ? One word and he can deliver us from our distress. But the Holy Father remained inactive. Alas ! he was weak in the presence of the laws of nature ! Joan could circumvent human minds, but blind natural forces mocked at her intelligence. The infuriated mob assembled at the gates of the Vatican. One could almost hear the voice of revolt which Luther, the son of the

[6] Griesinger, *Mysteries of the Vatican* (English trans., 1864), Vol. I, p. 314.

Thuringian peasant, was to raise six centuries later, resound in the distance. The hydrahead of revolution stared the Pope in the face. The rabble of Rome were convinced that a gesture of the Pontiff would suffice to deliver the city from the various sufferings. And they angrily asked why the Vicar of Christ held his hands in his pockets, when, like Moses, he needed only to extend it over the sea for the water to dry up, or to work similar miracles. The hostile and ambitious cardinals fomented the uproar. Working in obscurity, they at last contrived that the *canaille* appeared threatening before the gates of the Vatican.

Joan is then reluctantly persuaded to take part in a great religious function which is to put an end to these calamities. Dr. Rappoport describes the scene :

The church bells of Rome sounded the glad tidings and confidently everybody awaited the miracle. Bishops, priests, and monks assembled at the Vatican ; in their thousands the people had come to witness the wonder wrought by the Holy Father. In the last moment her lover implored her not to appear in public, but Joan could scarcely cancel her promise, although she had gloomy presentiments. The air was impregnated with holy incense, the church bells were ringing and announcing her doom to Joan. Slowly the successor of St. Peter advanced at the head of the holy procession, acclaimed by the masses. From a thousand throats the sounds of holy hymns mounted heavenwards, and the shout " *Ora pro nobis*," was re-echoed from Rome's seven hills.

Bearers of crosses, standards, and holy images marched in front, followed by monks and holy friars, bending low their heads, covered with ashes in sign of repentance. Nuns and deaconesses, virgins and married women, all in the attitude of sinners, walked behind ; and at last came the motley crowd of Romans interspersed with Eastern converts, Greek monks, English theologians, and other foreigners. But the private physician of His Holiness noticed a sudden faintness of Joan, and quickly advised some refreshment. Then the Pope blessed the fields and the harvests, making crosses into all directions. The procession now being over, Joan remounted the mule to return to the Vatican, but, alas, she was not destined to reach it.

The climax, in fact, had come. The Pope had prematurely given birth to her child.

The passages just quoted are not exceptional. They are a rather favourable specimen of the style of this " best seller " of its year, though it must not be forgotten that Dr. Rappoport also seeks to conciliate his Protestant readers by dealing out quotations from the Holy Writ, not, of course, omitting the favourite extract from the Apocalypse which speaks of the woman " arrayed in purple and scarlet colour " . . . " and upon her forehead was a name written, MYSTERY, BABYLON THE GREAT, THE MOTHER OF HARLOTS AND ABOMINATIONS OF THE EARTH," etc.—all in the largest of capitals.

The elaborate details supplied in the wretched fiction just quoted are, of course, a pure invention either of Dr. Rappoport or else of some modern romancer whom he has copied. The earliest known mention of Pope Joan occurs about the middle of the thirteenth century—more than 350 years after the date which he assigns to her—in the following simple form, which the author of this section of the Chronicle of Metz had set down in evident perplexity and doubt.

Query. With regard to a certain pope—or rather popess, because she was a woman who pretended to be a man. By his excellent abilities having been appointed notary at the papal court he became Cardinal and eventually Pope. On a certain day, when he was riding, he gave birth to a child, and straightway in accordance with Roman justice his feet were tied together and he was dragged for half a league at a horse's tail while the people stoned him. At the place where he expired, he was buried, and an inscription was set up :

PETRE PATER PATRUM PAPISSE PRODITO PARTUM.

H

Under him was instituted the fast of the Ember Days, and it is called the popess's fast.[7]

Another somewhat divergent account which occurs about half a century later in the Chronicle of Martinus Polonus runs as follows :

> After the aforesaid Leo, John, an Englishman by descent,[8] who came from Mainz, held the see two years, five months and four days, and the pontificate was vacant one month. He died at Rome. He, it is asserted, was a woman. And having been in her youth taken by her lover to Athens in man's clothes, she made such progress in various sciences that there was nobody equal to her. So that afterwards lecturing on the Trivium at Rome she had great masters for her disciples and hearers. And forasmuch as she was in great esteem in the city, both for her life and her learning, she was unanimously elected pope. But while pope she became pregnant by the person with whom she was intimate. But not knowing the time of her delivery, while going from St. Peter's to the Lateran, being taken in labour, she brought forth a child between the Coliseum and St. Clement's church. And afterwards dying she was, it is said, buried in that place. And because the Lord Pope always turns aside from that way, there are some who are fully persuaded that it is done in detestation of the fact. Nor is she put in the Catalogue of the Holy Popes, as well on account of her female sex as on account of the shameful nature of the episode.

As already stated, the story is on all hands admitted to be fabulous and without any foundation in authentic history.[9]

---

[7] See the *Chronica Universalis Mettensis* in Pertz, *M.G.H., SS.*, xxiv. p. 514. The story is told of the Pope in the masculine gender. The Latin words of the inscription should mean, " Peter, Father of Fathers, reveal the childbirth of the popess."

[8] The words " *Johannes Anglicus natione* (v.l. *nativitate*) *Margantinus*, or *Moguntinus*," are obscure, and might be variously rendered.

[9] For a fuller discussion of the legend the reader may be referred to the Catholic Truth Society's pamphlet *Pope Joan*, and to the excellent article by F. Vernat in the *Dictionnaire Apologétique de la Foi Catholique*.

The main point of interest concerning it is that this extravagant fiction which seems to reflect so discreditably upon the papacy was not a Protestant calumny but originated in medieval times and was universally believed for two or three hundred years. Nevertheless, all the various attempts which have been made to reconcile the supposed pontificate of Joan with the known facts of papal chronology have egregiously failed.   As Döllinger and many others have shown, the suggested dates (viz. 855, 915, 1099) are not only mutually inconsistent but separately impossible.   If it be urged that the wide diffusion of so scandalous a story proves that the Holy See had forfeited all title to respect and that the medieval world had learnt to regard the Popes as capable of every atrocity, there is, on the other hand, still stronger reason to argue that the agreement of numberless monastic chroniclers in repeating any malicious tale affords of itself no sure ground for concluding that the discreditable story is true.   This aspect of the question comes out strikingly in the case of Pope Sylvester II, a Pontiff whose life was passed in the very centre of that evil period from 900 to 1048 of which much was said in the first chapter of this book.   The story of " the Pope who was a sorcerer and sold himself to the devil " was a favourite gibe with Bishop Jewel, Bale and other Elizabethan controversialists on the Protestant side.   Nor has this fantastic legend entirely died down even in our day.   In the highly respectable columns of *The Times Literary Supplement*, a reviewer, not so long since, commenting upon Mr. Waite's *Book of Ceremonial Magic*, wrote as follows :

> The discovery of buried treasures was at all times an important part of the magician's business.   If the sorcerer engaged in this business for his own benefit, it was a case of black magic and punishable as such by the State.   But if— as often happened—he obtained the consent of some ecclesiastical dignitary to the experiment on condition that the whole of the proceeds (deducting what may be called his commission) went into the coffers of the Church, it was a case of white magic, and as such praiseworthy.   More

than one of the Popes dabbled in the black art (which became white as white could be in his sanctified hands) and was not blamed for it in his lifetime—though, to be sure, his reputation suffered in after ages. The alien Pope forced on Rome by the Emperor's power at the close of the tenth century when the whole of Christendom was expecting the end of the world, was thought in subsequent centuries to be the greatest magician who ever wore the Triple Crown. His progressive promotion from Rheims to Ravenna and from Ravenna to Rome had been foretold by a verse of diabolical ingenuity—

Scandit ad R Gerbertus ad R post Papa vigens R—

and it was only to be expected that he would scandalise even the tolerant aristocracy of Rome by his intrigues with demons when, under the title of Sylvester II., he became the third Otto's *âme damnée* in the eyes of all Italy. But other Popes followed his example part of the way, and the list of Cardinals, Archbishops, Bishops, and Abbots who were interested in magic would fill a folio page. Heresy was the unpardonable sin in the eyes of the Mediæval Church, which was infinitely tolerant as regards offences against discipline or morality. And the sorcerer was adjudged guilty of heresy—but only if he practised his art without her authority and connivance.

Now it seems fair to judge the importance of an insinuation of this kind by the reliability of the one definite instance adduced in support of it. The writer, it is true, refers vaguely to many examples of ecclesiastical dignitaries who were willing to acquire treasure by the use of any kind of magic whatever, black or white, but he tells us nothing definite on the subject, and certainly the facts cannot be said to be notorious in history. The one definite instance that he quotes of an exalted ecclesiastic dabbling in magic is the case of Pope Sylvester II (Gerbert), and if on the one hand he seems to allow, by referring to this story as the talk of " subsequent centuries," that the Pope's contemporaries knew nothing about it, he takes back any doubt implied in such a concession by declaring that many other Pontiffs "followed his example." If Gerbert himself did not deal in magic, it is obvious that he can have set no example for others to follow. Moreover, the *Times* reviewer clearly implies that the Church in a later age, while accepting the fact of Gerbert's necromancy, called it white magic, and passed no condemnation upon it. It seems worth while, then, to devote a little space to this notorious example of Papal sanction of the sorcerer's arts, the more so perhaps that, for some reason unexplained, English writers have contributed more than any others to the diffusion of the legend in its more aggravated form. The worst offender, though probably writing in all good faith according to the credulous ideas of the age in which he lived, was the well-known English historian, William of Malmesbury, who lived in the first half of the twelfth century, more than a hundred years after Gerbert's death. William of Malmesbury's narration is so characteristic of the age in which it was written and throws so much light indirectly upon the generation of such legends that at the risk of rather long quotations, it will be better, where possible, to keep to his actual words.

Gerbert, Malmesbury tells us, and in this he seems to be already following legendary sources, was a monk of Fleury, who, growing tired of religious discipline, and ambitious to acquire knowledge, ran away from his monastery and made his way to Spain. There, under Saracen teachers, he learnt arithmetic, astronomy, music, geometry, and also augury, necromancy and magic generally. Now, the master to whom he attached himself had a book of magical lore containing the most profound secrets of the black art, which he could not by any entreaties or inducements be persuaded to part with. Gerbert, accordingly, made love to the magician's daughter, and by her means contrived to make the old man drunk, and then to steal the precious volume from under his pillow. When the Saracen discovered his loss and found that his pupil had fled, he at once set out in pursuit, using his magical knowledge to ascertain the direction of his flight. But Gerbert also, by means of unholy arts, learned that he was being pursued, and to escape, hid himself between air and water under the beams of a wooden bridge. He avoided detection for the time being, but he was afterwards stopped by coming to the sea, which he had no means of crossing. Thereupon, in despair, he invoked the devil, and upon condition that he was carried safely across the water, agreed to become the devil's man, doing him homage in due feudal form. In this way he got back to his own country, and began the remarkable career which Malmesbury details at length.

But before proceeding further, Malmesbury inserts the following note, highly characteristic of the writer and of the tone of mind of the age in which he lived :

> Perhaps [he says] someone may think that this is but a vulgar fiction, because the common people often attack the reputation of the learned, accusing of dealing with the devil any one who excels in his art. I, however, am convinced of his impiety by the thought of his unheard-of death. For why should he, on his death-bed, as we shall relate hereafter, have caused his own body to be chopped up, if he had not been conscious of some unprecedented crime ? For this cause, in an old book which fell into my hands, in which all the names of the Popes are written, with the years of their reign, I saw these words : *Sylvester, qui et Gerbertus, annos quatuor, mensem unum, dies decem : hic turpiter vitam suam finivit.*[10]

After this Malmesbury proceeds to tell his readers how Gerbert returned to Gaul and became a most famous professor, having many illustrious men among his pupils. So far as the general outlines of the history are concerned, Malmesbury's account is fairly correct. It is quite true that he became

---

[10] " Sylvester, who was also called Gerbert [reigned], four years, one month, and ten days. This man ended his life infamously." (Malmesbury, *Gesta - Regum*, Stevenson's Translation, §§ 167–168.) It seems clear that the chance occurrence of some phrase like this in an anonymous summary of papal history made sufficient impression on the chronicler to induce him to accept a portentously improbable legend which his common sense would otherwise have rejected.

successively Archbishop of Rheims and of Ravenna, and that it was mainly due to the influence of his former pupil, the Emperor Otto III, that he succeeded Gregory V in the chair of St. Peter. Again, it is highly probable that Gerbert did derive his *abacus*, or calculating tablet, from the Arabs, through the Saracens in Spain, and we have satisfactory evidence that he was the most remarkable mathematician of his time. Once more, as Gerbert in two of his letters[11] speaks of the organs he had built, there may very probably be foundation for what Malmesbury tells us about his marvellous " hydraulic organs in which, after a wonderful fashion, by the violence of heated water, the wind emerging fills the concavity of the instrument, and brazen pipes emit modulated sounds through surfaces perforated with many holes." But the two special stories which the historian recounts to illustrate the Pope's unholy knowledge of magic bear every sign of having been derived, with the Spanish episode already summarised, from some collection or treasure-house of stories such as we find in the later *Gesta Romanorum*. Collections of this kind were familiar to all epochs, and despite their Christian colouring they commonly contain about the same admixture of fiction with the real names and facts of history as we find in the tales of the Arabian Nights. Be this as it may, here is Malmesbury's version of the two stories in question :

The Treasures of Octavian. There was in the Campus Martius near Rome, a statue whether of bronze or iron I do not know, with the index finger of its right hand extended and an inscription on its forehead " Strike here." Men of earlier ages had understood that they would there find a treasure and had battered the innocent statue with axes. But Gerbert, perceiving their mistake, gave to the inscription a very different meaning. At mid-day, when the sun was in the centre of the heavens, he noted the spot where the shadow of the finger fell and there set up a stick. Then, when night fell, with one attendant to bear a light, he came

[11] J. Havet, *Lettres de Gerbert*, pp. 70 and 91.

to the spot.   There he broke open the ground by his wonted
enchantments, and disclosed a broad entrance to their
approach.   They see a vast palace with golden walls, golden
ceiling, all of gold ;   golden knights playing with golden
dice, a king of gold feasting with a queen fashioned of the
same metal, with food before them and attendants standing
by, goblets of great weight and price in which the skill of
the workman outdid nature.   Within, a carbuncle dispelled the shades of night.   In the opposite corner stood a
boy, bow in hand, with arrow pointed and string stretched.
Yet they could touch nothing, for the moment one put
out his hand to touch anything, all the statues seemed to
rush forward and to attack the presumptuous man.   Gerbert
in fear repressed his desires, but the attendant could not
refrain from pocketing a golden knife of marvellous work-
manship, thinking it would not be missed.   Instantly all
the statues rose, the boy let go his arrow into the carbuncle,
and all was dark.   And had they not fled they would both
have perished there.   It is the common opinion that he
(? Gerbert or Octavian) had prepared it all by his diabolical
art.[12]

What object Gerbert could have had in preparing such a
demonstration to strike terror into the solitary youth who
accompanied him, Malmesbury does not suggest.   The second
story has a much more immediate bearing upon the legendary
history of the Pontiff, and runs as follows :

    The Speaking Head.   Gerbert, they say, fashioned the head
of a statue under a certain aspect of the stars—that is just
at the time when all the planets were about to begin their
course.   It would not speak except when questioned, but
would truly answer " Yes " or " No."   For instance
Gerbert asked it " Shall I be Pope ? "   " Yes."   " Shall I
die before I sing Mass in Jerusalem ? "   " No."   And with
that ambiguous reply they say that he was deceived, so

[12] Ibid., § 170.   Bishop Stubbs in his edition (Rolls Series, Vol. I, pp.
197–198) throws no light on the difficulty raised by this last sentence.

that he might take no thought of repentance while he flattered himself with the hope of a long life. For when would he think of going to Jerusalem only to hasten his death ? But he did not perceive that there was in Rome a church called Jerusalem (that is *visio pacis*, because whoever fled to it, of whatever crime he was accused, found help). There the Pope sings Mass on three Sundays of the year, which are called *Statio ad Jerusalem*. Wherefore as, on one of these, Gerbert was preparing himself for the Mass, he felt a sudden sickness, and as it increased he lay down. He consulted the statue and learned at once his mistake and his death. Calling, therefore, the Cardinals together, he long deplored his crimes, and then in his madness—for his reason was dulled with pain—ordered his body to be cut limb from limb and cast into the street, saying : " Let him have the use of my limbs who received homage from them, for my soul never loved that oath or rather sacrilege."

These are, then practically speaking, the only charges of necromancy alleged against Pope Sylvester II. It is upon just this evidence that the Middle Ages declared him to be a magician, and the uncritical chroniclers of later times, the devout as well as the irreligious, were content to pronounce judgment against him without further enquiry. But what in fact is the verdict of the scientific historian of the present day ? Is there the slightest inclination to concur in the insinuation of the *Times* reviewer, that Pope Sylvester did busy himself with the black art, and that, so far as he knew how, he invoked the spirits of evil to promote his ambitious schemes ?

To discuss the career of Gerbert, who was perhaps, as a man of intellect, if not as a prelate and a statesman, the greatest pontiff who ruled the Church from the time of Gregory the Great to that of St. Gregory VII, would be impossible here. The reader should consult the admirable account of him given in the fourth and fifth volumes of Mgr. Mann's *Lives of the Popes*. Be it sufficient to say here, that, so far as we are aware, there is not a single historian of any standing, whether his sympathies be Roman or anti-Roman, who attaches the least importance to the legends of Pope Sylvester's magical practices. The whole of this mythology, as Bishop Stubbs suggests, is probably to be regarded as no more than " the tribute which superstitious ignorance pays to genius or unexpected success in life."[13] No one is less likely to be prejudiced in favour of any representative of the Papacy than the German historian Gregorovius. Now Gregorovius says :

> A German and a Frenchman swept away the barbarism which so long prevailed at the Lateran. Gerbert in Rome is like a solitary torch in the darkness of the night. The century of grossest ignorance closed strangely enough with the appearance of renowned genius. . . . But Rome can merely claim the honour of having served as the scene of his studies which have met with no response. If the Romans noticed their aged Pope watching the stars from his observatory in a tower of the Lateran, or surrounded in his study by parchments and drawing geometrical figures, designing a sundial with his own hand or studying astronomy on a globe covered with horse's skin, they probably believed him in league with the devil.[14]

Professor Döllinger included the legend of Gerbert's necromancy in his volume of *Papst-fabeln*, and it is to be noted that in the second edition of that work, published after the author's death, the historian had apparently seen no reason to modify in any way the favourable judgment which he had originally pronounced. It would be ridiculous to multiply testimonies upon a point so generally accepted. Writers, no doubt, there have been who have severely criticised certain incidents in his career as an ecclesiastic and a statesman, but all are agreed, save apparently the *Times* reviewer, in dismissing the charge of dabbling in the black arts, as a matter unworthy of serious discussion. The majority seem disposed to agree in the high

---

[13] *William of Malmesbury*, Rolls Series, Preface to Vol. II, p. lxviii.

[14] *History of the City of Rome* (English trans.), III, 511.

eulogy pronounced by M. Julien Havet, the editor of the standard edition of Gerbert's letters :

> Gerbert has been very differently judged. In the Middle Ages legend represented him as an adept in Mohammedan necromancy or sorcerer, a limb of the fiend (*suppôt du diable*). Among modern writers some have done him justice, others have taken pleasure in repeating the old accusations of intrigue, duplicity, and treachery. . . .
>
> The fact is that in all the offices which he successively held, I do not believe that it would be possible to instance a single act done by his authority or due to his influence which was dictated by any other motive than a sense of duty, by zeal for justice, or by solicitude for the public welfare. Could we find higher praise to give to a prelate, who was at once Supreme Pontiff and the favourite of an Emperor ? [15]

But how, it may be asked, can legend have attached such a reputation so persistently to an able and high-minded Pontiff, if there were no sort of foundation for this suspicion of magical practices ? We may answer that quite sufficient foundation is provided by the simple and unquestioned fact that Gerbert in his professorial days had acquired a great reputation for experimental science. It will be remembered that some centuries later, not only was Friar Roger Bacon denounced for his supposed communications with the evil one, but that even Blessed Albertus Magnus, who had St. Thomas Aquinas for his pupil, has given his name to a whole flood of unsavoury literature, *Le Grand Albert, Le Petit Albert,* etc., of a more or less magical character. In Gerbert's case we have also the circumstance, that in all probability his arithmetical studies, as is proved by the figures which he used, were stimulated by some acquaintance possibly at second or third hand, with works of Saracen origin. Again, Gerbert as a man of low birth who had gradually climbed

[15] Julien Havet, *Lettres de Gerbert*, p. xxxviii. It may be added that the notices of Pope Sylvester II in Vols. III and V of the *Cambridge Medieval History* are hardly less appreciative.

his way upwards, and had become the favourite and counsellor of the Emperor, was bound to have many enemies. The earliest suggestion of magical practices comes, so far as we know, from Cardinal Benno, the supporter of the anti-Pope, Clement III (Guibert), who in the crisis of the violent attacks upon St. Gregory VII (Hildebrand) wrote a Life of that Pontiff, accusing him also of magical arts, and trying to make out that such unholy practices and compacts with the evil one had become a tradition in the Papacy since the low-born Gerbert had introduced these evil ways. It is likely enough that the legend began with some malicious insinuation of this kind on the part of Benno. But there must have been other elements that aided in the full development of the legend, not the least important of which was probably the mysterious line :

Scandit ab R Gerbertus in R, post papa vigens R.

We first hear of this supposed oracle from Helgald, who wrote about the year 1050, less than fifty years after Gerbert's death, and who tells us that the verse was a *jeu d'esprit* of Gerbert himself, playing on the letter R.[16] It is, perhaps, not wonderful that the precise point of the jest was misconceived. To simple people an oracular utterance of any kind seemed to bring the writer into close contact with the powers of evil. There is also considerable probability in the suggestion that Gerbert has had attached to his name stories which originally were either consciously fictitious inventions, or were told of somebody else. Bishop Stubbs, for example, shows very good reason for believing that there was a confusion in Malmesbury's mind, as also in that of another English writer, William Godel, between Gerbert and a far less reputable Pontiff, the anti-Pope, John XVI. It is certain that in some details both Malmesbury and Godel have confused the two, why not also in this ? Moreover, we have further confirmation in the fact that in a curious fourteenth century English poem, the greater part of the legend of Pope Sylvester II is told of another Pope who is called Celestine. The

16 *Inter cetera de se laetus et hilarus in R littera lusit " Scandit ab R, &c."* See Roland Allen in *English Historical Review*, October, 1892.

poem has been edited by Dr. Horstman in the periodical *Anglia* of Halle.[17] A few specimens may be acceptable on account of its connection with the subject, but the verse itself is wretched doggerel. This is how the poet describes the promise made by the devil in return for " Celestine's " undertaking to serve him as his vassal.

> I shall be by thee both early and late
> So that sickness shall thee not take,
> From death thou shall right well escape,
> More and less,
> Until thou in the chapel of Jerusalem have sungen a
>   Messe.

> He said : " that shall never betide
> Into that land will I never ride
> Ne further seek on no side,
> If that I may."
> " Then shalt thou live," the devil said, " till doomsday."

When " Celestine " is on the point of death the demons come from Hell to claim their bargain.

> So thick the devils came from hell
> That no tongue ne might them tell
> Fire and brimstone from them fell
> With stink of might ;
> The bright sun withdrew and gave no light.

But Clestine repents.

> The Pope kneeled down on the stone
> The blood burst through flesh and bone
> Wringing his hands he made his mone
> And wept well sore
> And prayed that Jesu should him save ; if His will wore.

Even more potent is his prayer to our Lady, which is thus worded :

[17] Vol. II, 1878.

> Queen of heaven, I pray with cheer
> To your son make for me your prayer
> As He bought us well dear,
> Upon the crois,
> If that it were His will, to hear my voice.

In return for this anguish of repentance the powers of Heaven intervene and Satan is defrauded of his bargain. Though the Pope's body is torn to pieces and left to the fiends to bear away, his soul is saved.

Lastly, it is very important to notice that this anguish of repentance is present in every form of the legend. Nothing could be more untrue, so far at least as the legend of Sylvester II is concerned, than the insinuation that magic used by a Pope for his own purposes at once becomes white magic and is accounted innocent of all offence. The supposed necromancy of Gerbert is everywhere represented as a crime of the deepest dye. This aspect of the case is curiously emphasised by the existence as late as the end of the sixteenth century of an inscription which was visible to all not only at the Basilica of the Holy Cross (or Jerusalem), where the Pope is supposed by the legend to have died immediately after singing Mass, but also by a duplicate of the same in the Church of St. John Lateran, where he was buried. Montaigne, in the Diary of his tour in Italy, remarks :

> I do not know why some people are so scandalised when they find accusations freely levelled at the life of some particular prelate, who is a public character and known to everyone, for both at St. John Lateran and at the Church of the Holy Cross in Jerusalem I saw the history of Pope Sylvester II. written up in a most conspicuous place, and it is the most discreditable story you can think of.[18]

The existence of the duplicate of this inscription has been disputed, but the description of Rome by N. Muffel in the fifteenth century seems to support Montaigne's statement, even

[18] " Qui est la plus injurieuse qui se puisse imaginer." (D'Ancona, *Giornale del Viaggio di Michele de Montaigne*, Ed. 1889, p. 297.)

though there was another inscription at the Lateran concerning Sylvester II which is still to be seen there to this day. The inscription which undoubtedly existed in the Church of Santa Croce, and most probably in substantially identical terms at the Lateran also, was to the following effect :

> In the year of our Lord MIII., in the time of Otto III., Sylvester, the second Pope of that name, who had previously been Otto's tutor, not having, it seems, obtained the Papacy by rightful means, after receiving warning from a spirit that he would die on the day that he came to Jerusalem, though he failed to understand that this sanctuary here was a second Jerusalem, in the fifth year of his pontificate, on the day determined, while offering here the Holy Sacrifice, died on that same day. But by the Divine grace, before the Communion, when he understood that he was near the point of death, he, on account of his worthy penance and his tears and the holiness of the place, was brought back, as we may piously believe, to the state of salvation. For after the Mass was ended, after disclosing to the people his crimes, and after giving directions that in punishment of these said crimes his lifeless body should be dragged by wild horses in any direction through the city, and should be left unburied, unless God in His mercy should otherwise dispose, when the horses, after careering far and wide, came to a standstill within the temple of the Lateran, he was buried in that spot by Otto. And Sergius IV., his successor, afterwards adorned his tomb in more seemly wise.[19]

No one could possibly say in the presence of such an inscription that the necromancy of Pope Sylvester was in any sense condoned and presented to the people as free from sin. Of course this inscription was of late date and founded entirely upon the legend. The other inscription, which, as just stated, still

---

[19] Graf, *Miti, Leggende e Superstizioni del Medio Evo*, II, p. 31. Like every other scholar, Graf ridicules the idea that these supposed magical practices of Gerbert were anything more than a myth (Ibid., pp. 1–75).

exists at the Lateran, is a serious historical document. Antiquaries are agreed that it is a copy probably of that which originally was engraved on the tomb itself. This certainly cannot be the inscription referred to by Montaigne, for no one could describe it as *la plus injurieuse qui se puisse imaginer.* It contains of course no reference to the legend of Sylvester's magical arts, but describes him to us as in the opinion of his successor he really was. The verdict which it pronounces has been of late more and more fully justified by all historians who have seriously investigated the question.

> This spot will yield up the remains of Sylvester
>> When the Lord cometh at the last trump
> This famous man was given to the world by a most learned virgin
>> And the seven-hilled city of Romulus head of all the world.[20]
> At first Gerbert was deemed worthy to rule
>> The Metropolis of Rheims, filling a Frankish See,
> And later to acquire the chief sway
>> For the noble city of Ravenna, thus waxing powerful.
> After a year under an altered name, he acquired Rome
>> And became the new Shepherd of the world.
> He to whom this loyal and friendly mind was all too dear—
>> Otto third Caesar of the name—has raised this tomb.
> Each of the two sheds lustre on the age by his conspicuous virtue and wisdom ;
>> The whole age rejoiced and every guilty thing was shattered.
> Like the Apostolic Bearer of the keys he gained a place in Heaven,
>> Having thrice been chosen to fill his place on earth.
> After filling the See of Peter for the space of five years,
>> Death carried him into eternity.

[20] These two lines are certainly a puzzle. History records nothing of this *doctissima virgo* who was Gerbert's mother. But the text, as shown by Gregorovius and Roland Allen, p. 668, is quite clear.

The world was stupefied by the loss of its peace,
> And wavering unlearned its repose and the triumphs of
> the Church.

Sergius the priest, his successor, had adorned this humble
tomb
> With gentle piety and as a sign of love.

Thou who mays't chance to turn thy gaze upon his tomb
> Pronounce the prayer : " Almighty God have mercy on
> him."

He died in the year of our Lord's Incarnation 1003, in the
first indiction,
> On the twelfth day of the month of May.[21]

There is no word here of any dismemberment of the body of
Pope Sylvester. Indeed, the first lines imply the contrary. And
if any further proof were needed of the utterly mythical character
of the legend which declared the self-imposed sentence of
mutilation to be the condition by which the compact with the
devil was rescinded, we are told that in the course of some necessary repairs in 1648 the tomb of Gerbert was opened. Canon
Cesare Raspo, who was present, asserts that the body of Gerbert
was found complete, dressed in full pontificals with ring and
crozier, though on exposure to the air it at once fell into dust,
emitting a sweet perfume, due, no doubt, to the spices with
which it had been embalmed.

Nevertheless the story of Pope Sylvester, the sorcerer, who
sold his soul to the devil and was torn to pieces by wild horses,
is repeated by nearly all the chroniclers of the later Middle
Ages without the least hint that any one of them doubted its
authenticity. Ralph Higden in his *Polychronicon*, Giraldus
Cambrensis, Matthew Paris, Walter Map, and the Malmesbury
monk who wrote the *Eulogium Historianum*, all of them amongst
the foremost representatives of English scholarship in the
thirteenth and fourteenth centuries, echo the same tale. Giraldus
in particular informs us that the reason why the Pope in a

[21] Gregorovius, *The Tombs of the Popes*, translated by R. W. Seton-Watson,
p. 34.

pontifical Mass consumes the Body of Christ facing the people, was because Sylvester II, conscious of his crimes, used to evade communicating by depositing the Host in a little bag hung around his neck. He further declares that whenever a Pope is about to die great drops of water are seen to trickle from the marble tomb at the Lateran where Gerbert lies buried.

No two legends could be more absolutely devoid of foundation than the two we have been considering—that of the woman Pope who never existed and that of the sorcerer Sylvester II, the Pontiff who in fact more than any other represented worthily the cause of his Divine Master in an age of exceptional licence and barbarity. Discreditable to the whole conception of the Papacy as these legends might seem, not a voice was raised in protest until they had been universally believed for many generations. No violent political antagonisms came in here. It was just the bizarre story which attracted. On broad lines both learned and unlearned understood that though the office of the Vicar of Christ was exalted in dignity above all others, no promise had been made that he who held it should be immune from human weakness or human passions. At the same time it is not improbable that the circulation of such fables did contribute to the readiness with which men believed evil of those who occupied the chair of St. Peter in their own day, and for that reason it seemed worth while to give them a prominence which intrinsically they do not merit. In the case of Pope Gregory VII, which we have next to consider, fierce political partisanship undoubtedly came into play, but the contemporaries who attacked him with bitter calumnies, do not provide any detailed narrative such as we may read in the *Love Affairs of the Vatican.*

CHAPTER VII

HILDEBRAND AND MATILDA OF TUSCANY

It will, no doubt, be inferred from what has been said above, that Dr. Rappoport, by reviving the absurd fable, long since discredited, of the female Pope, went far to prove that his book was too contemptible to be taken seriously. For scholars who have even an elementary acquaintance with medieval history, this is certainly true ; but it is obvious that *The Love Affairs of the Vatican* was not intended for that class of reader. There is, as the author and his publishers very well knew, a tolerably large public quite uncritical as regards evidence, but thoroughly persuaded that the Church of Rome is the source of all evil, a public also ready to welcome anything which promises scandal with a spice of pruriency. For such people it would mean much that Dr. Rappoport dates his preface from " Rome the Eternal City," claims to have written " in a spirit of impartiality," protests that he only desires, Jew though he may be, to mark " the discrepancy between the noble and sublime teaching of Christ and the practice of His disciples," and describes himself in *Who's Who* not only as Revising Editor of the *Times History of the World*, but as a contributor to the *Fortnightly Review*, the *Nineteenth Century*, and other journals of high respectability. Who would have the audacity to suggest that a bulky volume by this eminent scholar, published in pre-war days at sixteen shillings net, was nothing but a rather filthy lampoon which traded upon the ignorance and the bigotry of the average Protestant Englishman ? Was it not procurable at all the libraries, and did not the advertisement of it fill nearly half a column in the *Times Literary Supplement ?*

From the point of view of the damage likely to result, the revival of the Pope Joan fable was of very little consequence. This was not a matter in which people were likely to be misled, and it would have signified little even if they had been. But there were other falsifications of history in Dr. Rappoport's book which wore a much more serious complexion. Let us admit that men like Pianciani and Léo Taxil, who slandered the living or the recently dead, were guilty of a viler offence. It is a less crime to calumniate those whose memory only survives in history books or monuments of the past. But whereas, in the former case, intense party feeling and honest misconceptions may often be pleaded in excuse, there is something singularly cold-blooded and revolting in the conduct of a man of education who, knowing the truth, and in a quarrel which is not his own, sets out to bespatter with filth the great characters of long ago, regardless of the veneration in which they are almost universally held. A more flagrant case than that of Dr. Rappoport's treatment of Hildebrand (Pope Gregory VII) and Matilda of Tuscany it would be impossible to find. He could not conceivably be ignorant that this pontiff has been canonised, and is consequently venerated by all Catholics as a Saint. But so far from this consideration weighing with him to study the evidence more carefully, our impartial historian repeatedly goes out of his way to denounce St. Gregory as a man of immoral life, who enforced the law of clerical celibacy with no higher motive than to cover his own vices.[1] For example he says :

> But if Gregory was severe against others, he was not so against himself, and the mask of authority and austerity which he had put on was made a means to hide his own irregular life. His own love affairs and intrigues were well known to his contemporaries. . . . He had three mistresses, and was besides carrying on many other minor intrigues and love affairs. History mentions, as some of his favourites, Agnes, the mother of the Emperor of Germany, her aunt Beatrice, and above all, the famous Countess

[1] See Rappoport, pp. 26, 27 and 28 ; cf. also p. 6, p. 40 and p. 194.

Mathilda, the Sultana of the Holy Father. She was constantly in his company, and had been surnamed the "daughter of St. Peter." By this beautiful title the Holy Father had sanctified the object of his passion.[2]

All this, be it noted, is written, with a reiteration suggestive of something like personal vindictiveness,[3] outside the section professedly devoted to Hildebrand and Matilda.

Now here again one finds oneself baffled by the difficulty of discussing in a chapter of moderate length so considerable a subject as the moral character of Gregory VII. The best which can be done is to appeal once more to the verdict of non-Catholic scholars, whose authority is generally respected. Although St. Gregory was far too fearless and out-spoken a champion of truth in a corrupt and lawless age not to have been assailed by calumny, there is not a single modern historian of weight who has expressed a doubt of his moral integrity. Englishmen like Stubbs, Freeman, and Milman, Germans like Carl Mirbt, Gregorovius and Hauck, Frenchmen like Monod, and Duruy and Bayet may condemn Gregory's ecclesiastical policy, but they render homage to his private character. With regard to Matilda in particular, Gregorovius voices the judgment of all serious historians when he declares that "hatred and mistrust have in vain striven to besmirch her relations with the Pope."[4] To see if Dr. Rappoport had any extrinsic support for his slanders, I have once more consulted upon this point the popular Encyclopædias previously mentioned. There is not one that throws suspicion upon the sincerity and high personal character of Hildebrand, even though several of them condemn in strong terms what they regard as the arrogance of his pretensions as head of the Church. "He was himself pure and disinterested," said the *Penny Encyclopædia* nearly a century ago, and at the present day the *Nouveau Larousse* echoes an almost

---

[2] Ibid., p. 28.

[3] Compare what is said of Clement VI. "He was no hypocrite like Gregory VII," p. 194.

[4] Gregorovius, *Geschichte der Stadt Rom*, Vol. IV, p. 172, 5th Edn., 1906.

unanimous judgment when it declares : " Gregory VII is one of the greatest figures of the Middle Ages. Whatever may be thought of some of his ideas, we must do justice to the austerity of his life and to his extraordinary energy of character."[5]

If a more elaborate estimate be needed, let us turn to that in the eighth volume of the *Historians' History of the World*, upon the title-page of which, as already mentioned, Dr. Rappoport's name stands printed. There we read :

> The German line of pontiffs had done much to reinstate the papacy in its ancient sanctity. The Italian Alexander II. had been at least a blameless pontiff, and now every qualification which could array the Pope in imposing majesty, in what bordered on divine worship, seemed to meet in Gregory VII. His life verified the splendid panegyric with which he had been presented by Cardinal Hugo to the Roman people. He had the austerest virtue, the most simple piety, the fame of vast theologic knowledge, the tried ability to rule men, intrepidity which seemed to delight in confronting the most powerful, and stern singleness of purpose, which under the name of churchmanship, gave his partisans unlimited reliance on his firmness and resolution, and yet a subtle policy which bordered on craft.[6]

Let us supplement this by the verdict of an English non-Catholic historian of high standing, the late Professor Tout :

> The wonderful self-control which the new Pope had shown so long did not desert him in his new position. Physically there was little to denote the mighty mind within the puny body. . . . He was not a man of much learning or originality . . . But he was one of the greatest practical men in the Middle Ages ; and his single-minded wish to do what was right betokened a dignity of moral nature that was rare indeed in the eleventh century.[7]

[5] *Nouveau Larousse Illustré*, 1900, Vol. IV, p. 950.

[6] *Historians' History of the World*, VIII. p. 595.

[7] Professor Tout, *The Empire and the Papacy*, p. 125.

Even at the risk of superfluous reiteration, we cannot afford to pass over what seems to be the latest pronouncement on the subject, the chapter devoted to Gregory VII in *The Cambridge Medieval History*, by Mr. Z. N. Brooke, who is one of its editors.

He was, in fact, in temperament not unlike a prophet of the Old Testament—fierce in denunciation of wrong, confident in prophecy, vigorous in action, unshaken in adversity. . . . His enthusiasm and his ardent imagination drew all men to him ; that he attracted men is well attested . . . The keenness of his glance . . . was kindled by the righteousness of his aims and his determination, in which self-interest did not participate, to carry them into effect.[8]

And again in an eloquent passage describing the death of this great Pope.

The bitterness of failure hung heavily upon him. He, who had prayed often that God would release him from this life if he could not be of service to the Church, had now no longer any desire to live. He passed away on 25 May 1085, and the anguish of his heart found expression in his dying words : " I have loved righteousness and hated iniquity ; therefore I die in exile." The emphasis was on righteousness to the last. And it was justified. Had he consented to compromise his principles and to come to terms with Henry, he could have maintained himself unchallenged upon the papal throne.[9]

This is the man whom Dr. Angelo Solomon Rappoport, fresh from his studies in the history of artists' models, thought fit, with the support of a well-known English firm of publishers, to describe to the world as a hypocrite and a voluptuary. The form of the slander is almost as repellent as the substance. On the rare occasions when Dr. Rappoport happens to be composing at first hand, and not merely translating, this is the kind of drivel he produces :

[8] *The Cambridge Medieval History* (1926), Vol. V, p. 54.
[9] Ibid., p. 80.

The infallible, the tyrant, became submissive, the ruler a subject of the imperious woman. He who was supposed to possess the power of unlocking the gates of Heaven and of unchaining all bonds, became enchained himself by the shackles of love. The Pope was in love! Mathilda of Tuscany, with her dazzling appearance, her gleaming flesh, her glorious opulent beauty, had captivated the heart of Hildebrand. The proud monk, who was wont to command sovereigns and mighty warriors, was only too happy to obey the woman he loved.[10]

Of course if our historian had produced evidence for his allegations, we should be quite ready to consider it. But he offers us absolutely no evidence. He simply says it was so. He tells a long and revolting story of the attempt of the Pontiff, at a time when Matilda, according to him, was still Gregory's acknowledged mistress, to seduce a niece of Matilda's, named Theodorine, a girl of eighteen, who is, so far as we know, an absolutely fictitious personage. Dr. Rappoport introduces his narrative with the statement :

> Some historians, however, have proved, on the strength of contemporary documents,[11] that the relationship of Hildebrand and Mathilda had not been wholly mystic, platonic, and political. I shall relate some episodes of their lives as I have gathered them from ancient chronicles.

We could conceivably excuse a statement like this, if we were dealing with what was known to be, or might readily be guessed to be, a work of fiction. But Dr. Rappoport (and his publishers), exclude any such indulgent interpretation by the wording of the advertisement, and the Address to the Reader quoted above. It is our historian's high purpose to expose " the discrepancy existing between the noble and sublime teaching of Christ, and the practice of His followers." In

---

10 Rappoport, p. 121.

11 Why does not Dr. Rappoport tell us where these documents are printed, or where they are to be found ? His work does not exclude references and footnotes ; see, for example, pp. 21, 85, 213, etc.

the light of that moral pose, this pretence of citing contemporary evidence must be pronounced to be a deliberate untruth of an exceptionally nauseous kind, an untruth simply intended to blacken the fame of two very noble characters in history, and to discredit the religion which they both professed. For Dr. Rappoport in this chapter is not quoting " ancient chronicles." It does not contain a line taken from ancient chronicles. He is quoting most certainly, but the document from which he borrows or condenses is a romance written by a certain Madame Bédacier at the beginning of the eighteenth century, and entitled *Histoire des amours de Grégoire VII*. Let us examine a few specimens. Here is a passage which professes to describe the state of Rome under Gregory VII.

BÉDACIER IN 1700.	RAPPOPORT IN 1912
Rome n'avoit jamais été plus galante et plus magnifique sous Auguste qu'elle l'étoit sous Grégoire VII. La volupté étoit sa Déesse ; on ne voyoit dans son palais que des courtisans intéressez qui flatoient ses plus grands deffauts, et on entendoit bien plus souvent chanter des chansons amoureuses chez le Pape que des hymnes sacrez et de saintes litanies.[12]	Rome in the pagan days of Augustus had not been more magnificent and gallant than under the Christian rule of Hildebrand. Voluptuousness was the Goddess reigning supreme in the Eternal City ; favourites and courtiers crowded the papal palace, flattering the vanity of the Pontiff, and pandering to his weakness and to his passions. Love songs were as often to be heard within the precincts of His Holiness's residence as sacred hymns.[13]

Then for a little while Dr. Rappoport paraphrases more freely while he describes how Matilda tries to attract to herself her niece's lover, Hippolyte, in order that Theodorine, being disappointed in her own affections, may more easily listen to the Pope's advances.

[12] Bédacier, p. 26.   [13] Rappoport, p. 129.

Le Pape avoit véritablement brulé pour Mathilde, mais outre que ses premiers ardeurs s'étoient modérées dans la tranquillité d'une longue et facile possession, Théodorine lui donna d'autres fers ; et quoy qu'il eut tout lieu de croire qu'ils seroient plus pesans que ceux de la Comtesse, il fut cependant contraint de les porter. Pressé de ces désirs il inventa de nouveaux jeux pour plaire à Théodorine ; Mathilde y paroissoit parée comme une Impératrice qui va au Triomphe dans le dessin de tenter la constance d'Hypolite, mais elle étoit à l'épreuve d'armes beaucoup plus redoutables.[14]

Forgotten were the teachings of the Apostles, forgotten the noble life of the Founder of Christianity, forgotten the sublimity of the teaching of Christ. Gregory VII., who had ordained the celibacy of the priests, was burning with an unholy fire for Theodorine. And while he gave splendid festivals and receptions, Countess Mathilda put on Imperial raiment and appeared in all her dazzling beauty and tempting nudity to attract the reluctant Hippolyte. But the prince's heart belonged to his *fiancée*, and he pretended not to notice the advances made by the amorous aunt.[15]

We have quoted this passage that the reader may see how Dr. Rappoport improves upon his original by the addition of an unctuous appeal to the teachings of the " Founder of Christianity," and by the addition of touches such as the " tempting nudity " of Matilda, which are not in the original. But the close dependence of Dr. Rappoport upon Mme Bédacier comes out most markedly in the dialogue, of which we give a specimen or two. After a set of French verses which are supposed to have been sung at the banquet, and which Dr. Rappoport has naturally not taken the trouble to translate, we have the following scene which may also be given in parallel columns :

Théodorine avoit écouté ce qu'on venoit de chanter avant ce dernier couplet sans étonne-

The pure and innocent mind and the honest nature of Theodorine revolted at all that she

14 P. 26.   15 P. 130.

ment, . . . mais elle perdit alors patience. " En vérité," dit elle à une jeune Romaine qui était assise à table aupres d'elle, et qui se nommoit Flavie, " je commence à rougir de ce qui se dit icy, et ce n'est pas là le langage des cherubim et des seraphins qu'on y devroit parler ; diroit-on des choses plus libres dans un lieu de débauche ? Et pourroit-on s'imaginer que nous sommes chez le Lieutenant de Dieu ? "

" Vous êtes encore bien novice et peu consommée dans le commerce des Papes," repliqua Flavie, en souriant, " et je m'étonne que la fille de St. Pierre ne vous en aye pas mieux informée."

" Hé, qui est-elle," continua Théodorine, " cette scavante dont vous parlez ? "

" Quoy ? " poursuivit Flavie,

saw and heard. Her neighbour at table was a Roman girl named Flavia, with whom she had struck up a friendship and to whom she did not hesitate to communicate her thoughts.

" I blush," said Theodorine, " in listening to all that is being uttered within these sacred walls. Surely this is not the language of either the *seraphim* or the *cherubim* and is not fitted for such a place. Can one imagine more licentious conduct in any house of debauchery ? And it requires a great deal of imagination to feel oneself in the house of the Vicar of God." . . .

Flavia, born and bred in the Eternal City, and to whom the scandalous life led by the clergy and the Pontiffs of Rome was nothing new, smiled at the innocence of her friend.

" You are very young and inexperienced," she replied " and you seem to know very little about Pontifical Rome. I am rather surprised that the daughter of St. Peter did not teach you better."

" The daughter of St. Peter, and, pray, who is she ? " asked the bewildered girl.

" Don't you know that His

" vous ne scavez pas que Sa Sainteté a adopté Mathilde ? "

" La fille de St. Pierre," interompit Théodorine, " devroit s'employer à faire marcher Hildebrand sur les traces des Apôtres, puis qu'elle a tant de crédit auprès de lui, et je vous avouë que je suis confuse de ce qui se passe icy."[16]

Holiness has adopted the Countess Mathilda ? "

" Then the daughter of St. Peter," replied Theodorine, " ought to endeavour to lead Hildebrand in the footsteps of the Apostles and the path trodden by the Saviour. I am ashamed and indignant."[17]

It is of course important to note that not the slightest indication is given by Dr. Rappoport that these portions of his text are merely translations. True, he tells us in his prefatory note, already quoted, that " the principal sources upon which this study has been based," are enumerated in the bibliography, and among the one hundred and eight different works there set down (some of them in ten or twelve volumes), there appears, along with many other books on Gregory VII, an entry of " Durand, Catherine Bédacier : *Histoire des Amours de Grégoire VII.*, Paris, 1702," but there is not, of course, a hint that this wretched fiction has been selected to be not only consulted, but translated, while all the rest have been ignored. We call it fiction, for *roman* is the name the authoress herself gives to it, when she says in the first sentence of her Preface :

> C'est une grande témérité, ce semble, que de choisir des Papes et des Cardinaux pour en faire les sujets de ce que l'on appelle roman.

It is true that the lady afterwards alleges that there is nothing fictitious in her stories, but Bayle, her contemporary, Protestant and anti-clerical as he was, laughs at the idea. " *C'est là le comble de la hardiesse,*" he remarks, and in a footnote to his account of Gregory VII he declares that Madame Bédacier's story of *les Amours de Grégoire VII.* is a pure work of the imagination. In any case, it is plain that when Dr. Rappoport professes to take his narrative of Hildebrand's alleged intrigues with

[16] Bédacier, p. 31.   [17] Rappoport, p. 132.

Matilda and Theodorine from "ancient chronicles," he is roundly lying. He has given us nothing but a rough paraphrase or translation from Madame Bédacier's romance. Even his consistent spelling of the name Matilda with an *h* (Mathilda) is highly significant of the source from which he has been borrowing. For anyone who will take the trouble to examine Madame Bédacier's novel, the plagiarism cannot remain a moment in doubt. It will be enough to supply one final illustration. The style of the presentment alone would be sufficient to dispose of the claim that the story was derived from "ancient chronicles."

Pendant qu'elles parloient ainsi le Pape eut toujours les yeux sur Théodorine, et Matthilde qui avoit Hypolite à son côté tâchoit par ses regards et par ses actions de lui faire entendre mille choses : mais il fut sourd à tout, et la Comtesse en soupira de chagrin. Le repas étant fini, le Pape fit disposer les places de manière qu'il se trouva au bal derrière Théodorine, et si commodément qu'il pouvoit se faire entendre d'elle, sans être entendu des autres, pour peu qu'il baissât la voix. Elle eut du chagrin de se voir dans une situation si contrainte. Et comme elle tournoit souvent la teste d'un autre côté :

" Est-ce que je vous fais peur, Madame," dit le Pontife en luy pressant un peu le bras, "et que vous avez juré de ne me point regarder ? Si c'est un vœu, je

Whilst the two girls had been conversing the Pope had eyes only for Theodorine, whom he was devouring with ardent glances, whilst Countess Mathilda was trying the influence of her charms on Hippolyte, prince of Arimini. At the close of the banquet, when the guests had left their seats, His Holiness seized the first opportunity to place himself near Theodorine, so that he could talk to her undisturbed. The girl was compelled to remain and to listen to his words, but her gaze often wandered away, as if looking for some help or for some one to rescue her from her pursuer.

"Am I frightening you, madam," asked Hildebrand, "that you avoid looking me in the face ? If it is a vow you have made, I, who am all powerful, have the power to

puis vous en dispenser, et vous n'ignorez pas que je lie et délie quand il me plaît."

" Comme Votre Sainteté ne doit penser qu'au ciel," répondit Théodorine, " mes regards ne lui sont pas fort nécessaires."

" Ma Sainteté," reprit le Pape, " en a plus de besoin que vous ne pensez, et je n'ôteray rien au ciel en admirant une beauté céleste."

" Vous avez des expressions bien étranges," continua Théodorine, " et que l'on n'apprend sans doute pas au Collége de St. Pierre. C'est apparemment pour m'éprouver que vous vous en servez ! mais je n'en abuserai point et je ne demande pas mieux qu'à les oublier, puisque je les trouve si opposées à votre charactére."[18]

break it, for, as you know, mine is the prerogative to ' bind and to loosen ' ' "

" As your Holiness ought only to be thinking of Heaven," replied the girl with some spirit, " my gaze is quite unimportant to you."

" My Holiness requires the lustre of your eyes more than you can imagine, and I am in no way depriving Heaven of its due in contemplating and admiring your heavenly beauty."

" The expressions your Holiness deigns to employ sound somewhat strange to my ears ; I am sure they are not those used in the college of St. Peter. I fancy the Holy Father only wants to try me and is therefore showing himself in a light and in an attitude so opposed, and contradictory to his dignity and to his holy office."

All this is an abominable perversion of truth, where no good faith can be pleaded, but in which religious fanaticism and mercenary greed have combined to produce a book which it was hoped would produce a *succès de scandale*. Such tactics would be contemptible, were it not for the acute trouble of mind which fictions like that of Dr. Rappoport cause to simple Catholics, too honest themselves to suspect anyone of reckless mendacity, and incapable of investigating the matter on their own account. That there have been bad and unworthy Popes, they are well

18 Bédacier *Histoire des Amours de Grégoire VII*, Cologne 1700, p. 33.

aware. But when they find a canonised Saint like Gregory VII, charged with keeping three mistresses while actually Pope, it becomes to them a matter of real concern. Moreover, there is something peculiarly despicable and cowardly in besmirching the fair fame of a noble woman like the Countess Matilda. This is the account of her death, given by a modern biographer in a work of most painstaking and conscientious research :

> As the watchers stood round her bed, the Modenese bishop, seeing her sufferings, held to her lips a crucifix. Kissing this repeatedly, the dying woman exclaimed : " O Lord Christ ! Because I have always loved Thee, I pray Thee now to forgive me my sins ! " And almost immediately afterwards she breathed her last.
>
> So there passed from this life one of the greatest and noblest spirits the world has ever known.[19]

Is there not something peculiarly vile in Dr. Rappoport's attempt to represent this woman to the world as a lustful and vindictive courtesan, intriguing to bring about the moral ruin of her own niece for the benefit of her paramour the Pope ? Here is the account of Matilda's last moments taken from the pages of another recent biographer :

> Though endowed with a princely patrimony, Matilda had, throughout her life, denied to herself the comforts with which it was her pleasure to surround others. Notwithstanding that she lived in an age of unrestrained appetite, she observed a simplicity of diet that almost amounted to austerity, and daily at her well-spread table set an example of self-mortification. Not even in illness did she allow to her body the ease which is not only at such times permissible but even desirable. When her attendants, we are told, attempted to place her pain-racked limbs in postures which would afford them some relief, she begged them to desist. Her Redeemer had for hours suffered the pain of a fixity of position in addition to His other agonies upon the cross, and Matilda desired to imitate

[19] Nora Duff, *Matilda of Tuscany*, pp. 273, 274. Methuen, 1909.

her dear Lord. " How properly all the beatitudes in the Sermon on the Mount seemed, as it were, to belong to her," piously remarks the historian ; " She had indeed broken her box of precious ointment and poured forth its fragrance at her Saviour's feet."—So calmly ended the eventful life of Matilda that her friends, waiting to hear the parting words from her smiling lips, were unaware when the last moment came. Without a sigh or regret her pure soul winged its flight from the sunny land she loved so well to the eternal reward she merited. Thus on the 8th July 1115 followed by the prayers and blessings of a people for whom she had often prayed and blessed soared the spirit of the greatest and noblest woman of her age.[20]

The very fact that two long and enthusiastic English biographies of this noble Princess have appeared within a few years of each other would alone constitute an argument in her favour. Further, when we remember that she survived Gregory VII for thirty years, and during all that time continued to be the same loyal champion of the successive occupants of the See of St. Peter, we must judge that this circumstance alone would be sufficient to establish the purity of her motives, even if we were not abundantly assured upon the point by the testimony of contemporary writers. No serious work of reference suggests a single word of scandal against the moral integrity of " the Great Countess."

[20] M. E. Huddy, *Matilda Countess of Tuscany*, London, John Long, 1905, pp. 338–339.

Chapter VIII

PAPAL FORGERIES

One is glad to dismiss for a time the crude mendacities of such people as Pianciani, Léo Taxil and Dr. Rappoport, and to turn to a somewhat different kind of attack, in which the assailant, however reckless and misleading the charges he makes, may be assumed to have written in good faith. The fabrication of the False Decretals, a collection of spurious papal letters and decrees of councils purporting to have been made by a certain Isidore, popularly identified with St. Isidore of Seville, is a topic upon which we are never likely to hear the last word. It holds a foremost place among those weapons of the Protestant armoury which are from time to time refurbished for use in anti-Roman controversy, whenever circumstances provide opportunity for fresh hostilities. Some few years after the War there was mention in the newspapers of certain alleged negotiations between France and Japan, the documents connected with which were found, when produced, to be a barefaced forgery. Straightway the incident was exploited to revive all the old allegations about the unscrupulous methods of papal Rome. "A Correspondent," unnamed, contributed to *The Times* an article headed " False Documents—Historical Forgeries Recalled." His selection was varied, but one historical forgery which the writer strangely omitted to recall was that connected with the publication by *The Times* in 1887 of the famous series of articles on " Parnellism and Crime." *Per contra*, we find a great deal said about all those other forgeries which could be regarded as reflecting discredit upon the Church of Rome, and in particular, emphasis is laid upon the momentous consequences

which resulted from the False Decretals and the spurious
Donation of Constantine. Not content with stating that the
Papacy was "buttressed upon forgery," the writer went on
to declare that these fabrications "followed one another in
relentless succession," and that if in the tenth century the
Pope was incomparably superior to the Patriarch of Constantinople, this pre-eminence, which, he alleges, did not exist
in early times, was due to the influence of Rome's unscrupulous
exploitation of documents which were at least known to be of
doubtful authenticity. On the next day *The Evening Standard*
chimed in, and in view of the real scholarship of the writer of
the article, who was no other than the Dean of St. Paul's, a
former Lady Margaret Professor of Divinity and a Vice-President
of the Royal Society of Literature, the reckless inaccuracy of
the statements contained therein is a curious revelation of the
attitude of certain Anglican Modernists of whom he is the
mouthpiece. If Dean Inge had been criticising the position of
Buddhists, or Jews, or sceptical scientists, he would probably
have taken pains to refresh his memory of the points in dispute, so
as to save himself from saying anything too foolish. But in the
case of Catholics he is apparently persuaded that a pose of
complete indifference to details is the most effective check he
can offer to the Romeward movement. And just as the climax
of studied rudeness is achieved by the man who manages to
convey to his interlocutor that he has not listened to a word he
has been saying, so it is Dean Inge's amiable habit to let his
Catholic opponents understand that he does not trouble to
consider accuracy when he is dealing with *them*. St. Isidore of
Seville or Isidore "Mercator," seventh century or ninth century,
what does it matter ? Anyway, Dean Inge writes :

The shameful story of the False Decretals is a monumental
example of the way in which successful forgery may affect
the history of the world for centuries. The guilt is distributed over many Popes and ecclesiastical statesmen,
among whom Isidore of Seville, in the seventh century, is
conspicuous. The body of forged documents continued to

be added to and formed the chief argumentative support of the Papal claims to rule the world. Only the Renaissance brought the monstrous imposture to light, and at the present time even a Jesuit would not defend the Decretals.[1]

Now if there is one thing certain with regard to the False Decretals, it is that St. Isidore of Seville had nothing whatever to do with them. The bitterest assailants of the papal system have not pretended that they came into existence until a century after his time. Moreover, modern scholarship is now agreed that the collection was fabricated about 850, that is to say, at a date when St. Isidore had been just two hundred years in his grave. Obviously Dean Inge, sitting down to write his article about "Hoaxes on the Public and Literary Forgeries," has been haunted by a vague recollection that he has somewhere heard the False Decretals spoken of as the "Isidorian Decretals," and also, that being forgeries, they were, of course, very infamous. On the strength of some such sketchy acquaintance with the Church Law of the early Middle Ages he considers himself justified in preaching a homily to his miscellaneous readers on this "shameful story" of successful forgery and on the "monstrous imposture" of the papal claims. Some of those readers who happen to have studied the facts and to know the trend of modern expert opinion regarding them, may be disposed to ask themselves whether such phrases as "shameful story" and "mostrous imposture" should be confined to denouncing the pseudepigraphic literature of Carolingian times. There are other insincerities and other pretences for which lack of competent learning or the tardy development of a literary conscience cannot so easily be pleaded in excuse as in the case of the ill-educated and sorely oppressed ecclesiastics of the ninth and tenth centuries.

It will be the main object of this present chapter to state briefly the conclusions arrived at by modern scholars, and notably by non-Catholic scholars, concerning the False Decretals. It is remarkable that so far as regards the essential facts of the

[1] *The Evening Standard*, January 5, 1922.

problem there is a very general agreement between the representative Catholic authorities in this matter and those who approach the question from outside. The differences which divide Hinschius, Maasen, R. Simson, Hauck, and Seckel from the Ballerini, Lapôtre, de Smedt, Schrörs, and Paul Fournier are of a quite secondary order, and regard not so much the facts themselves as the interpretation of motives and the influence of earlier precedents. In point of fact, however, almost every quotation in the pages which follow is taken from non-Catholic scholars, all of them of recognised authority.

Let us take first the question of the origin of the Decretals and the responsibility for the forgery. No casual reader, previously unacquainted with the subject, could fail to infer from the newspaper articles cited above that the Popes, speaking generally, were the chief culprits. " The *guilt*," writes Dean Inge, " is distributed over many Popes and ecclesiastical statesmen," and the motive, we learn, was " to support the papal claim to rule the world." The papal power, says *The Times* writer, " was based on forgeries which followed one another in relentless succession." It is plainly insinuated that the weapon of forgery was systematically employed by the Holy See, and the impression is given that the Decretals were only the most important item in a series of fabrications all concocted with the same motive. There is a sense in which this last assertion is true. The false capitularies of " Benedict Levita " and the *Capitula Angilramni* are both closely related to the False Decretals, and they are undoubtedly fabrications, but the vital fact to be noted is that none of these collections originated in Rome or could conceivably have been produced at the instigation of the Roman Pontiffs then reigning. Indeed, it is not, and cannot be, pretended that the " Benedict Levita " or Angilramnus capitularies were intended to further in any way the interests of the Papacy.

The influences which brought about the production of this series of fabrications culminating in the False Decretals are very well sketched by Professor Seckel in the great Lutheran

Encyclopædia of Germany, Herzog-Hauck, *Realencyklopädie für protestantische Theologie und Kirche*. One may quote for convenience sake the abbreviated English edition produced in America by Professor Schaff, but the abridgment reproduces the original with all reasonable fidelity. The author of the forgery is here always spoken of as the Pseudo-Isidore, and Professor Seckel is satisfied, like nearly all other modern scholars, that the Decretals were compiled in the Frankish empire about the year 850. The substance of Seckel's account of the circumstances which led to the forgery is thus presented : [2]

The Pseudo-Isidore's attitude and activity find their explanation only in the general conditions of the West-Frankish Church at the middle of the ninth century ; and when these are understood, he appears in his true light, not one aiming to serve the ambition of any individual or to advance himself, but as the representative and spokesman of a party. The harmonious co-operation between Church and State under Charlemagne had given way under his successors to an antagonism between the secular and spiritual authorities. Disturbed conditions resulted from the civil wars under Louis the Pious and his sons. The bishops suffered in consequence and found themselves compelled to seek protection from the civil power, where they were exposed to false accusations prompted by avarice, while the imperial synods before which they were tried were political and partizan. Between 818 and 835 several bishops were deposed and others through fear fled from their sees. A reform party arose and at various synods (Paris 829 ; Aachen 836 ; Meaux—Paris 845—846) sought to remove the intolerable conditions by an appeal to the old canons. At the Diet of Epernay (June 846) the insolence of the predatory nobility and its disregard of just demands made at the Synod of Meaux, passed the limit of endurance in the estimation of the reform party. Redress by secular legislation was hopeless after the division of the Empire in

[2] Herzog-Hauck, *RE*. XVI, pp. 283-284.

843, and in their need the reformers grasped at falsification as a last resort. The (false) capitularies of Benedict (Levita) had already sought to promote their cause by misuse of the authority of the great Charlemagne, and now the Pseudo-Isidore attempted to cast the highest ecclesiastical authority in the scale of reform. From his point of view the Gallic Church had to choose between two evils—either to secure unity and strength by submission (with proper restrictions) to the pope, or to be involved in the downfall of the Carolingians ; and he chose the former as the lesser. Perhaps, also, by this fictitious ancient law he hoped to convert the obstinate nobility and proud metropolitans, and animate cowardly synods. At any rate he made the venture in spite of the fact that he must have known it was dangerous and probably futile.

Obviously, if this account of the genesis of the False Decretals is in any way correct, the Holy See had nothing to do with the matter. The forgery was perpetrated not in the interest of the Papacy but in that of the Episcopate, and this is explicitly affirmed by Seckel himself. " The consolidation and the extension of the primacy of the Pope," he says, " was certainly not the main purpose of the system of procedure set out by Pseudo-Isidore," and he declares that the opposite view, formerly maintained by Blondel, Febronius, Theiner, etc., is not now held by anyone. Even " Janus " leaves no doubt upon the point. Speaking of the compilation of the False Decretals, he remarks : " Rome, as we have seen, had no part in that," and Hauck so far excuses the fabrication as to admit that " it was not lust of power, but dire necessity (*nicht die Herrschsucht sondern die Not*) which converted one or more of the learned theologians of the ninth century into forgers."[3] Seckel even goes further and denies that the forged Decretals effected any change or altered in any substantial way the conditions of papal authority.

[3] Hauck, *Kirchengeschicte Deutschlands*, II, 533. He adds that, though the forgers cannot be held guiltless, their fabrications were directed to enforcing principles which they believed to be just and necessary.

Only when the pseudo-Isidorian ideas accorded with the spirit of the time and had external support did they prove of practical moment. If they augmented the papal power, they were not the only or the chief factor which produced that result. The attempts to exalt the bishops, to free the Church from lay domination, and to make all synods dependent on the Pope proved abortive. The primacy constructed by the Pseudo-Isidore had no influence on the Church constitution.[4]

It is quite plain, therefore, that when the *Times* writer declares that the power of the Pope in the tenth century (!),[5] i.e., a century before Hildebrand, had enormously increased and was based upon forgeries, he can find no support for such views amongst the most representative scholars of Lutheran Germany.

The principal point with regard to which a difference of opinion is still expressed is the problem of the precise birth-place of the Pseudo-Isidorian Decretals. All authorities are now agreed that they saw the light in the Frankish empire, and also that they cannot be dated earlier than 847 or later than 852, but three separate localities have been suggested for their compilation, and the question cannot be said to be finally decided. Hinschius, who was the first scholar to produce a really satisfactory critical edition of the text, argued strongly for the probability that they were concocted in the province of Reims, where the Archbishop Hincmar showed himself strongly opposed to the presence and action of chorepiscopi (auxiliary-bishops). Other eminent authorities such as Seckel, Friedberg and A. Tardif have adhered to the same view. On the other hand, the indications which Pseudo-Isidore gives of his acquaintance with the correspondence of St. Boniface, and also his use of the capitularies of Benedict

---

[4] *The New Schaff-Herzog Encyclopædia of (Protestant) Religious Knowledge,* IX, p. 349.

[5] It would be hard to imagine anything more preposterous than the supposition that the power of the papacy had increased in the tenth century.

Levita which purported to emanate from Mainz, have induced
Baluzius, Wasserschleben and others to look for the native
home of the Decretals in eastern Franconia. More recently,
however, Paul Fournier has argued very strongly in favour
of the diocese of Le Mans on the borders of Brittany and
in the province of Tours. The political conditions of the times
seem to fit this locality, which was the scene of great disorder
and many outrages upon ecclesiastics, better than any other,
and there has long been a considerable body of critics, including
R. Simson, Mgr. Duchesne and J. Havet, who have warmly
favoured this solution.

But obviously, for our present purpose, the discussion as to
the exact birthplace of the Decretals is of altogether secondary
interest. We are only concerned with the object the forger had
in view, and with regard to that there is agreement. English
scholars, while often repeating, like Hallam, Milman and Lord
Selborne,[6] that the entire edifice of mediæval and modern papal
supremacy was built up upon the False Decretals, have never
even pretended to make them the subject of serious investigation.
A few words, however, may be quoted from Pollock and Maitland's *History of English Law*, seeing that these high authorities
have had the breadth of mind to study this and other problems
in the light of continental research :

> The false decretals [we read] are elaborate mosaics made
> up out of phrases from the Bible, the fathers, genuine
> canons, genuine decretals, the West-Goth's Roman law-
> book ; but all these materials wherever collected, are so
> arranged as to establish a few great principles ; the grandeur
> and superhuman origin of ecclesiastical power, the sacro-
> sanctity of the persons and the property of bishops, and,
> though this is not so prominent, the supremacy of the
> bishop of Rome. Episcopal rights are to be maintained
> against the *chorepiscopi*, against the metropolitan and against
> the secular power. Above all (and this is the burden of
> the song), no accusation can be brought against a bishop so

---

[6] See Moore and Brinkman, *The Anglican Brief against Roman Claims*, p. 170.

long as he is despoiled of his see ; *spoliatus episcopus ante omnia debet restitui.*[7]

The whole position may be summed up in yet another extract from Professor Seckel's article as abbreviated in Schaff-Herzog :

His (the forger's) main object was to emancipate the episcopacy, not only from the secular power, but also from the excessive influence of the metropolitans and the provincial synods. Incidentally as a means to this end, the chorepiscopi were to be suppressed and the papal power to be exalted. . . . The papal power is exalted, but solely as a means to the end desired, viz : to protect the bishops against the political and ecclesiastical parties of West-Franconia and make them supreme.[8]

But even if the Pope had nothing to do with the concoction of these forgeries, and even if the purpose of the forger was entirely selfish and interested, Rome, we are told, has turned the imposture to her own profit and unscrupulously made it the basis of her extravagant claims. As the late Father Ryder [9] well puts it, if the Pope be not a coiner, he is accused of being at least the conscious utterer of false coin. If he is not the thief, he is at least the receiver of stolen goods. It is difficult to return a wholly conclusive answer to this objection, because in order to do so we ought to go into the details of each alleged example of dishonest dealing, and that is impossible in such a book as this. Dr. Littledale—followed, of course, herein by a whole series of controversialists of kindred spirit—declares that no sooner had the Decretals been fabricated than they " were eagerly seized upon by Pope Nicholas I, an ambitious and perfectly unscrupulous pontiff (858–867) to aid in revolutionising the Church, as he, in fact, largely succeeded in doing." To discuss the action of Pope St. Nicholas in relation to his alleged use of the False Decretals would require a chapter to itself. Let us

---

[7] Pollock and Maitland, *History of English Law*, I, p. 17.

[8] Schaff-Herzog, IX. pp. 345, 346.

[9] See his admirable little handbook, *Catholic Controversy*, 10th Edn., p. 177.

note that such writers as Dr. Littledale and Mr. Denny [10] do not hesitate to charge the pontiff, in the words of the former, with " solemnly and publicly lying," seeing that he " assured the Frankish bishops that the Roman Church had long preserved all these documents with honour in her archives and that every writing of a Pope is binding on the whole Church," even though he knew " that not one of the forgeries had ever been laid up in those archives." No one who looks at the Pope's actual words can possibly justify language of this sort. His sentence is vague and involved. He makes no mention of the Pseudo-Isidorian Decretals as such. It may be that his words mean no more than that the Holy See claims in general to preserve the papal letters, though not necessarily any particular letter, among her official records. He does not suggest that he had caused search to be made. He might very well have assumed it was there, believing the document to be genuine. Moreover, as the most distinguished and representative Lutheran historian of our day, A. Hauck, suggests in his *Kirchengeschicte Deutschlands*, it is quite possible that a copy of the Pseudo-Isidorian Decretals had in fact been brought to Rome shortly after 850 in the brief pontificate of one of his two immediate predecessors.[11] When Nicholas declares that such documents were preserved with honour, he need not necessarily be understood to mean that the copies were really ancient copies made at the time. In fact, Hauck, who is little disposed to favour the Roman Church or her pontiffs, goes so far as to say that he finds it easier to believe some such solution as this last, than to suppose that such a man as Pope Nicholas had deliberately lied. In the eyes of German Protestant scholars like H. Boehmer and Hauck, Nicholas was by no means " an ambitious and perfectly unscrupulous pontiff." The former tells us that " his wisdom and eloquence had long been noted," and also that, on his election in 858, " he soon won the affections of the people, maintaining a monastic simplicity in his life and devoting himself to works

---

[10] Littledale, *Plain Reasons*, § 54, e ; Denny, *Papalism*, p. 111.

[11] Hauck, *Kirchengeschicte Deutschlands*, II, p. 542, note 4.

of charity, to well-considered government and to the erection of new churches." With regard to his views of the papal prerogative Boehmer declares :

> His historical importance, however, lies in the facts that he established a wholly new conception of the dignity and power of the papacy and that he made this theory practically felt throughout the West. Gelasius I., indeed, had given a standard expression to the papal claims, as they had developed in course of time, in the famous decretal *Duo quippe*, asserting that the pope, divinely chosen ruler of the Church was, as such, equal in rank to the emperor and independent of him, though in temporal matters his subject, as the emperor was of the Church in spiritual things. But these claims had been of no effect in practice ; it was Nicholas who made them effective and drew their logical consequences. The pope, he asserted, was the absolute ruler of the universal Church, the bishops were his officers, and synods but instruments to express and register the papal will ; church law is not law except when approved by the pope, who is the supreme judge, the personal representative of Christ. These far-reaching claims would probably not have found acceptance, if the most powerful western church, that of the Frankish empire, had not been prepared for them by the Pseudo-Isidorian Decretals. But these were not the sources from which Nicholas derived them ; it was not until after 864 that he ever used this support for them. And he goes even beyond the assertions of the forged decretals, assuming not merely a precedence of etiquette over all secular princes, but the power of commanding them as seems good to him. . . . In a word, it is not too much to say that Nicholas created the medieval papacy.[12]

Not without reason have Catholic apologists always insisted that the claims made for the Papacy in the False Decretals were

[12] Schaff-Herzog, VIII, 116 ; cf. Hauck, *Kirchengeschicte Deutschlands*, II. p. 542.

not new or without earlier precedent.[13]   All who have studied
the recent literature of the subject outside the circle of those
religious controversies which nearly always prejudice discussion in
England, will attest that the trend of competent opinion is to make
less and less of the influence practically exercised by the Decretals
in augmenting the weight of the Pope's authority.   Professor
Seckel declares that the mischief done by the forgery, so far as
canonical procedure was concerned, was relatively inconsiderable (*Der Schaden . . . ist verhältnismässig nicht sehr bedeutend*).
The counterpoise provided by the fact that brute force was
arrayed on the other side must always be borne in mind.[14]
Even " Janus," who uses such exaggerated language about the
harm wrought by Pseudo-Isidore, is constrained to delay the
practical working out of these evil results until the time of
Gregory VII, that is to say, two hundred years after the forgery
had been perpetrated.   Harnack opines that the worst that can
be said of the False Decretals is that by persuading men who
believed in the genuineness of these pretended enactments of the
early Popes, they blinded the learned world to the fact that the
whole history of Christianity had been a process of development
and led to the belief that the Church had been organised from
apostolic times in the form in which she revealed herself in the
Middle Ages.[15]   Hauck candidly admits that to sift out the
spurious from the genuine in such a compilation as the Pseudo-
Isidorian collection was a task which in the ninth or even in
the twelfth century was beyond the capacity of all but a very few.

[13] The question is too intricate and the precedents too numerous to be
debated here.   There are unquestionably authentic letters of Pope Gelasius
(492–496), as Boehmer admits in the above extract, which claim the same
pre-eminence for the Holy See as we find emphasised in the False Decretals.
See Ryder, *Catholic Controversy*, pp. 43–44, 17, and 177–187.   The whole
subject of Psuedo-Isidore is admirably treated by Paul Fournier in the *Revue
d'Histoire Ecclésiastique*, from Jan. 1906 to Jan. 1907, where, on the point now
before us, see especially Jan. 1907, pp. 26–27.   Upon these papers of Paul
Fournier is based the excellent article on the " Decretals " in the *Encyclopædia
Britannica*, 11th Edn., Vol. VII, pp. 915–917.

[14] *Realencyclopädie*, XVI, pp. 303, 306.

[15] Harnack, *Reden und Aufsätze*, I, pp. 7–8.   He adds that the Decretals were
like a winding sheet laid over the features of actual history.

Apart from the extremely obscure and controverted problem of the use made of the Decretals on one or two occasions by Pope Nicholas I [16] there is no reason to believe that these forged documents were made any account of by the Roman Pontiffs during the fifty years which follow this first appearance in history. There is no Pope of that age of whose letters so large a collection has come down to us as John VIII (872–882), but it is noteworthy that there is not a single citation of the False Decretals in any document belonging to this pontificate. Even in the tenth century they are appealed to but rarely, and it was only after that date that they seem to have become widely known, and, as must almost inevitably have happened in so uncritical an age, to have been accepted on all hands without suspicion. To show by quotations from the pronouncements of earlier Popes and councils that most of the claims made for the papal authority by Pseudo-Isidore were not by any means new, would take too much space, but the following words of a recent English essay on the subject are worth citing :

> The immediate influence of the False Decretals in their aggressive character on the Church at Rome was almost as negligible as on the Church in Gaul. They happily confirmed and strengthened three Papal principles which had been alive before they reached Rome, but their part in the development of Papal supremacy was comparatively insignificant. Without the False Decretals Nicholas I. was sure to have effected the same mode of government, and the principles of Nicholas I. were the principles of Gregory VII. and Innocent III. After all, it was not unreasonable. The False Decretals were based upon ancient custom : so were the doctrines of papal supremacy. There was no need for them to be based on the False Decretals.[17]

The same view of the relatively slight importance to be attached to these forgeries is maintained by that distinguished

---

[16] On this see especially Schrörs in the *Historisches Jahrbuch*, 1904, pp. 1–33. He quotes the texts in full, in a more critical form than that supplied in Migne.

[17] G. H. Davenport, *The False Decretals* (1916), p. 57.

student of medieval conditions, the Rev. A. J. Carlyle, of University College, Oxford. In reference more especially to the Donation of Constantine he declares that this fabrication, though it must have been some time in existence, " produced no appreciable effect upon the political theory of the ninth century," [18] and he uses language which implies that the same judgment may safely be passed upon the whole collection of similarly fabricated documents.

Again, Professor Louis Halphen, of the University of Bordeaux, writing in the *Cambridge Medieval History* on " The Church from Charlemagne to Sylvester II," says in connection with the False Decretals : It is a much disputed question to what extent the papal doctrine was influenced by this famous collection." Further, after giving a reference to the articles of M. Paul Fournier, mentioned above, he remarks : " M. Fournier estimates their influence at practically nothing. His arguments appear to prove his case. It is certain that the papal theory had been formulated in its main outlines before Nicholas had cognizance of the False Decretals." [19] Testimonies like these, emanating from scholars who have given their lives to the study of medieval history and law, but who are quite beyond suspicion of any controversial purpose, must surely outweigh the vague references to " monstrous imposture," the " guilt of successful forgery," etc., etc., made by men whose anti-papal animus betrays itself in every line. Seckel, Hauck, Böhmer, Pollock and Maitland, Halphen, Fournier and A. J. Carlyle are names held in reverence by every serious student of history. On the other hand it would hardly be possible to prove more completely that even elementary knowledge of the subject was lacking than the phrases let fall by Dean Inge and the *Times* contributor, as quoted above. No sane person has ever contended that St. Isidore of Seville was guilty of the forgery or that the power of the Roman Pontiffs dominated the Eastern Empire in the tenth century. As would sufficiently appear from what has

---

[18] *Mediæval Political Theory in the West*, I, p. 290.
[19] *Cambridge Medieval History*, Vol. III (1922), p. 453 note.

been written here in our first chapter, the papacy in the tenth century was at its lowest ebb.

Although we are told that the forgeries " followed one another in relentless succession," the only other forgery of consequence which is laid at the door of the See of Rome is that of the so called " Donation of Constantine." Dante has made the Donation (*quella dote*) famous when, in speaking of the fate of the simoniacal Popes, he writes :

> *Ahi, Constantin, di quanto mal fu matre*
> *Non la tua conversion, ma quella dote*
> *Che da te prese il primo ricco patre !* [20]

It was, of course, in Dante's time accepted universally as authentic, like the False Decretals, and it was associated by the wording of the document itself with the fable of the conversion of Constantine, the healing of his leprosy and his baptism by Pope St. Sylvester I. In gratitude for such services the Emperor confirms to the Pontiff and his successors the primacy over the four Patriarchs of Antioch, Alexandria, Constantinople and Jerusalem, and also over all the bishops of the world ; he endows the Roman basilicas with rich possessions, invests the Pope with the imperial insignia, and makes over to him the Lateran palace, the city of Rome and the provinces, districts and towns of Italy and all the Western regions, transferring on the other hand the seat of the Imperial government to a new capital in the East, which is to be called by his name, Constantinople. That this document was a forgery was already seen in the fifteenth century by Cardinal Nicholas da Cusa, by Lorenzo Valla, by Æneas Sylvius (Pope Pius II) and by the Englishman Reginald Pecocke, Bishop of Chichester. The only points which concern us here are the origin of this *Constitutum* and the use that was made of it. As might be expected, it has become the subject of a vast literature.

Despite all the researches devoted to it, the origin of the

---

[20] *Inferno*, XIX, 115 : " Ah, Constantine ! To how much ill gave birth, not thy conversion, but that dower which the first rich Father took from thee ! "

Donation of Constantine is still wrapped in complete obscurity. We have nothing but more or less well-founded conjecture to guide us. The earliest manuscript which contains the text seems to have been written in the Frankish dominions and to date from the early years of the ninth century, but even this is not quite certain. No one can pretend to say that the fabrication of the document was commissioned by any particular Pope. The official style in which it is drafted points, we are told, to the forger's familiarity with the forms employed in the papal chancery about the year 760 ; but this is by no means adequate ground for asserting that it was drafted in Italy. The first writers to notice it are not Italians, and the early manuscripts which contain it are not Italian manuscripts. A wide divergence of opinion concerning the purpose of the forgery has prevailed and still prevails among competent scholars, and this alone shows that the problem has never been solved. On the other hand, while we may conclude with some probability that the document was in existence before the year 800, the first Pope who quite definitely appeals to it, in any Bull or letter preserved to us, is St. Leo IX in the year 1054, when writing to the Patriarch Michael Cœrularius. Surely if such a forgery had been concocted at the instigation of the Holy See it would not have been suppressed for nearly three centuries. It is true that Döllinger and others have professed to find a reference to it in a letter of Pope Hadrian I to Charlemagne in 778, but this, says the article in the *Encyclopædia Britannica* " is now largely rejected ; there is nothing in the letter to make such an assumption safe." Mr. A. J. Carlyle also rejects this interpretation, and he adds that " it is certainly perplexing that there should be no satisfactory evidence that the document was known in Italy until the latter part of the tenth century."[21] Dr. Hodgkin is so much impressed by the little use to which the Donation was put for several hundred years after this date of its fabrication that he suggests that it may originally have been a mere pious romance, recognised as such by its author and his contemporaries,

[21] *Medieval Political Theory in the West*, I, p. 290.

and laid up in the papal archives until its origin was forgotten.[22] Finally, a writer in the *English Historical Review*,[23] points out that until the middle of the fifteenth century the Popes very rarely made appeal to this document, and when they did it was not " to enlarge their own territorial possessions, but rather to dispose of lands newly acquired." In view of these facts, which are attested by historical scholars whose authority and good faith are undisputed, it is a pity that such people as Dean Inge and the *Times* writer, who tell us that the Papacy was " buttressed upon forgery," that " these fabrications followed one another in relentless succession," and that such " successful forgeries affected the history of the world for centuries," do not take the trouble to supply a little evidence in support of their gratuitous assertions.

It is, of course, a great deal too much to expect that the denunciations of the " monstrous imposture " upon which the papal authority has based its claims will ever cease to be popular with the journalist or with the ardent champion of the blessings of the Reformation. But it is a pity that our sensitive moralists do not sometimes vary the theme of their diatribes. They might, for example, occasionally give a turn to the *Monita Secreta*, which for more than two centuries was cited as an exposure of the infamous plottings of the Society of Jesus and which is still treated as an authentic document by certain representatives of extreme Evangelicalism, or they might call attention to " the Papists' Bloody Oath of Secrecy," that forgery of Robert Ware, refurbished by Bolron and Titus Oates, which, thanks to popular credulity, sent scores of honest citizens to prison or to death. Even to this day the Oath continues to be circulated in various forms and it has been repeatedly certified to be the authentic engagement undertaken by the members of different Catholic societies. It is only within the last few months that Sir Edward Parry, in his book *The Bloody Assize*, has expressed his conviction that the oath is an authentic document.

[22] Hodgkin, *Italy and her Invaders*, VII, p. 153.

[23] Vol. IX, 1894, p. 632.

I fail to see [he writes] how Bolron, the colliery manager, could have imagined or learnt it, and woven the strands of the secret treaty into a long and elaborate religious oath, which has the outward literary form of a responsible official production.   This seems to me so improbable that I prefer the simple explanation that there was such an oath, and that the priests on the left wing of the plot were administering it to persons they thought suitable to their ends.[24]

If Sir Edward would take the trouble to consult the article by Father John Gerard, S.J., in the April number of *The Month* for 1901 (pp. 405–413), he would find that the mystery can easily be explained.

[24] *The Bloody Assize* (1929), p. 66.

CHAPTER IX

THE FORGERIES OF CARDINAL VAUGHAN

THE conviction that the whole authority of the Roman See is based on forgery, when once firmly rooted in the Protestant mind, is apt to lead to curious developments. To illustrate the point, it may not be out of place to call attention to a similar imputation which some few years ago was repeatedly made against the late Cardinal Vaughan, the rest of the Catholic episcopate in this country being cited as his aiders and abettors. It is true that in this case the Popes themselves were not the object of attack, but the matter is not alien to our present subject, for the document which occasioned the outburst was a vindication of England's ancient devotion to the Holy See in the shape of a joint pastoral letter signed by the whole hierarchy. This embodied a form of dedication by which the bishops in a solemn function were to consecrate England to our Lady and St. Peter, and in explanation of the ceremony a brief historical sketch laid stress upon the homage paid by the Anglo-Saxon Church to the Prince of the Apostles from the time of the coming of St. Augustine. For some reason or other Dr. George Forrest Browne, then Bishop of Stepney and afterwards of Bristol,[1]took violent exception to this manifesto of the Catholic episcopate. During the years which followed he directed attention to the matter again and again, in published books, pamphlets and lectures.[2] His main contention was that the devotion of the

[1] Bishop Browne resigned the See of Bristol in 1914, but I gather from *Who's Who* for 1930 that he still survives at the age of 96.

[2] Bishop Browne reverts to the same topic in each of the following publications : *The Church in these Islands before Augustine*, p. 15. S.P.C.K. Second

Anglo-Saxon people was not concentrated upon St. Peter as Head of the Church, but was divided impartially between the Holy Apostles, St. Peter *and* St. Paul. The plea itself, as a little examination will show, was singularly weak, but Bishop Browne did not hesitate to urge it in language which was beyond measure extravagant and discourteous. The tone of this Anglican dignitary, who was a Fellow of the Society of Antiquaries and claimed to write with authority on early British history, affords an interesting illustration of the prejudice which often seems to paralyse the reasoning faculties of so many of our fellow-countrymen in their opposition to the Church of Rome.

As a specimen of Bishop Browne's many diatribes, it will be convenient to quote a lecture delivered in South Kensington in May 1897, first because it covers the whole ground, and secondly because, in spite of its quite unpardonable language, it was reprinted in several editions without the alteration of a word.[3] Here is the passage.   We take the liberty of inserting a few numerals to distinguish the different points raised.

> As to the dedication to St. Peter, I shall have to use stronger language.   Leo XIII (*Tablet*, June 3, 1893) spoke of " the special worship always paid by the English to the Prince of the Apostles as primary patron of their kingdom." I would call special attention to that word " worship." Perhaps it, too, is a mistake of the *Tablet*.   Cardinal Vaughan and the fourteen Roman Catholic Bishops in England issued a pastoral in support of this statement, which was published in the same number of the *Tablet*.

Edition. 1895. *St. Augustine and his Companions*, p. 130. S.P.C.K. 1895. *On what are Modern Papal Claims founded?* p. 91. S.P.C.K. Second Edition. 1897. *The Conversion of the Heptarchy*, pp. 51–55. S.P.C.K. 1896. *Theodore and Wilfrith*, pp. 62–70, and pp. 229–231. S.P.C.K. 1897. *St. Aldhelm*, pp. 98 and 252. S.P.C.K. 1903. *What is the Catholic Church in England?* p. 157. S.P.C.K., Fourth Edition. 1905. Most of these are not mere pamphlets, but substantial books. The idea of laying stress upon the distinction between dedications to St. Peter and those to SS. Peter and Paul seems to have been borrowed from Mr. Henry Soames, a rabid opponent of Dr. Lingard, who wrote in the first half of the nineteenth century.

[3] *What is the Catholic Church in England?* p. 157.

(I.) In it they spoke of Caedualla, King of Wessex, and his visit to Rome, as an evidence of the *cultus* of St. Peter. But, unfortunately, Bede states (*E. H.* v. 7) that Caedualla went to Rome that he might be " cleansed by baptism at the threshold of the Apostles " ; that is, it is an evidence of the *cultus* of St. Peter and St. Paul. (II.) They proceed to say that Ina went to Rome " to visit the blessed Apostle," and they proceed—quoting Bede, v. 7—" the same thing was done through the zeal of many of the English nation." Will it really be believed that Bede says Ina went to Rome in order that he might go " to the threshold of the blessed Apostles "—that is, of course, Peter and Paul, not Peter only, and the same thing was done through the zeal of many of the English nation ? I call that scandalous. Here we have *what is practically forgery* [4] to support Roman claims in the nineteenth as in so many an earlier century. (III.) They proceed—" The second monastery at Canterbury was dedicated to St. Peter himself." I call that scandalous. It was dedicated to St. Peter and St. Paul, and this Mr. Rivington has at last allowed. (IV.) They proceed further—" The royal Cathedral of Winchester bore the same patronal title." I call that scandalous again. It was dedicated to St. Peter and St. Paul. No doubt the Cardinal is not personally responsible for these false assertions advanced in support of the claim he is arguing, but he is officially.

It was no doubt very generous of Bishop Browne to excuse Cardinal Vaughan from personal responsibility, but the concession could hardly make matters much better ; for at the foot of the page of *The Tablet* from which the Bishop is quoting, a note is printed giving the immediate authorities for this section of the Pastoral on St. Peter's Patronage in old England. It runs as follows :

[4] The italics of course are mine. We may note that the words " forgery —I can call it no less"—are used of this assertion again later on in the same pamphlet.

See *The English People and Blessed Peter*, by the Bishop of Salford (now the Cardinal Archbishop of Westminster), Catholic Truth Society ; two articles by the same in the *Dublin Review* for January and April, 1892, respectively, entitled " England's Devotion to St. Peter during a Thousand years," and an article by the Rev. Dr. Moyes in the same *Review* (April, 1893) on " Early English Pilgrimages " (to Rome).

Of the four papers mentioned, three, it will be noticed, are by Cardinal Vaughan himself, written not officially, but in his private capacity. Clearly the subject was one to which we may presume that he had paid special attention, and for which he was prepared to take all the responsibility. If the arguments of the Pastoral were based on what was practically forgery, the Cardinal cannot be exonerated. But let us discuss these four points in order, before we touch upon the remainder of Bishop Browne's criticisms.

I. CÆDWALLA

Bede's language about Cædwalla, Bishop Browne tells us, shows that his journey to Rome was evidence of the *cultus* of SS. Peter and Paul. We will not say that this statement is " scandalous," but it is certainly an astonishing instance of the power of preconceived ideas to warp the understanding of very plain language. It is quite true that Bede states that Cædwalla went to Rome that he might be baptised at the threshold of the blessed Apostles (*ad limina beatorum apostolorum*), but we can hardly suppose that Bede meant that he was to be baptized both at St. Peter's Basilica and at St. Paul's. Obviously the phrase is only an ornamental synonym for Rome, the city of Peter and Paul. What Dr. Browne did not tell his audience, who were not likely to look up the original for themselves, was that a few sentences lower down Bede proceeds as follows :

At his baptism the aforesaid Pope (Sergius) had given him the name of Peter, to the end that he might also be united in name to the most Blessed Prince of the Apostles, *to whose most holy body his pious love had brought him from the utmost bounds of the earth.* [5]

Here, then, we have in Bede two remarks about this journey, one, the phrase *ad limina apostolorum*, in itself a formula absolutely vague and colourless, the other a definite and explicit statement. Dr. Browne proposes that the definite statement should be entirely ignored and the passage interpreted according to his own peculiar understanding of the vaguer of the two phrases. But there is more than this. An epitaph was inscribed upon Cædwalla's tomb, and this Bede inserts in his history. The lines of which it is composed are exactly known to us from many different sources, [6] and we also know who the poet was— St. Benedict Crispus, Archbishop of Milan. If Bede goes out of his way to incorporate such a document, he surely was in sympathy with it. If he had wanted to express disagreement, he would have contrived to do so more clearly than by saying that Cædwalla desired to be baptized *ad limina apostolorum*. Now that epitaph begins thus :

Sovereignty, wealth, kindred and kingdom ; triumphs and spoils, nobles, cities, camps and home—all that the worth of ancestry had brought to him and all that he himself had won—Cædwalla, mighty in arms, gave up for the love of God, that he as a royal pilgrim might visit Peter and Peter's see.

Further, the epitaph tells us that he rejoiced to change his name to Peter, and that he gazed upon " the august temple of Peter, bringing mystical gifts." Throughout there is not the least allusion to St. Paul. To me it seems that the one conclusion which may fairly be drawn from this passage is precisely this, that the phrase *apostolorum limina* possessed just the same connotation for Bede that it has for us at present. It involved no conscious reference to the duality of Rome's patrons.

[5] Bede, *Hist. Eccles.*, v, 7.

[6] De Rossi has edited it carefully in the second volume of his *Inscriptiones Christianae*. For the author, see Gregorovius, *Geschichte der Stadt Rom*, 4th Edit., Vol. II, p. 184.

II. INE

If this be true, the misrepresentation concerning Ine's visit to Rome could not be very serious even if it had been intentional. The words used are almost the same : *Ad limina beatorum apostolorum profectus est*—" He (Ine) set out for the thresholds of the Apostles." All that Bede wishes to lay stress upon is that Ine gave up his kingdom and went to Rome to prepare for death. What the motive of this journey was, he leaves us to infer, but it is surely not unreasonable to discern in this extraordinary attraction towards the Holy City some sort of tribute to the See of Peter. No one would wish to regard this as a conclusive argument that England was formally dedicated to St. Peter, but it is not without its value amid a crowd of similar indications. And it is just this which makes the Bishop's imputation of fraud so uncalled for. Whether Bede represented Ine as journeying to the thresholds of the Apostle, or the thresholds of the Apostles, can hardly make a feather's weight of difference in the argument, and yet Dr. Browne did not hesitate to use in connection with a man of Cardinal Vaughan's position and well-known integrity so uncompromising a phrase as forgery. Most assuredly one may admit that where the original text bears *apostolorum* in the plural, it ought not to be translated as if the reading was *apostoli* in the singular. But there is no reason to say either that the Pastoral was, as asserted by Bishop Browne, " a highly controversial " document, or that, even if the change were deliberate, any substantial misrepresentation had been introduced.

Further, the most ordinary courtesy, not to say Christian charity, surely requires that so slight an alteration should not without good reason be assumed to be a deliberate act. There are many bad handwritings, my own for example, in which a final *s* is continually being mistaken for a comma, and *vice versa*. If in the manuscript of the Pastoral, the sentence had been written thus : *Then he gave up his crown and went to Rome* " *to visit the Blessed Apostles* " *and there he died ;* it is surely very intelligible that this should be printed : " *to visit the Blessed Apostle,*" *and there he died.* Neither would such a change readily attract notice in proof. What is more, in Cardinal Vaughan's article in the *Dublin Review*[7] to which the footnote of the Pastoral makes reference, the passage from Bede is translated in full and the words are correctly printed " to visit the Blessed Apostles." Moreover the same is true in the case of Monsignor Moyes' article to which reference is also made,[8] and the Presidential Address delivered before the Catholic Truth Society by Cardinal (then Bishop) Vaughan in 1891, upon which the pamphlet was founded, does include the passage ; and here again it is accurately translated " to visit the Blessed Apostles." [9]

III. ST. PETER AND PAUL, CANTERBURY

We come, then, to the third offence, which Dr. Browne also calls " scandalous." He asserts that the second monastery built at Canterbury was not, as the Pastoral stated, " dedicated to St. Peter himself," but to Saints Peter and Paul together.[10] Now, first of all, even had the fact been as the Bishop supposed, there was nothing " scandalous " in the statement of the Pastoral. So far as can be learnt, hardly any writers, before the Bishop of Bristol, had taken up or laid much stress upon this distinction between St. Peter alone and SS. Peter and Paul jointly. If this matter were one which was known to be keenly debated, it would certainly not be very straightforward to withhold the fact that St. Paul was included in the dedication. But the point was not a matter commonly called in question, and even now the dedication to Peter and Paul seems every bit as significant of strongly Roman sentiment as the dedication to Peter

[7] P. 20.   [8] *Dublin Review*, 1893, p. 255.

[9] See *The Tablet*, July 4th, 1891, p. 35.

[10] It is important to notice, as I have pointed out further on (p. 162), that the words " dedicated to St. Peter himself " are not the equivalent of " dedicated to St. Peter alone," as the reader would inevitably infer from Dr. Browne's way of putting it. The antithesis lies between a dedication to St. Peter himself, and a dedication which, while not mentioning St. Peter, was significant of dependence upon St. Peter's See.

alone. No doubt an exact reproduction of the wording of one's
authorities is always desirable, but in a man like the late Cardinal,
whose tastes did not specially lie in the direction of historical
research, it cannot appear so very shocking that, being for
the moment intent on the dedication of England to St. Peter,
he should regard the insertion of St. Paul's name, when it
occurred, as irrelevant.

Moreover, there remains the question of fact. Was that second
monastery of Canterbury, afterwards known as St. Augustine's,
really dedicated in the first instance to SS. Peter and Paul
jointly ? In spite of the statement to that effect in Bede's
Ecclesiastical History, there is strong evidence that it was not. The
inquiry is rather instructive, and it is curious that Bishop
Browne, while recurring so often to the same point and making
the most categorical assertions, should never have given his
hearers the slightest inkling that there was anything to be said
on the other side. Earlier than the time of Bede we find in the
chartulary of St. Augustine's, Canterbury, a number of documents
(" land books ") detailing donations of land to the monastery.
A large proportion of these are unquestionably spurious, and
it is curious that in nearly all these grants of late manufacture
the monastery is described as dedicated to SS. Peter and Paul.
But in the year 686 under King Eadric we light upon a grant to
the monastery of land at Stodmarsh. The authenticity of the
document is admitted by Kemble,[11] by Earle,[12] who prints it at
length among his *Genuine Records*, by Plummer and by Stubbs.[13]
Now this deed twice over describes the monastery as St. Peter's—
" *monasterium beati Petri, apostolorum principis, quod situm est juxta
civitatem Dorovernis*," and again " (*terram*) *beato Petro ejusque
familiae, in qua nunc praeesse Adrianus abbas dinoscitur.*"[14]

Again, there is a grant by Oswyni, King of Kent, to the

---

[11] *Cod. Dip.* No. 108.　　　　　　[12] *Land Charters*, No. 6, p. 10.

[13] Plummer's *Bede*, II, p. 204. Haddan and Stubbs, *Concilia*, III, p. 169.
No one, as far as I know, has contested this decision.

[14] Birch, *Cartularium Saxonicum*, No. 67 (i, p. 102). In this and similar
examples there can be no question of abbreviation. It is no shorter to write
beati Petri apostolorum principis, than to write *beatorum Petri et Pauli apostolorum*.

same Abbot Adrian, of an iron mine near Lyminge, in A.D. 689, of which the highest authority on Anglo-Saxon charters, the late Mr. W. H. Stevenson, remarks that " it seems to be genuine."[15] though Kemble has asterisked it. Here too we have mention of St. Augustine's as " *monasterio beati Petri Apostoli.*"[16] But what is perhaps still more striking, a privilege of Pope Adeodatus to Adrian, Abbot of St. Augustine's, in 673, which Stubbs accepts as genuine while rejecting other similar Papal documents professing to be addressed to the same monastery, again bears the inscription, " *Adriano Abbati Monasterii Sancti Petri.*"[17] In the spurious documents, however, the inscription is " *Adriano religioso Abbati monasterii Sanctorum Apostolorum Petri et Pauli.*"[18] Now the Stodmarsh charter, the Oswyni charter and the Adeodatus bull are the only early documents relating to the abbey which are accepted as authentic, and they all without exception omit any reference to St. Paul. Hence, we are surely justified in regarding this as satisfactory evidence that in the most official records the abbey in the seventh century was known to be dedicated to St. Peter. All these documents were drawn up a good many years before Bede wrote his *Ecclesiastical History ;* indeed it is noteworthy that in the earliest reference which Bede himself makes to the monastery—it occurs in the *Historia Abbatum,* compiled several years before the *Ecclesiastical History*—he tells us that Benedict Biscop " undertook the government of the *Monastery of St. Peter,* of which Adrian was afterwards Abbot."[19] Moreover, it should be noticed that in his *Ecclesiastical History* itself, Bede several times refers to the same abbey under the name of St. Peter alone.[20] There are no signs in these passages of any effort after brevity, and it seems simplest to suppose

---

[15] Stevenson, *Asser's Life of Alfred,* p. 220.

[16] *Cartularium Saxonicum,* No. 73 (i, p. 107).

[17] Haddan and Stubbs, III, p. 123. It would be ridiculous, it seems to me, to regard these forms as mere abbreviations. There is no sign of any striving after brevity in the rest of the privilege.

[18] *Ibid,* p. 124 ; cf. p. 58.   [19] Plummer, I, p. 366.

[20] *Ibid,* pp. 93, 95, 204, 294.

that this is not a mere contraction, but that in the notes supplied
to Bede the name of St. Peter was alone to be found. The
expanded title was probably due to some accidental misconception of the historian, who might easily be misled by the
analogy of the official designation of his own community,
divided as that was between the two houses of Wearmouth
(St. Peter's) and Jarrow (St. Paul's).[21]

IV. SS. PETER AND PAUL, WINCHESTER.

But if Bede was mistaken in the case of Canterbury, it is
just possible that he may also have followed the same misleading analogy in the case of Winchester, which he mentions
but once.[22] We need not maintain that this was so, but it is
a possibility, and the possibility is certainly not overthrown by
the evidence adduced in Dr. Browne's *Conversion of the Heptarchy*.[23]
The really astonishing thing is to find two Anglican scholars of
the standing of Bishop Browne and Dean Kitchin appealing on
such a point to an array of notoriously spurious charters. " A
charter of 672," wrote the Bishop of Bristol, " describes the church
as ' dedicated in honour of St. Peter, the chief of the Apostles,
and St. Paul,' a charter of 737, Peter and Paul," etc. But
unfortunately these documents form the earliest stratum of
rubbish contained in the Winchester chartulary. They were
probably fabricated long after the time of St. Æthelwald, and
consequently the idea of a dedication to SS. Peter and Paul
may very well have been derived from what Bede himself has
written. Some charters there are in the same collection which
Kemble was inclined to accept and which bear the title Peter
and Paul, but they are all much later than Bede. Of this
Winchester chartulary, to which the Bishop of Bristol appealed
as irrefragable evidence, Bishop Stubbs remarks that it " is a

---

[21] *Ibid*, p. 357, and note the variants of the MSS.

[22] *Hist. Eccles.*, III, 7 ; Plummer, I, p. 140.

[23] *Conversion of the Heptarchy*, p. 52 and p. 53, note. Bishop Browne states
that Dean Kitchin has supplied these references.

chartulary of the lowest possible character,"[24] a verdict which Dr. F. R. Maitland, one of the most eminent authorities on the history of English law, quoted and adopted as his own. Again, Dr. Maitland, alluding to some later and rather better documents in the same collection, spoke of certain " charters of the tenth century which are not (if anything which comes from Winchester is not) suspected,"[25] while Mr. W. H. Stevenson described the contents of the Winchester book as " of such indifferent repute that little confidence can be placed in them."[26] Consequently we may well doubt whether the dedication to St. Peter and St. Paul which appears in the Winchester charters is at all more reliable than the description of the church of Winchester as dedicated to St. Peter which is found in not a few charters and in certain later manuscripts of the Anglo-Saxon Chronicle.

Be this, however, as it may, the chief ground of objection against the Bishop of Bristol's criticism under this fourth heading lies in the impression which he gave to his readers that these were the primary arguments of the Pastoral, and that immense stress was laid upon the fact that the early churches of Canterbury and Winchester were dedicated to St. Peter alone. Those who may examine for themselves either the Pastoral under discussion or the other articles cited in its footnote, will find that this is not the case. The appeal lay entirely to the numerical predominance and to the generally early character of dedications to St. Peter. Under these circumstances the fact that some of the dedications may have been made not to St. Peter alone but to the not less distinctively Roman combination of St. Peter with St. Paul, in no way invalidates the argument. From a painstaking work on *Church Dedications* which was published some years ago by a fervent Anglican and which still holds the field, one may learn some interesting facts. This writer says, for example :

[24] Haddan and Stubbs, III, 638.

[25] *Domesday Book and Beyond*, pp. 330 and 499, cf., p. 497.

[26] *Op. Cit.*, p. 151, cf. *ibid.*, p. 149, note 6, pp. 227 and 246.

Perhaps no chapter in the history of English dedications exemplifies so markedly as the present, the curious fluctuations of feeling towards the various saints. For example, the pre-Reformation churches dedicated to St. Peter outnumber all those to St. John Baptist, St. Paul, and St. John the Evengelist put together. Whereas if we reckon the nineteenth century dedications only, we find St. Peter occupying the third place, after St. John and after St. Paul, and we feel at once that the change is not purely accidental.

Again, the same conscientious student remarks :

The dedications to St. Peter as they are by far the most numerous of the four, so are they—speaking generally— the earliest, and the name when once given has been seldom altered.[27]

In point of statistics we learn from the same authority[28] that the existing pre-Reformation churches in England dedicated to St. Peter, including St. Peter ad Vincula, number 730. Of churches at some time or other dedicated to SS. Peter and Paul jointly we have 275. But of churches older than the Reformation dedicated to St. Paul alone, we have only 29, and indeed, as some of them are doubtful, we have only about 10 of which we can speak with certainty. Needless to say that the dedications to St. Peter alone far outnumber any other dedication except those to our Lady.

Before quitting the subject it seems desirable to say a few words about the refinement so vehemently insisted on by Bishop Browne, which attempts to establish a distinction between the honour shown to St. Peter and that shown conjointly to SS. Peter and Paul. The prevalent impression is that any devotional tribute paid in common to SS. Peter and Paul was much the same thing as a tribute paid to St. Peter himself. With regard to the practice of the present day there seems no room for doubt. The Bishops of the Catholic world who at stated intervals make their prescribed visit *ad limina apostolorum* (to the thresholds of the

---

[27] Arnold-Forster, *Church Dedications*, Vol. I, pp. 51, 52.
[28] *Ibid.*, Vol. III, p. 22.

Apostles), as the phrase still runs, unquestionably regard this as a mark of veneration paid to the See of Peter, the centre of Catholic unity. To set up a distinction between the two associated Apostles and the Prince of the Apostles, between the basilicas of SS. Peter and Paul and the Confession in St. Peter's would never occur to anyone. For long ages the effigies of Peter and Paul have been to Christian Rome what Romulus and Remus with their wolf foster-mother were to the Rome of pagan times.[29] The figure with the keys and the figure with the sword which are impressed side by side upon many Papal decrees, or the still more ancient leaden *bullae* stamped with the portrait-busts of the two Apostles, are just as intimately identified with Roman pontifical authority as the single-figure device of St. Peter upon the ring of the fisherman. The two Apostles are, in fact, the twin patrons of the See of Rome, and from the earliest times their joint praises have been sung, their help implored, or on occasion their malediction invoked upon wrong-doers, in the most solemn Papal letters. But the situation is modified by the fact that St. Peter is recognised as the superior and the source of jurisdiction. It was to him that the power of binding and loosing was directly committed by our Lord. Hence, it has always been the practice to invoke Peter alone quite as commonly as the two Apostles together. The Popes use one form or the other indifferently. What we never do find is an appeal to St. Paul as distinct from St. Peter. Even our homely phrase about "robbing Peter to pay Paul," which in slightly varying forms exists in other European languages,[30] bears witness to our deep-rooted sense of the substantial identity of the two great patrons of Rome. Of course this may not have been so in the days of Bede and Alcuin. It is just conceivable that in that age, when it was said of a man that he had gone to Rome to the thresholds of the Apostles, this gave quite a different colour to his act, and that it was by no means the same thing

[29] Both in the letter of St. Clement, Pope, to the Corinthians, and in that of St. Ignatius of Antioch to the Romans, SS. Peter and Paul are associated. "I do not command you," writes the latter, "as Peter and Paul did."

[30] *E.g.*, in modern French, *décoiffer Saint Pierre pour coiffer Saint Paul.*

as if his object had been to visit the body of St. Peter. It may
be so, and Bishop Browne apparently thought it was so. But
here again we had better allow him to state the case in his own
words. What follows is simply the continuation of the passage
previously quoted.

As a matter of simple fact [he wrote], the first dedications
of churches by the Italian mission sent by Gregory were to
the Saviour and to St. Andrew and to St. Paul ; Augustine
dedicated no church at all to St. Peter.[31] No such dedication is recorded till a generation after his time. It may be
said, that is merely the silence of history. But, unluckily,
the " dedication to St. Peter " must be shown from history,
if it exists. As a fact, it does not. There is more to say
for St. Andrew in the way of primary dedication than for
St. Peter ; and more for St. Paul.

This same combination of the names of St. Peter and
St. Paul, to the exclusion of the name of St. Peter alone,
reaches its climax perhaps exactly where you might have
expected that St. Peter's name would be specially pushed
to the front, viz., in the letter which Pope Vitalian wrote
to the English kings when they had referred to him the
task of finding for them an Archbishop of Canterbury.
Three times over in that letter the Pope speaks most emphatically of Peter and Paul, and only once of Peter alone.[32]
He bids King Oswy follow the pious rule of the chief of
the Apostles in celebrating Easter, and in all things delivered
by the holy Apostles Peter and Paul, who give light to the

[31] The Bishop here adds a footnote of some length, part of which will be
quoted later on. St. Augustine did not live to see the church of St. Peter
dedicated, but he had begun to build it and was buried in it.

[32] For a man who is complaining of inaccuracy of statement and attaching
rather ugly names to it where he finds it, Bishop Browne is surely a little careless
in reading his documents. This letter of Pope Vitalian contains not one but
two references to St. Peter. He tells the King first that he ought " *piam regu-
lam sequi perenniter* PRINCIPIS APOSTOLORUM, *sive in pascha celebrandum*," etc.
(Haddan and Stubbs, III, p. 111.) Secondly, he informs him that he
(Vitalian) has duly received " *munuscula a vestra celsitudine* BEATO PRINCIPI
APOSTOLORUM *directa pro aeterna ejus memoria*." (*Ibid.*, p. 112.) The word
ejus, it should be noted to prevent misconception, apparently refers to *celsitudine*, not to *principi apostolorum*.

hearts of men as the two luminaries of the heaven illumine the world. And he sends to King Oswy relics of the blessed Apostles Peter and Paul, and to Oswy's queen a cross made of the most sacred chains of the blessed Apostles Peter and Paul. And as we are speaking of the forgery of documents by the Romans—for I can call the statement about Ina and Bede no less—even the forged Donation of Constantine itself, by which Constantine was made to give, as we are told, to the see of St. Peter his various possessions, the very forgery, as a matter of fact, gives the property to his holy lords, the Blessed Apostles Peter and Paul, and it assigns as a reason for the gift that when he was cleansed in baptism he was cleansed by the merits of Peter and Paul.[33]

It would be interesting to comment upon the whole of this passage in detail, but a few disconnected remarks must suffice. Let us begin with the reference to the forged donation of Constantine. Bishop Browne fails to see that the terms used emphatically contradict the view that the mention of Peter and Paul was a tacit protest against the supremacy of Peter. Here we have a document, forged, so the scholars unfriendly to the Papacy maintain, about 753 in Rome itself,[34] with the express object of glorifying and extending the authority of the Holy See, and yet this fabrication " makes Constantine declare that in his baptism at Rome he was cleansed by the merits of St. Peter and St. Paul, and makes him give his palaces, &c., &c., to the holy Apostles my lords the most blessed Peter and Paul." Bishop Browne considers that the forger " is so far sound in tone."[35] In reality the forgery proves that in the eighth century, as in the twentieth, no distinction was recognised between what was given to SS. Peter and Paul and what was given to St. Peter. Then as now in the Catholic idea the two great Apostles were completely identified with the See of Rome of which they were

---

[33] *What is the Catholic Church in England?* p. 159.

[34] See Hauck, *Realencyklopädie fur protestantische Theologie und Kirche*, Vol. XI (1902), pp. 6, 7.

[35] *Theodore and Wilfrith*, p. 16.

the patrons. The evidence for this conclusion is overwhelming. Let us take a few examples ; and first of all one or two which, like the last, are supplied by the Bishop himself.

In a lecture delivered at Stafford House in November 1896 on the Church in the eighth century, Bishop Browne had occasion to speak of Pepin's conquest of the Lombards. He told his audience how Pepin collected the keys of the gates of the various Lombard cities and sent them to Rome. Whereupon the lecturer continued :

> There is a curious difference in detail here and I have not had time to look it up. One set of historians say that he had them laid on the altar of St. Peter and St. Paul, and declared that he gave the territories of the Lombards as a possession to the holy Apostles St. Peter and St. Paul. Others say that he had them laid on the altar of St. Peter and he gave the lands to St. Peter.[36]

The writer speaks as if this were a matter calling for much research. It does not seem to occur to him that a very simple solution may be found in the supposition that practically speaking no distinction was made between what belonged to SS. Peter and Paul, the joint patrons of Rome, and what belonged to St. Peter, the first Bishop of the See.

Again, in a footnote to the passage quoted above, Bishop Browne added the following comment :

> Pope Boniface V., in writing to Edwin and Ethelburga in 625, used a phrase which Gregory had not used in writing a generation before to Ethelbert and Bertha, " your protector, the blessed Peter, chief of the Apostles." But, a hundred and thirty years later still, Pope Paul wrote to Eadbert, King of Northumbria, of " your protectors the blessed chiefs of the Apostles, Peter and Paul."[37]

Obviously, Dr. Browne wished his readers to notice how Pope

---

[36] *Stafford House Lectures* (S.P.C.K.), p. 83. We cannot turn aside to follow up this trail ; but the case is full of interest for anyone who cares to examine the evidence. See Hodgkin, VII, pp. 219–229.

[37] Haddan and Stubbs, III, p. 395. *What is the Catholic Church in England ?* p. 158.

Paul also is " so far sound in tone," and corrects, as it were, the language of his predecessor. " The earlier Popes," he says in another place, " in trying to frighten or awe the English into attending to them, spoke time after time of the Prince or chief of the Apostles. But Pope Paul used the true phrase which alone really expresses the view of Catholic times, ' the princes (or chiefs) of the Apostles, Peter and Paul.' "[38]   Unfortunately it has not occurred to the Bishop to examine the other letters of Pope Paul, of which we possess nearly forty, directed for the most part to King Pepin. In these letters there are more than sixty-five references to St. Peter alone, who is often called Prince of the Apostles, but we have not been able to find a single reference to SS. Peter and Paul together, except that now in question.

More than half a century earlier we have a noteworthy letter included among the documents relating to St. Boniface, the apostle of Germany. It appears that shortly before the year 713, Ælfled, abbess of Whitby, sent a nun with a letter of commendation to the abbess of Pfalzel, near Treves. In this epistle she explains that the Sister is on her way to the thresholds of the Apostles for the love of Christ and for the honour of the holy Apostles Peter and Paul (*pro Christi caritate et pro honore sanctorum apostolorum, Petri videlicet et Pauli, ad ipsorum limina ire cupientem*). Thereupon she begs the abbess to entertain her and to help her on her journey, " so that with the good favour of the holy and key-bearing Prince of the Apostles, Peter," she may happily accomplish her design.[39] Surely this combination of the veneration of the twin Apostles with an appeal for the special aid of St. Peter alone is very striking.

Or again, let us note one or two of the many examples in the writings of Bede, whom Bishop Browne commends for dealing out in his Latin poems equal praises to both " the chiefs of the Apostles."[40]   Take the famous speech of St. Wilfrid at the

[38] *Theodore and Wilfrith*, p. 230.
[39] *Monumenta Germaniae Historica*, Epistolae, iii, p. 249.
[40] *St. Aldhelm*, p. 255.

Synod of Whitby in 664, where he won King Oswy over to the loyal acceptance of Roman traditions, by quoting the words " Thou art Peter and upon this rock will I build My Church, and the gates of hell shall not prevail against it, and to thee will I give the keys of the Kingdom of Heaven." When Oswy, Bede informs us, had satisfied himself by the admission of Celts and Romans alike that these words were really spoken to Peter and that to him the keys of Heaven were given by the Lord, he came to this decision :

> And I say to you that this is the door-keeper whom I will not gainsay, but in so far as I have knowledge and strength I desire to obey his decrees in all things, lest perchance when I come to the gate of the Kingdom of Heaven I find no one to open to me, should he not be my friend who is acknowledged to hold the keys.[41]

And thus in Bede's phraseology the counsellors of the Northumbrian king along with him " chose the better part," giving up their Celtic traditions and embracing those of Rome. But the point of special interest is that Wilfrid, with all his devotion to Papal authority, begins his speech with a reference to Rome not as the See of Peter, but as the city " where the blessed apostles Peter and Paul lived, taught, suffered, and were buried." He evidently had no suspicion that by so doing he was weakening the appeal he was about to make in behalf of the Papal claims to jurisdiction.

At the risk of exhausting the reader's patience, two other illustrations ought to be mentioned, because they throw a good deal of light upon the question we are investigating. The first is from Arbeo's Life of St. Emerammus or Haimhrammus, a biography composed about the year 770 and relating to a Saint who lived in the middle of the preceding century. The Saint wished to leave the city in which he dwelt, and made a pretext of a journey to Rome. The phrase used by his biographer in his narrative is " to seek the thresholds of the Apostles," or, in another place, " to go to Rome to the thresholds of the blessed

---

[41] *Hist. Eccles.*, III, 25 (Plummer, I, p. 188).

Apostles Peter and Paul." [42] This, Bishop Browne would say, is quite clear ; it was to be a visit to St. Peter and St. Paul, not to St. Peter only, a visit inspired by devotion to " the actual remains of the two twin-chiefs of the Apostles." [43] But a little further on in the same biography we have what is, or professes to be—it does not for our present purpose matter which— St. Emerammus's own account of the motive which inspired such a pilgrimage :

> I promised [he says] that I would journey to Rome to seek as a suppliant the threshold of Peter the prince of the Apostles, whose Church is known to be founded by Gospel authority, in whose habitation of this world it is undisputed that a judge now sits who by God's appointment has succeeded to Peter's prerogative (*honorem*). He is an apostolic man and a most holy one who holds the primacy, being invested with sacred orders.

Neither here nor in what follows is there any mention of or allusion to St. Paul.

Now this passage may not reproduce the language of St. Emerammus, but it represents the ideas of abbot Arbeo as to the motives which in those days took pilgrims to Rome. Clearly the attraction was not merely archæological or even devotional. The person of Peter's successor counted for something, and the phrase about " visiting the thresholds of the Apostles " was, as it is now, little more than a formula, an ornamental synonym for any Romeward journey. In point of time Arbeo was in some sense the contemporary of both Bede and Alcuin, but he was nearer Bede than he was to the younger English scholar. His ideas of the Roman pilgrimage, so far as we can judge, were those common to all Christians at that period, as many other examples would prove.

The other illustration brings us back again to the question of Church dedications. I have already mentioned that in the

---

[42] I quote from Krusch's edition in the *Monumenta Germaniæ Historica*, Scriptores Ævi Merovingici, IV, pp. 480, 483, 487.

[43] Cf., *St. Aldhelm*, p. 99.

case of the monastery of St. Peter at Canterbury,[44] Bede, though he states formally that it was dedicated to SS. Peter and Paul, also speaks of it in other places of his History as the monastery of St. Peter. Bishop Browne has a characteristic reference to this, which is also interesting as adding yet another item to the long list of the Bishop's comments upon Cardinal Vaughan's Pastoral He tells us that sometimes

> the usual dedication to St. Peter and to St. Paul came by colloquial use to be regarded as a dedication to St. Peter alone. It was probably a curt use of this title on one occasion by Bede, in connection with the Abbey Church of Canterbury, which laid the trap so fatal to all of the Roman Catholic Bishops in England when they put forth their strange and historic though unhistorical document about the dedication of England to St. Peter.[45]

Evidently the reader who seeks information from Bishop Browne upon controversial questions must be prepared for a little generalising. When Dr. Browne talks of " a curt use of this title by Bede on *one* occasion," this is not to be understood quite literally. In point of fact Bede speaks of the Canterbury abbey as St. Peter's abbey not once only but six separate times.[46] Moreover, when he speaks of it as *monasterium beatissimi apostolorum principis*, he certainly cannot be aiming at brevity. We are led, then, to the conclusion that in the eyes of Bede himself a dedication to SS. Peter and Paul was simply a variant of the ordinary dedication to St. Peter.

Finally, it must not be forgotten that, in the words of the late Professor Godefroid Kurth, a high authority on Merovingian history, " the immense majority of churches in the early middle ages were dedicated to St. Peter either alone or in company with other apostles." [47] Hence it would be quite permissible

---

[44] At a later date known as St. Augustine's. I may remind the reader that, as shown above, charters and Papal letters earlier than Bede uniformly give to the abbey the title of St. Peter's.

[45] *St. Aldhelm*, p. 116.

[46] *Hist. Eccles.*, II, 6 ; II, 7 (bis) ; IV., 1 ; V, 8 ; *Hist. Ab.*, 3.

[47] Kurth, *Clovis*, Vol. II, p. 245 (Edit. 1901).

for a critic to quarrel with Cardinal Vaughan's Pastoral on the ground that there were no signs in early Saxon England of any *exceptional* devotion to St. Peter, but to attempt to disprove the prevalence of Petrine dedications simply argues ignorance of the ecclesiastical conditions universal in Western Europe at the time. Bishop Browne quietly ignores all that had been going on in Gaul one hundred and fifty years before the days of Augustine. He forgets what the Bishops assembled at Arles wrote in 450 to St. Leo the Great addressing him as *Apostolatus Vester* (Your Apostleship), and formally recognising that " through the most blessed Peter, the prince of the Apostles, the most holy (*sacrosancta*) Church of Rome held the supremacy (*principatum*) over all the churches of the entire world."[48] And this, be it noticed, was written three hundred years before the fabrication either of the Donation of Constantine or the False Decretals which are supposed to be the main foundation of Papal authority.

[48] See the *Monumenta Germaniæ Historica*, Epistolæ, III, p. 19.

Chapter X

THE POPES AND THE BIBLE

No matter has more frequently been made a subject of reproach against the Roman Pontiffs than their alleged withholding of the Bible from the laity. It was the theme of endless diatribes in the early Reformation period. Under Elizabeth the *Homilies*, so warmly commended in No. XXXV of the *Thirty-nine Articles of Religion*, describe how Satan hath always stirred up tyrants "to pull with violence the holy Bibles out of the people's hands." To this day the charge is still reiterated with manifold embellishments, not only in the more rabid Evangelical journals and from the platforms of Hyde Park, but also by scholars at the Universities and by contributors to our leading reviews. Quite at the end of his life, James Anthony Froude, then Regius Professor of Modern History, in a series of Lectures on the Council of Trent delivered at Oxford, had occasion to sketch the career of Martin Luther. After telling his hearers that as a lad Luther had been sent to Erfurt to study law, he went on to describe how " the Bible was a rare book in Germany, but Martin found a copy of the Vulgate in the Erfurt library. He devoured it day and night. The world assumed a new aspect to him,"[1] etc., etc. Although this represents a relatively mild form of the legend extensively circulated, the statement that the Bible was a rare book in Germany is so contrary to the truth as to be absolutely preposterous. Between the date of the discovery of printing and the beginning (1501) of Luther's studies at the University of Erfurt we know for certain that more than 100 editions of the Latin Bible had been published—most of them in

[1] *Lectures on the Council of Trent*, p. 31.

Germany.[2]   When Brother Martin, having entered the August-
inian monastery at the same place, began his ecclesiastical
studies, we learn from himself that a Bible was given him for
his own private use, and there is no reason to believe that he
was exceptionally treated.   But the legend beloved by Protestant
tradition tells us that when he first discovered that rare work,
an entire copy of the Vulgate, he found it *chained*, so that the
normal reader is left to infer that it was kept as a precious
curiosity which was to be gazed at, not studied.   The truth
being of course that in the monastic scriptoria the more important editions of works in great demand were secured by a chain
attached to the binding so that they might not be carried away
by individuals but preserved where they could be consulted by
all in the interests of the general convenience.[3]   All genuine
students of the Middle Ages are now satisfied that the Latin
text of the Bible was in an extraordinary degree familiar to the
writers of nearly every period before the Reformation.   A
generation earlier than Wyclif, Richard Rolle, the Yorkshire
hermit, as Miss Hope Allen has lately shown, was simply
saturated with Scriptural knowledge, and he was but one of a
hundred others whose whole learning seems to have centred in
their devotion to Holy Writ.   It is true that Dr. G. G. Coulton,
with that charming urbanity which makes him unique among
University scholars, dissents from this view.   " When Dr. Pope,"
he writes, " asserts in the *Dublin Review*, that before the Reformation, ' the Latin of the Vulgate Bible was extraordinarily familiar
to all who could read or write,' he is making an assertion which
nothing can excuse but the ignorance of actual medieval documents which transpires from every paragraph of that article." [4]
Without necessarily endorsing all that Father Hugh Pope has
maintained in the article complained of, one may point out

[2] See W. A. Copinger's essay in *Incunabula Biblica* on the first half-century
of the Latin Bible, and his continuation of Hain.

[3] Mr. J. Willis Clark in his various essays, on *The Care of Books*, gives interesting photographs of the chained books still existing in English cathedral
libraries, etc.

[4] Coulton, *The Roman Catholic Church and the Bible*, 1921, p. 24.

that there are German non-Catholic scholars whose reputation for scholarship is certainly not inferior to Dr. Coulton's, but who speak almost as strongly as Father Pope. "We must admit," wrote E. von Dobschütz in 1900, "that the Middle Ages possessed a quite surprising and extremely praiseworthy knowledge of the Bible such as might in many respects put our own age to shame," and again, "we have to acknowledge that the Bible at the present day no longer forms the foundation of our knowledge and civilisation to the same extent as it did in the Middle Ages."[5] No end of similar testimonies from modern Lutheran theologians might be quoted in the same sense. But it must suffice to refer the reader to the article "Bibellesen und Bibelverbot" in the great Protestant *Realencyclopädie*, re-edited by Professor Hauck, which surely is open to no suspicion of Romanist sympathies. In this contribution the late Professor Rietschel, a high functionary in the Lutheran Church, declared in complete accord with the Protestant Walther and the Catholic Janssen, that "if one considers the whole period of the Middle Ages there is no question of any general prohibition of Bible-reading for the laity." When, he says, heretical tendencies manifested themselves, restrictions were imposed, but in Germany a lively interest was taken, from the end of the fourteenth century onwards, in the multiplication of Bibles in the vernacular. This movement was not of heretical origin. The Church silently tolerated these efforts so long as no abuses followed, without on the other hand lending any active assistance. This is a very different presentment of the case from that of Dr. Coulton—that "until comparatively recent times the Bible was steadily kept away from the people by Popes and clergy."

But it is, of course, the question of the rendering of Holy Scripture into the vulgar speech, and in particular of the Wycliffite version, which has attracted most attention. Whatever view may be taken regarding the existence of a pre-Wycliffite translation of the Bible into English, it must be plain to all upon

[5] See the article of von Dobschütz in the *Deutsche Rundschau*, 101 (1900), pp. 61 *seq.*

reflection that the problem, though most interesting in itself, is essentially a matter of detail, and that it does not touch any point of theological principle. From the absence of such a rendering it could not legitimately be inferred that the Popes or the Church had kept away the Bible from the people. Neither, on the other hand, would the production of a multitude of pre-Wycliffite English Bibles be able to set aside the fact that a Provincial Council in 1408 prohibited the reading of any version of the Scriptures, in whole or in part, which was circulated without episcopal authorisation. The whole question, indeed, of the attitude of the Catholic Church to the Bible may be stated in a very few words, and, despite many efforts to insinuate the contrary, the considerable variations which circumstances have at different times introduced into the Church's practice have been quite consistent with an inflexible adherence, throughout, to the same fundamental principle. For faithful Catholics the Bible is not the supreme, much less the only, rule of faith. Tradition, preserved and communicated through the magisterium of lawful ecclesiastical authority, must always take precedence of Scripture. Moreover, it is from tradition alone that we obtain sure guidance regarding the content of the Canon of the Bible and the nature of its inspiration. The Church has never been wanting in respect for Holy Writ. From the apostolical age down to that in which we live, she has always urged the study of the Bible upon her ministers as a perennial source of truth, as a fountain which springeth up into life everlasting. None the less, she has with equal persistency denied that an acquaintance with the letter of the sacred page was in any way necessary for salvation. How otherwise would the illiterate, who for more than a thousand years constituted the majority of the *ecclesia discens*, and who in her missions to barbarous peoples form the sole audience to which her message is delivered, how could they hope, if this were a necessary wedding garment, to be qualified to take their seats at the supper table of the Lamb ? As a source of edification, of counsel, of knowledge, as a revelation of God's merciful dealings with His people throughout the ages, and above all, as a portrayal of the life and teachings of the Redeemer upon whose Death and Resurrection all our hopes of salvation are based, the Scriptures are infinitely precious and infinitely to be honoured. But as long as the Church claims to be a teaching body, as long as she repudiates and utterly rejects the principle of private judgment, so long must she claim to interpret authoritatively the true meaning of the Written Word, and so long must she continue to exercise a certain control over the dissemination of the Scriptures, when the conditions are such as she deems likely to lead to misunderstanding and abuse.

Even a very elementary acquaintance with the Catholic position should suffice, one would think, to make this attitude intelligible. Can any reasonable man, confronted with the divisions of Christendom, maintain that the Scripture is easy of interpretation. Our Saviour thought it needful to expound the Old Testament to the two disciples on the way to Emmaus. The Eunuch of Queen Candace, asked whether he understood what he was reading, cried out : " And how can I unless some man show me ? " And this was before the Epistles of St. Paul and the Apocalypse of St. John were ever penned. By many non-Catholics the attitude of the Church to the Scriptures has been quite fully grasped. One would ask for nothing fairer or more discerning than the late Dr. James Gairdner's treatment of the subject in the first volume of his book, *Lollardy and the Reformation in England*. Speaking of the medieval Church, he says :

> The feeling was that Scripture was a thing too sacred to be handled by any but a sacred order of men trained to use it properly ; and familiar as we have become with a vernacular Bible, if we could only transfer ourselves backwards some centuries to a period when the sacred text had always been studied in Latin, and when laymen who could read had been accustomed to quite other literature, we might not feel on reflexion that the vulgarisation of Holy Writ was a thing altogether free from objection.

Again, on a later page of the same work, we may read this correction of what Dr. Gairdner calls " a vulgar error which was sedulously propagated by some even in Sir Thomas More's day, and which has been current ever since—that the Church of Rome was always opposed to any translation whatever of the Bible and to its use by laymen."

The truth is [he continues] the Church of Rome was not at all opposed to the making of translations of Scripture, or to placing them in the hands of the laity under what were deemed proper precautions. It was only judged necessary to see that no unauthorised or corrupt translation got abroad, and even in this matter it would seem the authorities were not roused to special vigilance till they took alarm at the diffusion of Wycliffite translations in the generation after his death. . . . The clergy, in short, as they were charged with the care of men's souls, were bound, according to the prevailing view of their duty, to see that what men read was entirely wholesome. We may well feel in the twentieth century, as we have done for some centuries past, that the law of perfect liberty is best, and the attempt which Rome still keeps up to control such matters by the " Index " deserves as little sympathy as it commands. But if we would understand the history of past times, we must enter into the spirit of past times. We must conceive of the clergy as a self-governing body having a divine commission to guide, direct and even control the laity in all that concerned the welfare of their souls, expounding Scripture to them according to their several needs, while inculcating the principles of the faith and commanding obedience to Church ordinances as the necessary means of grace. To allow the use of Scripture to get out of their control when it was easy to keep it under their supervision would have been on their part a manifest dereliction of duty.[6]

All this seems to me temperate and just, as we should expect

6 Gairdner, *Lollardy*, Vol. I, pp. 105-106.

the conclusions of an able and sober-minded Anglican scholar
to be who had for fifty years devoted his time and his energies
to the study of one particular period of English history. Further,
Dr. Gairdner undoubtedly puts his finger upon the point which
was uppermost in the minds of the orthodox ecclesiastics of the
early fifteenth century when he says :

> That which made Wyclif's translation so objectionable
> in the eyes of his contemporaries was not corrupt renderings
> or anything liable to censure in the text, but simply the
> fact that it was composed for the general use of the laity,
> who were encouraged to interpret it in their own way
> without reference to their spiritual directors. To the
> possession by worthy laymen of licensed translations the
> Church was never opposed ; but to place such a weapon
> as an English Bible in the hands of men who had no regard
> for authority, and who would use it without being instructed
> to use it properly, was dangerous not only to the souls of
> those who read, but to the peace and order of the Church.[7]

In close accord with the general trend of Dr. Gairdner's
observations, we find another Anglican scholar, the Rev.
Professor J. P. Whitney, in the authoritative *Cambridge History
of English Literature*, expressing an equally temperate view
regarding the medieval Church's attitude towards the Bible.
It is worth while also to notice that, as Prof. Whitney's essay
was contributed to a volume, the preface of which is dated
March, 1908, his views can hardly have taken their colour from
Dr. Gairdner's monograph which was only published in the
same year. Be this as it may, Prof. Whitney remarks that
among Wyclif's opponents " men like Bishop Brunton of
Rochester also had a deep love for the Scriptures," and he adds
that " the language often used as to ignorance or dislike of the
Bible at the time is much exaggerated and mistaken, as the
works of Rolle indicate." Further, speaking of Wyclif's own
treatise, *De Veritate Sacræ Scripturae*, the same writer notes
that here,

[7] Gairdner, *Lollardy*, Vol. I, p. 117.

while there are already complaints that preaching is inter-
fered with, there are no complaints that the Bible in the
vernacular is prohibited : indeed, the history of the English
translations before Wyclif show that such was not the case.
We have already seen in the case of Rolle how translations
were made for dwellers in religious houses. . . . The
translation of the Bible into English was not prohibited,
but the use now made of it was leading to a claim for
stricter control. . . . The changed attitude of the Church
—the way in which it laid stress upon its right of controlling
the reading of vernacular translations, and was led to regard
popular literature, when likely to supersede its own teaching,
with suspicion—was due to the history of Lollardy.

The Church, which had been so long the guardian of
unity, found itself confronted by forces forming nations and
tending to disruptions. To control and guide these forces
would have been a noble work, but it was a work of supreme
difficulty, not to be wrought by short-sighted or selfish
men. . . . The claim made by the Lollards that " each
lewd [*i.e.*, uneducated] man that shall be saved is a real
priest made of God," tended to weaken the power of the
Church, its power for good as well as for evil, and naturally
made " worldly clerks cry out that Holy Writ in English
would make Christian men at debate, and subjects to rebel
against their sovereigns, and therefore ought not to be
suffered amongst lewd men." Medieval notions of freedom differed from our own, and, as a rule, freedom to do
any special work was held to belong only to a corporation
licensed for the purpose.[8]

For our present purpose it does not seem necessary to quote
the criticisms with which Prof. Whitney—very naturally from
his standpoint—tempers his account of the attitude of the
medieval English Church in this matter, but he clearly has no
sympathy with the statement recently made that " until comparatively recent times the Bible was steadily kept away from

[8] J. P. Whitney in *The Cambridge History of Eng. Literature*, Vol. II, pp. 58–63.

the people by Popes and clergy." It was Wyclif himself, he reminds us, who pointed to other nations with translations of the Bible in their own tongue, and asked why England should not have the same. Dr. Gairdner quotes the passage here referred to in full, and at the same time answers Wyclif's question with true insight into the mind of the clergy and the conditions of the times.

> The worthy realm of France [says Wyclif] notwithstanding all lettings hath translated the Bible and the Gospels, with other true sentences of Doctors, out of Latin into French. Why should not English men do so ? As lords of England have the Bible in French, so it were not against reason that they hadden the same sentence in English ; for thus God's law would be better known.[9]

The answer returned by Dr. Gairdner is twofold, and it seems to me that the two points he makes have not in general met with the full attention they deserve. Even Miss Deanesly's conscientious discussion of the whole subject in *The Lollard Bible* (with its valuable appendices, notably the treatise of William Butler), gives the impression of being too intent upon a controversial purpose to attach full weight to such considerations. Anyway, Dr. Gairdner, to our thinking very rightly, insists that an extensive scheme of translation of the Bible into English before Wyclif's time was not to be looked for simply for the reason that English literature (as distinct, of course, from Anglo-Saxon literature) was only then at its birth. " No considerable work of either Chaucer or Gower had appeared in their own mother-tongue before the death of Wyclif." French, as he goes on to remark, was still the language of the Court and cultivated people. When he cites " Mandeville's " travels as written originally in Latin by an Englishman, and then translated into French, Dr. Gairdner seems to have overlooked the results of recent research, but

[9] Mathew, *English Works of Wyclif* (E.E.T.S.), p. 429. The note upon this passage, p. 530, might now be much expanded from S. Berger's *Bible française*.

there is a sound basis for the general conclusion that "an English reading public could hardly have existed very long when Wyclif began to set on foot the translation of the Bible." No doubt it would be rash to dogmatise, but the evidences which exist in abundance down to the middle of the fourteenth century of the domination of French, or more correctly of Anglo-Norman, among the more educated classes in England are such as to incline to the belief that, if it had not been for some convulsion of a social nature—perhaps the Black Death or the Peasants' Revolt—which occurred towards the latter half of the same century, the prevalent language in this country under the Tudors, and perhaps down to our own day, might have been not English but Anglo-Norman. Surely it is a striking fact that when so typically English a prelate as Bishop William of Wykeham in 1378 wanted to ask a little service of the not less typically English Sheriff of Oxfordshire, Edmund Stonor of Stonor, he writes to him in French ; and such portions of the Stonor correspondence as are preserved from the fourteenth century show that this was not peculiar to William of Wykeham, but was a common practice. It would be possible to give many similar illustrations, but I prefer to quote from a recent utterance of Professor Studer, of Oxford, who possesses a special competence in this matter :

Until the middle of the fourteenth century [he writes] Anglo-Norman remained in every sense of the term a living language, and the natural medium of expression of a considerable portion of the population, of the king's household, the nobility, the clergy, and even the merchants. Nay more, it was steadily gaining ground. A recent investigation [by F. J. Tanquerey, *Recueil de lettres anglo-françaises*, Paris, 1916] has shown that before 1300 few letters were written in Anglo-Norman except by members of the aristocracy, but fifty years later all but the lowest classes of the community conducted their correspondence in that language. . . . For a long time Anglo-Norman maintained itself as the language of the aristocracy. In

N

the 14th century it was used by William Twich in his *Art de Venerye* (a treatise on hawking), by Sir Thomas Gray in his *Scalacronica* (1355), and in many satires and political songs. The regulations of the University of Oxford were drawn up in Latin and French, and students were forbidden to converse in any other language ; and when Bishop Stapeldon (A.D. 1319) wished the nuns of Polsloe Priory fully to understand his meaning, he drew up his injunctions not in English but in Anglo-Norman.[10]

Professor Studer further reminds us that Anglo-Norman, though differing, like the speech of Chaucer's Prioress, from " French of Paris," was not a jargon, but an independent language, as homogeneous in character as the majority of French dialects ; and also that it was closely related to continental Norman, from which it derived its phonetic system and the bulk of its vocabulary. Further he declares :

> The earliest translation into French of any section of the Bible, that of the Books of Kings, was made in this country. Versions of the Psalter, the Gospel of Nicodemus, the Book of Revelation, etc., followed in course of time. Poems based on Biblical stories are numerous and still imperfectly known, but they are surpassed in number by treatises on the deadly sins, the follies of mankind, poems on the love of God, exhortations to saintly life—dull reading when judged by modern standards, but not devoid of interest as the source of some of the earliest Middle English writings.[11]

But apart from the fact that before the close of the fourteenth century there was hardly any reading public to which an English translation of the Bible could have been addressed, Dr. Gairdner is undoubtedly right in his contention that according to medieval views there was a certain desecration of sacred things involved in the idea of rendering the words of Holy Writ,

[10] Paul Studer, Taylorian Professor of the Romance Languages, *The Study of Anglo-Norman* (1920), pp. 11–12.

[11] *Ibid.*, p. 19.

the simplest of prayers of the Church, or even any unfamiliar philosophical conception into the speech of the people. To us who now for centuries have prided ourselves upon the possession of so noble and vast a storehouse of words, capable of expressing the sublimest speculations and the deepest pathos of the human mind, the suggestion must seem preposterous that any sense of profanation or incongruousness could have been associated with the idea of translations into the vulgar tongue. Nevertheless, the doubt whether such a process was quite fitting and reverent was unquestionably real enough. Neither is the point of view so wholly incomprehensible, when one recalls the jarring sensation one has often experienced in hearing noble thoughts, whether they belong to the domain of literature or of religion, associated with some vulgarity of accent or manner which seemed to rob them of all their sublimity. One thinks of rich textures trailing in the mire, of sensitive and refined innocence in the atmosphere of a pot-house. But whether we can analyse it and explain it to ourselves or not, the feeling was undoubtedly there. It comes out very strongly in the decree of Archbishop Berthold of Mainz in 1486 ; it meets us in certain contemporary comments on Archbishop Arundel's action in 1408, and, in fact, in the constitutions then drafted by the Provincial Council. But perhaps no more significant evidence of the persistent survival of the same instinct can be produced than a few stanzas appended by R. Pynson, the printer, by way of *envoi* to the edition of the *Calendar of Shepherds*, which he published in 1506. I quote, in modernised spelling, the first two stanzas, which are alone relevant :

> Remember clerkés daily do their diligence
> Into our corrupt speech matters to translate ;
> Yet between French and English is great difference,
> Their language in reading is douce and delicate ;
> In their mother tongue they be so fortunate
> They have the Bible and Apocalypse of Divinity
> And other noble books that in English may not be.

Wherfore with patience I you all desire,
Beware of the rising of false heresy,
Let every perfect faith set your hearts afire,
And the chaff from the corn clean out to try.
They that believeth amiss be worthy to die,
And he is the greatest fool in the world ywis
That thinketh no man's wit is as good as his.

The verses are rather halting and confused, but they evidently strive to convey two separate trains of thought, ideas which were probably dominant in the minds of many ecclesiastics at this period. The first is that French being a more literary language, and itself of Latin stock, was a fitter vehicle for the communication of spiritual ideas than the barbarous speech of the northern islander. The second was the danger of misuse by private interpretation. The man who trusted his own judgment might easily fall into heresy and come to a bad end. As regards the former difficulty there was undoubtedly some difference of opinion among ecclesiastics regarding the propriety of using translations—the feeling seems to have been analogous to the divergent views of school-masters as to the admissibility of " cribs." Even those who tolerated the vernacular versions regarded their action as a condescension to weakness and strove to give the impression that to use such aids was not quite playing the game. An extract taken by Dr. Gairdner from the *Chastising of God's Children*, a work, written for nuns early in the fifteenth century is, as he says, highly instructive and interesting :

Many men reproveth to have the Psalter, or Matins, or the Gospel, in English, or the Bible, because they may not be translated into no vulgar word, as it standeth, without circumlocution after the feeling of the first writers which translated them into Latin by the teaching of the Holy Ghost. Natheless I will not reprove such translations, ne I reprove not to have them in English, ne to read on them where they may stir you to more devotion and to the love of God. But utterly to use them in English and to leave the Latin I hold it not commendable, and namely in them that been bounden to say their Psalter or Matins of our Lady. For a man's confessor giveth him in penance to say his Psalter withouten any other words—and [i.e., if] he go forth and say it in English and not in Latin, as was ordained, this man, I ween, doeth not his penance. Skills [i.e., reasons] I may show reasonable and many ; but because that I trust to God that ye will not use your Psalter in that manner, therefore I leave off to speaken of this matter, and counsel you, as I said before, that ye pray entirely in time of your service whereto ye been bounden by the ordinance of Holy Church and in the manner as it was ordained by our holy fathers.[12]

It was undoubtedly this spirit of conservatism, at the back of which lay an obscure realisation that the unity of the Western Church was immensely strengthened by the fact of its possessing one common liturgical language, which led many ecclesiastics to look askance at all vernacular translations, even of such simple formulæ as the " Our Father " and the Creed. And their mistrust was in some measure justified by the facts. Probably the most lasting step towards a final breach with Rome which was brought about in the reign of Henry VIII was the abolition of Latin for the public and private prayers of the people. Down to the date of Henry's open defiance of the papacy, out of over a hundred editions of the *Prymer* (the layman's prayer-book), printed for the English book trade, not one is known to contain the Office or the Psalms in English. It was not, most assuredly, that the bishops wished to put difficulties in the way of the people understanding the prayers they said, but they wished them to be familiar with the Church's liturgy in her own chosen ecclesiastical language. Once the practice of using translations became universal, it was felt that it would be very difficult to maintain the same acquaintance with, and interest in, the ritual of the altar, and still more of the Office. When we speak of the restrictions laid by Roman authority

[12] Gairdner, I, p. 112.

upon the free circulation of the vernacular Scriptures, it must not be forgotten that the same rather jealous control was maintained over all versions of the Missal, Breviary, and Books of Hours. The Bull published by St. Pius V on March 11th, 1571, is of considerable interest in this connection.

In this document the Pope absolutely and unequivocally forbids the use of any translation of liturgical prayers even by those who were in no way bound in conscience or by rule to say such prayers. Even the *Horae*, the Little Office of the Blessed Virgin, must not be printed in the vulgar speech or with any part of the text in the vulgar speech. What is more, the officials of the Inquisition are directed to confiscate all books of this kind, though if the substance of the volume were Latin with only a few insertions of vernacular prayers, the books, after correction, might be restored to their owners.[13] This prohibition has long since fallen into desuetude, but it was not a dead letter from the first. We have proof of this ten years later in the pontificate of Gregory XIII, the successor of St. Pius. The decree forbidding translations of the Little Office had entailed particular hardship upon the suffering Catholics of the British Isles. Not only were they by ancient custom peculiarly attached to that manual of devotion, long familiar to them under the name of the *Prymer*, whose most conspicuous element was the Little Office of Our Lady, but they had lost to a much greater degree than other nations the practice of reciting their more familiar prayers exclusively in Latin. No feature of Henry VIII's ecclesiastical legislation was more far-reaching in its effects than the royal ordinances which required that the Pater, Ave, Creed and other such formulæ, not to speak of the psalms and collects of the Church offices, should be recited and taught to the children in English. Even by the

---

[13] It may be interesting to reproduce the text of this last injunction : *At ut ipsorum Officiorum vulgaris idiomatis et sermonis abusus re ipsa penitus aboleatur eadem omnia per omnes et singulos saeculares, etiam ad recitationem antedictam nequaquam adstrictos, Inquisitoribus haereticae pravitatis absque spe illorum unquam recuperationis, alia vero Latino sermone et aliis libris inserta ad effectum emendandi et a maculis seu erroribus expurgandi, sibi postmodum cum sic per eosdem Inquisitores expurgata fuerint, restituenda, consignari quam primum jussit.*

time that Queen Mary Tudor came to the throne, a generation had grown up which was no longer familiar with the Latin prayers, and the result was that, though in her reign Catholicism was restored, a compromise was arrived at by which henceforth the Office of the Blessed Virgin and the other quasi-liturgical elements of the Prymer were printed in Latin *and* English, side by side, in the manner now familiar to Catholics everywhere.

It will be seen, in the light of this explanation, that Pius V's prohibition of any translation of liturgical prayers into the vernacular was felt by English-speaking Catholics with peculiar intensity. If that legislation was maintained, no new edition of the Prymer, practically speaking the layman's only prayer-book, could be issued in the form which had now grown familiar to all the younger generation. From this position of affairs we may realise the peculiar interest of a document which though it has been in print for more than forty years, seems to have escaped the notice of such investigators as Hoskins, Maskell, Littlehales, and others, who have specially concerned themselves with the editions of the Prymer. The whole consists only of a clause in a paper described as " A Petition for Faculties addressed to Pope Gregory XIII by Dr. William Allen [afterwards Cardinal] and the Jesuits on the English Mission." It is dated January 1582 and may be found printed in the supplementary matter added to the first volume of the *Douay Diaries*, edited by Father Knox (p. 365). Translating from the Italian original, one of the sections of the petition addressed to the Pope represents that—

> Whereas a custom has existed up to this among the Catholics in England of using certain little office books (*officioli*) of the Madonna, in Latin and English together, of which there was formerly a good supply dating from the time of Queen Mary but which are now all exhausted, and whereas on account of the reverence they bear to the Holy See they have not ventured to get them reprinted without the express permission of your Beatitude, the priests of the Society of Jesus now on the mission there, being

importuned by the pressing solicitations of these good and devout Catholics, who would derive unspeakable consolation from such a favour, humbly supplicate your Beatitude to grant them this permission, believing that it would be a service to Almighty God and a great help to these souls.

This clause is marked in the margin—the petition was printed by Father Knox from an (intercepted?) copy at the Record Office—*Concessit*, *i.e.*, " he granted it." [14] At what date the permission thus accorded was carried into effect it is difficult to decide with any certainty. Probably whole editions of prayer-books of this kind have perished without leaving a trace. But we know that a new edition of the Prymer was printed by Richard Verstegan at Antwerp in 1599, and there may have been others still earlier.

Now it must be clear that the Popes could have had no conceivable motive in wishing to deter the laity from reciting the Little Office of the Blessed Virgin. There was no danger to faith to be apprehended in this quarter—very much the contrary. No doubt there were a multitude of excrescences which had attached themselves to the *Horæ* and Prymers printed at an earlier date. Amongst these were superstitious devotions and endless apocryphal indulgences. Pius V, as he clearly says, was bent on eliminating all this matter ; but he went much further and forbade any translation of the approved text of the Office itself. It was his manifest purpose to constrain the laity to say the Office in Latin, not assuredly because he wished them to use words which they did not understand, but simply from an intense conservatism which persuaded him that there was a certain disrespect shown to Catholic tradition by using a language other than the liturgical language of the Church. In his idea translation cheapened and vulgarised that which was regarded as especially sacred and which constituted not only

---

[14] The late Father J. H. Pollen was kind enough to point out a reference to this petition in More's *Historia Provinciae Anglicanae S.J.* (p. 121), and to show from an unprinted letter addressed by Father General Acquaviva to Father Persons that the petition must have been presented to the Pope before Dec. 23, 1581.

a symbol of unity, but a real bond, holding together in fellowship the faithful of many nations.

For those who have been at pains to study the conditions of the time, the persistence of this point of view will not seem so extravagant as it might at first sight appear. Down to the end of the Middle Ages everywhere, and in southern Europe very much longer, the man who was able to read at all was able to read Latin, and roughly at least to understand it. What is so constantly overlooked is the fact that every child who was taught to read had his first lessons, not in his own vulgar tongue, but in Latin. He began with the *Pater noster*, the *Ave*, the *Credo* and a few of the psalms. The elementary school-books printed in England at the beginning of the sixteenth century prove this clearly. Very few survive, but we know that thousands were sold. For Italians, Spaniards, and Frenchmen a Latin vocabulary presented no great difficulty. It was easy to recognise the identity of the Latin words with those which they themselves habitually employed in a slightly modified form. For Germans and Englishmen it was otherwise. But even as between England and Germany there was a notable difference. In the speech of the Teuton the percentage of words which could readily be identified with their Latin equivalents was very small ; moreover the whole population spoke German and wrote in German. In England there was not the same uniformity ; the more cultured classes, as we have seen, even in the fifteenth century, often used French. Down to a relatively late date the reports in the law courts and the Acts of Parliament were drafted in French. Corresponding in a remarkable way to this distinction, we find that the need of a vernacular Bible was much more widely realised in Germany than in any other part of western Europe. Apart from the numberless " Plenaries " or " Postils," *i.e.*, translations for the use of the people of the extracts from Holy Writ read in the liturgy, more than 200 manuscripts of the Scriptures in German have so far been enumerated. Sixteen of these contain, or originally contained, the whole Bible, ten others the whole of the Old Testament ; the rest enshrine smaller collections of the books of which the Bible is made up. As for printed editions, seventeen were published between 1450 and 1520 containing the whole Bible, and besides these there were numerous other works which rendered the text of Scripture accessible to the laity of Germany in their own language.[15]

There can be little doubt that this multiplication of translations in countries of Teutonic speech was due to the fact that though a certain proportion of the laity had learned to read, they did not easily read Latin. The vocabulary of the Vulgate was too dissimilar to their own native tongue. The Roman Pontiffs, on the other hand, living under quite different conditions, were prone to assume that the people who were sufficiently educated to read at all would have little difficulty in comprehending the Latin version of the Bible which the Church officially took under her sanction. They did not forbid the use of translations as long as they were approved by the local Ordinaries, but they did not encourage them, for they were persuaded that the Vulgate sufficed, and that this did not lend itself in the same degree to falsifications and incongruities dishonouring to the dignity of Holy Writ.

To sum up. It is the general opinion of those who have paid most attention to this special branch of research—not only of Catholics like Janssen and Jostes, but also of such non-Catholic authorities as Walther, Gairdner, Rietschel, and S. Berger—that the Popes before the Reformation did not systematically keep the Bible out of the hands of the people or forbid vernacular renderings on principle. As Samuel Berger has shown, a version of the entire Bible in French was produced at Paris between 1226 and 1250, while another complete translation into Anglo-Norman was written, probably on English soil, in the early part of the next century ; numerous printed editions followed when this method of multiplication became available.

---

[15] W. Walther, *Die deutsche Bibelubersetzung des Mittelalters*, pp. 709 *seq.* and *cf.* p. 613. The numbers here given have been added to since Walther wrote. See Grisar's *Luther* (Eng. Trans.), V, pp. 536–544.

In Germany, as stated above, there were certainly translations of the whole Bible in use before the invention of printing, and we know of fourteen printed editions in High German and of four in Low German, which all appeared before Luther's translation of the New Testament. In relation to all these renderings, the Church for the most part refrained from any official interference. Some individual ecclesiastics encouraged the movement, others opposed it and held it to be dangerous. When, however, as in the case of the Albigenses in Provence, of the Beghards and Béguines in Germany or the Lollards in England, these translations of the Bible into the vernacular began to serve as an instrument for the undermining of the Faith and the propagation of heresy, the Church imposed stringent restrictions ; but no general prohibition of such versions was ever incorporated in the text of the Canon Law. As for the study of the Latin Vulgate, this has always been encouraged by the Church, practically without restriction. It is interesting to note that Chaucer and Gower, Wyclif's contemporaries, and both of them laymen, possessed an excellent knowledge of Scripture. " He has a deep sense of religion," says Mr. G. C. Macaulay, speaking of Gower, " and is very familiar with the Bible." Yet he had no liking for John of Gaunt, and he calls Wyclif " a new Jovinian and a sower of heresy." No more absurd calumny was ever perpetrated than that which maintains that to the average student of the Middle Ages the Bible was a sealed book. In modern times, now that a certain level of education is generally prevalent, that good Catholic translations are everywhere procurable and that the more active propaganda of heresy has spent much of its fury, the attitude of ecclesiastical authority towards the reading of the Scriptures in the vernacular has passed to a new and much more approving phase. Writing to Cardinal Bourne, in his capacity of President of the Catholic Truth Society, on March 2nd, 1915, the late Pope Benedict XV, through his Secretary, strongly commended the work of the circulation of the Gospels in the vernacular :

The work of opening a way into every Christian household

for the books of the Holy Gospels is one to which assuredly the highest possible praise is due, for thus, as we see, are made known the words of life which tell of all that was said and done by God our Saviour, to the end that men by faithfully giving heed to them as to a light shining in a dark place, may be led nearer to the true light of our souls and aroused to follow Him more closely. . . . It was with no little gladness of heart that the Holy Father learned of the work of the Society and of its diligence in spreading far and wide copies of the Holy Gospels, as well as of other books of the Holy Scriptures, and in multiplying them so as to reach all men of good will. Most lovingly, therefore, His Holiness blesses all who have put their hand to this very excellent work.

It would not be easy to express approval in more emphatic terms than these. Neither can it be said that this encouragement on the part of the Holy See was reserved for the twentieth century. In 1778 Pius VI wrote to the Bishop of Florence, who was active in circulating Bibles in the vernacular :

You judge wisely that the faithful should be encouraged to read the Holy Scriptures, for these are inexhaustible fountains which ought to be left open for every one to draw from them purity of morals and of doctrine, and to eradicate the errors which are so widely spread in these corrupt times. This you have seasonably effected by publishing the sacred writings in the language of your country suitable to every one's capacity.

Similarly in 1820 Pius VII urged the English Bishops " to encourage their people to read the Holy Scriptures ; for nothing can be more useful, more consolatory, and more animating ; because they serve to confirm the faith, to support the hope, and to inflame the charity of the true Christian."

In the face of such considerations as those which have occupied us in this chapter it is difficult to see anything but bitter anti-papal and anti-Catholic bias in the statement that " the Popes and the hierarchy who often dealt so carelessly and ignorantly with their own Vulgate steadily denied the Bible to the people." [16] They did not deny the Bible to the people ; if only because, throughout the whole pre-Reformation period, the immense majority of those who could read at all were able to read the Latin Vulgate. It is again anti-papal prejudice which prompts the assertion that " from 1080 onwards we *frequently* find Popes, Councils and Bishops forbidding such versions." Such official prohibitions were not frequent, and they were always occasioned by some special abuse or danger to the faith ; moreover they were not absolute but conditional. Only prejudice, once more, could inspire such an " interested mis-statement "—the phrase is dear to Dr. Coulton—as the following : " Even in Germany, an Imperial decree was published under Papal influence in 1369 forbidding vernacular Bibles, ' since it is not lawful, according to Church law [*canonicas sanctiones*] that layfolk of either sex should read any books of Holy Scripture whatsoever in the vulgar tongue '." [17] The document is not a decree—not, that is, a piece of legislation. It is simply a commission to certain officials to take steps against heretical suspects, including among a multitude of other provisions a censorship of books. It does not speak of the books of Holy Scripture, but of " books dealing with Holy Writ " (*libri vulgares de sacra scriptura*) which very probably means works concerned with theology, neither is there any reason to suppose that " papal influence " was specially operative in the matter. Still more indefensible is the carelessness through which Dr. Coulton, in his breathless haste to denounce everything Catholic, averred that Janssen " in his enormously bulky " *History of the German People* devoted only two and a quarter pages to the Bible question, and that his treatment is " a masterpiece of the suppression of truth without too definite assertion of falsehood." [18] The facts are that Janssen's *History* gives not two and a quarter, but more than fifty pages to the subject, recurring to it in three separate places, of which Dr. Coulton had only noticed the least important.

[16] G. G. Coulton, *The Roman Catholic Church and the Bible*, p. 24.
[17] *Ibid.*, p. 25. [18] *Ibid.*, pp. 25–26.

Moreover the matters which Janssen is charged with suppressing are duly noticed and commented on in their proper order. The suppressions of which Dr. Coulton is constantly guilty, owing to the fact that prejudice has blinded him to every consideration which tells against his own prepossessions, are far more noteworthy than those on the Catholic side against which he so constantly inveighs.

CHAPTER XI

THE EXTERMINATION OF HERETICS

In connection with this matter of suppression just referred to, a striking instance may be cited from the same pamphlet of Dr. Coulton entitled *The Roman Catholic Church and the Bible*. It has to do with Innocent III, who, he says, " is often spoken of as the greatest of all the Popes." A letter of this Pontiff is appealed to by Dr. Coulton as an illustration of the practice of Catholics in misusing the Bible and in begging more than half the question at issue. But it will be best to quote the whole passage.

In 1199 [says Dr. Coulton], Innocent demanded formally of the Patriarch of Constantinople that he should submit himself and his Church to Rome. The Pope, in this celebrated letter, undertook to prove that " the primacy of the Roman See, constituted not by man but by God—nay, by the God-man—is proved by many evangelical and apostolical testimonies." Here are two of these evangelical testimonies. (1) St. Peter once leapt into the sea. (John xxi, 7) ; now *sea* stands symbolically in Scripture for the whole world (*see* Gloss on Ps. ciii, 25) ; by that action therefore it is signified that Peter took the whole world for his spiritual province. Still more plainly is this proved by Peter's walking on the sea on a previous occasion (Innocent conveniently ignores the unfortunate sequel to this adventure) ; " for seeing that *many waters* [in the Psalm] signifieth ' many peoples ' and that *the gathering together of the waters is the seas* (Gen. i, 10) therefore Peter, in that he walked over the waters of the sea showed that he had received power over all peoples whatsoever." The rest of this long letter, in the light of modern Catholic or non-Catholic thought, is almost as absurd as the foregoing specimen ; Innocent follows faithfully all the forms of scholastic logic, but is fundamentally unreasonable because he postulates instead of proving, all his premises.

Not one out of a hundred of the readers to whom this pamphlet is addressed will trouble to look up the reference to Innocent which Dr. Coulton supplies.[1] But those who do will find that the suggestion conveyed by the words " the rest of the letter is almost as absurd " is entirely without foundation. The Pope appeals to the texts upon which every Catholic controversialist at the present day bases the scriptural proof of the Petrine claims. " Thou art Peter, and upon this rock," etc., stands in the first place, with " to thee will I give the keys," etc. Then he speaks of the injunction, " Feed my lambs, feed my sheep," and later on of the striking words, (R.V.) " I made supplication for thee that thy faith fail not ; and do thou when once thou hast turned again, stablish thy brethren." He pursues the argument through the Gospels, the *Acts of the Apostles*, and the Epistles, pointing out how Peter always figures as the representative and spokesman of the rest. It is true that he also appeals to the mystical interpretations cited by Dr. Coulton, but there is no " still more plainly " when he passes to the walking on the waters—that little touch is supplied out of his own head by our conscientious censor. No doubt such mystical interpretations in these days make little appeal and are disregarded, but they abound in all the patristic literature which the Patriarch held in honour not less than Pope Innocent himself. Indeed it was St. Paul who set the example. What does Dr. Coulton make of *I Cor.* ix, 4 : " And they did all drink the same spiritual drink : for they drank of a spiritual rock that followed them : and the rock was Christ " ? But the point, of course, upon which I lay stress is that this stickler for accuracy and denouncer of suppressions quotes a few sentences which he knows will seem

[1] Migne, *P.L.*, Vol. 214, col. 758 ff.

extravagant to his readers and tells them unblushingly that the rest of the letter is almost equally absurd.

Strangely enough, the letter does not sound ridiculous to other scholars who have read it, even though they own no allegiance to the Catholic Church. In the sixth volume of the *Cambridge Medieval History*, published in December 1929, Professor E. F. Jacob remarks : " He (Innocent) had a noble conception of his office, a keen sense of his responsibility. His favourite metaphor was the fisherman's boat on Gennesaret. ' By Peter's boat is figured the Church,' he wrote to the Greek Patriarch in 1199 [this very letter], ' Peter, then, according to our Lord's command, launched out his ship into the deep, letting down his net for the draught, and thus placed the supreme command (*principatum*) of the Church in the region where temporal power flourished at its highest, the home of the imperial monarchy to which the various nations at fixed times paid their tribute, as the waves go to make up the sea.' " [2]

But being thus brought into relation with Innocent III, my aim in the present chapter is to discuss his alleged ferocity in the persecution of heretics. Once more it will be convenient to cite Dr. G. G. Coulton, the depository of so much of the anti-papal prejudice which has accumulated since the Reformation. In a contribution of his to the volume entitled *Anglican Essays* he wrote :

> The greatest of all the ecumenical Councils held in the West previous to Trent had been Innocent III's Fourth Lateran Council (1215). In the 3rd Canon of that Council it is enacted that bishops should inquire at least once a year in every parish, with power, if need be, to compel the whole community on oath to name any heretics whom they knew. An aider or abettor of a heretic is himself *ipso facto* excommunicate ; if discovered and publicly excommunicated, he incurs civil death, and those who communicate with such abettors shall themselves be excommunicated.

[2] *Cambridge Medieval History*, Vol. VI, p. 7.

For the heretics themselves, they are to be " exterminated,"
and any prince neglecting to exterminate them is to be
deposed by the Pope, who will release his subjects from
their allegiance.   Even if we would otherwise have doubted
what " extermination " means in its final implications,
the word is clearly glossed by St. Thomas Aquinas
(*Summa* 2–2, xi, 3) " remove from the world by
death." [3]

The ordinary reader would infer that St. Thomas was quoting
the canon of the Council and that he definitely pronounced
that " extermination " meant in this particular context " remove
from the world by death."   That is not the case.   He is only
laying down the principle, then generally received, but not
now sanctioned by the Canon Law, that a contumacious heretic
might rightly suffer capital punishment.   It was precisely
because the Latin word *exterminari* did not of itself imply any
loss of life that he adds the words *per mortem*, " be put out of the
way by death." [4]   It is true that, as Dr. Coulton argues, the Vulgate often uses the word in the sense of " destroy " or " make
an end of it," but we have quite clear examples in documents
of another class which plainly exclude that meaning.   Take
for example this pronouncement in the so-called Penitential of
Theodore, Archbishop of Canterbury.   It is attributed to St.
Gregory the Great, but we cannot be sure that it is older than the
eighth century.   In any case it is thus worded, and it may be
found in the same form in a number of manuscripts of later
date :

> If anyone breaks an appointed fast and does this in the
> church and contrary to the decrees of the Elders, outside
> of Lent, let him fast 40 days.   If in Lent, let him do penance
> for a year.   But if he frequently does this and it has become
> habitual with him, let him be put out of every church
> (*exterminetur ab omni ecclesia*), for our Lord has said, " he who

[3] *Anglican Essays* (1923), pp. 113–114.

[4] *Medieval Studies*, No. 17 : " Roman Catholic Truth," An Open Discussion
between Dr. Coulton and Father Leslie Walker, p. 39.

shall scandalize one of these little ones who believe in Me," etc. [5]

Now it is quite impossible to believe that any death penalty was imposed for a breach of the law of fasting, and in fact we frequently find the same canon with a change of wording—*separetur*, let him be excluded from every church. Here, then, is proof positive that in ecclesiastical legislation *exterminari* does not mean "killed." Still, those who framed this ordinance had the Vulgate before them and were just as familiar with its language as the canonists of the time of Innocent III.

It is interesting also to notice the reason alleged for this " extermination " of the offender who persistently sets the law of fasting at defiance. It is the fear that he may " scandalize the little ones," or as the Revised Version translates, " cause others to stumble," and especially the weaker brethren. A scabby sheep may infect the whole flock, and it is the duty of the vigilant pastor to protect those under his care from such contamination. The source of danger must be driven out, just as the leper had to be segregated, but not necessarily by such gentle means as in the latter case, for the leper is an innocent offender. This is the dominating idea which governed the Church's legislation against heretics for many centuries. We shall have to come back to this matter, but first let us notice that this use of the term *exterminari* as the equivalent of " banish " lasted in papal documents for over a thousand years. In the official *Codex Juris Canonici*, the complete revision of the Canon Law, published in 1917, there is an appendix of eight documents, the last of which reproduces a constitution of Pope Gregory XIII, dated January 25th, 1585. The purpose of this instrument is to make provision for the hard case of negro slaves who, after being kidnapped when they were pagans in Africa or elsewhere, have been torn from their wives and families, but, coming under the ownership of Christian masters, have been converted

[5] See Haddan and Stubbs, *Concilia*, Vol. III, p. 186 ; and cf. Wasserschleben, *Bussordnungen*, pp. 167–168 ; Schmitz, *Bussbucher*, I, 619, 641, 674 ; II, 248, etc.

to the Faith. The Pope, seeing the impossibility in such cases of any communication between those so transported and the wives whom they had taken to themselves in paganism, grants faculties for the annulment of these former pagan marriages so that the parties may be free to marry anew. Now the point of interest in the present connection is the phrase used to describe those who have thus been transported far from their native land. The Pope says : *saepe contingit multos infideles ab hostibus captos a patriis finibus et propriis conjugibus in remotissimas regiones exterminari*— " it often happens that many pagans, taken prisoners by their enemies, are exterminated from their native land and their own proper wives into regions far distant." [6] Obviously those so " exterminated " have not been killed, for the purpose of the Constitution is to allow them to marry again ; they have simply been transported from their homes by force.

Anyone who will study at all carefully the language of the Fourth Lateran Council and the papal documents of the same epoch will see that this is the sense in which *exterminari* is uniformly employed, *i.e.*, it means " to be expelled " or " driven out." It is the duty, these injunctions insist, of the bishop and secular rulers to see that the districts committed to their charge are kept free from infection. Contumacious heretics, who are deaf to every appeal, must be induced to betake themselves elsewhere, or else they must be cleared out by force. It would be impossible here to examine a tithe of the passages which make this plain. At the very beginning of his pontificate Innocent writes to the Archbishop of Auch (April 1st, 1198) pointing out how the plague of heresy is spreading in Gascony, urging him to extirpate these evil doctrines and " by every possible means to shut out from the limits of his province those who are infected," having recourse in the last resort to the sword of the secular arm to constrain them. [7] A few weeks later he writes to the Archbishop of Aix admonishing him to welcome the papal commissaries he was sending, and if any of the heretics

---

[6] *Codex Juris Canonici*, Edition 1917, p. 510.
[7] Migne, *P.L.*, Vol. 214, col. 71.

cannot be converted they must be banished from your territories (*de vestris finibus excludantur*).[8] Similarly Honorius III,
writing to Philip of France in 1222, insists that it is his duty
haereticos de regno tuo expugnare, to uproot heretics from the
kingdom.[9]

Perhaps the clearest case of all occurs in a letter of Pope Innocent
written to the King of Aragon on June 1st, 1213. The Pope
there explains that those heretics of Toulouse who honestly
and in good faith wish to return to the Church may be recon-
ciled by their bishop, but, the Pope goes on, we order that
those whom he (the bishop) brands as infected by heretical
pravity and who persist in their errors, are to be " exterminated "
from the said city (*exterminari praecipimus a civitate jam dicta*) and
that their property is to be confiscated and that they are never
more to be admitted into the town, unless afterwards, touched
by grace, they give proof by their deeds that they are true
adherents of the orthodox belief.[10] It is hard to see how even
Dr. Coulton can suppose that a man who has been exterminated
by death should be able afterwards to repent and be allowed to
return to his home again. Nevertheless, when this same bitter
assailant of the papal system was reminded by Father Walker
that Luchaire, whose life work was centred in Innocent III and
his period, acquits the Pope of any intention of exterminating
heretics by putting them to death, Dr. Coulton contrives to
suggest that Luchaire, as well as Havet and Ficker, had not
really looked at this decree, and that they were unacquainted
with the use of the word *exterminare* as used in the Latin Vulgate.
The truth is that they *had* studied the vast collection of Innocent's letters, and had seen enough to convince themselves that
the *expulsion* of the contumacious was the point primarily
aimed at. Thus Luchaire writes that " in the legislation of
Innocent III, as well as in his correspondence, there is no

[8] Migne, *P.L.*, Vol. 214, col. 82.

[9] Migne, *Honorius*, Vol. IV, col. 144.

[10] Migne, *P.L.*, Vol 216, col. 850. Cf. in the same volume, col. 125 and
col. 155 ; and regarding the general question of banishment Vol. 214, vol.
1109 ; also Harduin, *Concilia*, VI, 2, pp. 1031, 1986, 1997.

question of death for heretics. He never required more than
their banishment and the confiscation of their property," and
he adds a little further on that the Pope " forbids haste in
punishing." [11] With this estimate Professor Jacob is evidently
in full agreement. " Innocent, reasonable and judicial as ever,"
he remarks in one place, and, a little further on, " he had no
sympathy with summary justice."

Of the Inquisition, the beginnings of which date from
Innocent's time and which may in that sense be called his work,
there is no room to treat in a book like this. In any case its
extreme developments met with little encouragement from the
Holy See itself. The tribunal of the Holy Office in Rome—
though it is absurd to pretend with some apologists that it was
never responsible for the infliction of the death penalty—was
by comparison equitable in its procedure and merciful in its
punishments.[12] More in accord with the scope of the present
volume is a charge against Pius IV more than once reiterated
by the late Lord Acton, Regius Professor of Modern History at
Cambridge.

Writing to Mary Gladstone (Mrs. Drew) in 1884, Lord Acton
says in the course of some rather bitter comments upon the
tone of such Catholic apologists as Manning and Newman :

> I will show you what Ultramontanism makes of good
> men by an example very near home. St. Charles Borromeo,
> when he was the Pope's nephew and Minister, wrote a
> letter requiring Protestants to be murdered, and com-
> plaining that no heretical heads were forwarded to Rome
> in spite of the reward that was offered for them. His editor
> with perfect consistency, publishes this letter with a note of
> approval.

It must of course be remembered that these words occur
in the course of a brilliant and lively epistle to an intimate

[11] Luchaire, *La Croisade des Albigeois*, pp. 57–58.

[12] For a summary account of the Roman Inquisition I may perhaps be
allowed to refer to my article on the " Holy Office " in the *Encyclopedia of
Religion and Ethics*, Vol. IX, p. 450. Fuller details will be found in Pastor,
Geschichte der Päpste, Vol. XIII, and later volumes.

friend which was certainly not intended for publication. The writer would hardly have permitted himself such exaggerations of phrase in a public lecture, much less in any serious contribution to history. We know in point of fact the letter of St. Charles to which Lord Acton refers, and it contains no mention of murdering Protestants and no expression of dissatisfaction at the shortage of heretical heads. All this is simply the historian's purposely grotesque interpretation of a letter of remonstrance which Borromeo had addressed to the magistrates of Lucca, complaining of their slackness in looking after the heretical leanings of their fellow-citizens resident in Lyons. But it will be well to quote the text of the document :

> 1563, Dec. 18th, Rome.

Cardinal Borromeo to the Ancients [13] (*Anziani*) of Lucca. —I have written on previous occasions to your illustrious Lordships by the express command of our Lord (the Pope), and His Holiness in his briefs had admonished you, with that fraternal charity with which he regards the peace of your Republic and still more the salvation of the souls of its inhabitants, that you should make opportune provision that your citizens and subjects who are in France may live as good Catholics—indeed I remember that you were much commended for the godly measures (*santa provisione*) you adopted in consequence. But now since we hear anew from many quarters that your fellow-townsmen of Lucca, residing in the said Kingdom of France, and in particular at Lyons, are either doing their very worst against religion (*o fanno il peggio che sanno*), or have fallen under such suspicion in the matter of faith, that Catholics are rather scandalized than edified by them, His Holiness by this letter of mine admonishes your illustrious Lordships again, that now particularly when by the grace of God the Council (of Trent) has come to an end, you should see to the renewal of the decrees which have been passed about this matter, and rigorously

---

[13] This was the title of the chief magistrates of the free Republic of Lucca.

carry them out against offenders [14] in order that the evil and the decay of faith may not spread further, but in time be remedied, and that what still remains may be preserved intact. Your illustrious Lordships may be assured that such action will be infinitely agreeable to His Holiness, and that you can do nothing which will give him greater satisfaction than to apply a remedy as speedily and as efficaciously as may be possible. Indeed we are eagerly expecting to hear that you have made suitable provision. As this letter is written for no other purpose, I take my leave and commend myself very heartily to your Lordships.[15]

Clearly there is nothing here about murdering Protestants or sending heretical heads. All that the writer asks is that certain decrees may be renewed which had previously been passed to safeguard the Catholicism of a colony of Luccan merchants who were resident in France. What were these decrees? Canon Sala, Cesare Cantu,[16] Mazzarosa, and more recently Dr. Lazzareschi,[17] all assume that reference is made to a *Bando* passed by the magistrates of Lucca on January 9th, 1562,[18] which set a price of 300 gold crowns upon the head of certain heretics. No doubt this sounds sufficiently startling, especially when we are told that the *Bando* in question was warmly commended in a brief of Pope Pius IV, and in a covering

[14] " Con esseguirli severamente contro li delinquenti." This seems to be the true reading. It appears that one or other of the copies of this letter leaves out the word *contro*, and reads " et eseguiti severamente li delinquenti."

[15] *Documenti circa la Vita e le Gesta di S. Carlo Borromeo* pubblicati per cura del Canonico Aristide Sala, archivista della curia arcivescovile di Milano, Vol. III, p. 289, Milano 1861. It has also been printed by Dr. Lazzareschi in *La Scuola Cattolica*, July, August, 1910, p. 282.

[16] Cantù, *Gli Eretici d'Italia*, II, pp. 471, 478.

[17] *La Scuola Cattolica* for July, August, 1910, pp. 281, 282.

[18] That this was the document exclusively or even primarily commended is not clear to me. It is certain that there were other measures enacted on the 19th of December previous, making provision against the infiltration of heretical teaching into Lucca itself. A phrase in the Pope's Bull of commendation (*ad civitatem ipsam integram conservandam*) seems clearly to allude to these provisions.

letter from his nephew St. Charles.[19] But to say, as Lord Acton and others have said, that this decree was nothing but an incitement to assassinate heretics, amounts to what one can only call a very serious misrepresentation of its purport. At the very worst it was in no way a project for the promiscuous slaughter of Protestants, but a threat directed against certain individuals, *already condemned by the legislature or contumacious and proscribed by name* warning them that *if after a certain date they again set foot upon Catholic territory* a reward would be paid to anyone who took their lives.

To print the text of this long *Bando* would be impossible, but a summary of it will not be out of place. The wording shows that it was aimed at a few individuals who strove to pervert their fellow-Catholics *in Catholic countries*, and were thus carrying on an active propaganda of heresy. The death penalty applied only to those who were proscribed by name after a vote of the council and whose names were posted up publicly in Lucca. We know from existing documents that there were at that time only six such persons, and that in the course of seven years (1558 to 1565) only one name was added to the list.[20] By the aforesaid decree of January 9th, 1562, these men were solemnly warned that they must quit Catholic territory by a certain date, *i.e.*, the middle of February. If found in France, Spain, Italy, or Flanders after that time, a price was set upon their heads. But they were perfectly free to withdraw to Geneva, where in point of fact most of the Lucca Protestants were residing, or to settle in any part of Switzerland or Germany. It was, be it noted, the propinquity of Lyons to Geneva, and the fact that Lyons was then the frontier, which caused the former town to be a rendezvous of heretics. There is not the slightest suggestion that an assassin who struck his victim down in Geneva itself could claim any reward. The aim of the proclamation was not vindictive or punitive, but preventive, as the document explicitly

[19] The letter has been printed by Dr. Lazzareschi, in *La Scuola Cattolica*, 1910, July, August, p. 282.

[20] See the paper copied by Tommasi in the *Archivio Storico Italiano*, Vol. X, p. 450 ; and cf. *Inventario del R. Archivio di Stato in Lucca*, Vol. I, p. 355, note 1.

stated, and in this way it amounted to a general decree of banishment under penalty of death from certain specified Catholic countries.[21]

No one can possibly wish to apologise for such barbarous methods of enforcing stern decrees, but every honest-minded critic will acknowledge that this is something utterly different from a deliberate policy of assassination.

But, what is an even more serious misrepresentation, St. Charles is denounced as if the whole decree were concerned with setting a price upon the heads of heretics. By far the greater part of the proclamation is occupied with practical expedients to secure that the Lucchesi residents in Lyons should lead good Catholic lives. There are prohibitions concerning the reading and keeping of heretical books, the maintaining of correspondence with heretics, and the hearing of heretical sermons. There are other injunctions concerning the observance of the Lenten fast. Most noteworthy of all, the proclamation requires that all the Lucchesi shall make their Easter Communion publicly and together.[22] Information, enforced by heavy pecuniary penalties, is to be given of all transgressions, and a representative body, the *Commissi della Natione*, are to forward periodical reports to Lucca concerning the behaviour of their townsmen in all these particulars. Yet when St. Charles, two years later, complains that the Luccan merchants in Lyons

[21] I venture in spite of its length to give here the more relevant portion of this proclamation : " Che per ovviare che li ribelli et dichiariti heretici, descritti nella tauletta in Cancelleria de' magnifici Signori non infettino nè macchino li altri cattolici . . . statuito s'intenda et sia, che detti heretici et ribelli come di sopra, per l'avvenire, passato mezzo ferraio prossimo, non possino andare, stare, o vero habitare in qualsivoglio parte delle iefrascritte provincie et luoghi, cioè d'Italia, Spagna, di Francia et suo dominio, di Fiandra et del Brabante : luoghi ne'quali la natione nostra suole conversare, habitare et negociare assai. Et per questo ogni volta che saranno ritrovati, o alcuno di loro sarà ritrovato, passato detto tempo, in qualsivoglia de'sopra-detti luoghi, chiunque l'amasserà, guadagni . . . scudi trecento d'oro . . . et in oltre, se sarà bandito, purché non sia bandito del magnifico consilio, sia rimisso et libero di tal bando, et non essendo bandito possa rimettere un altro bandito." (Tommasi e Minutoli, *Sommario della Storia di Lucca*, App. p. 177).

[22] Che siano tenuti et debbino, sotto le pene contenute in dette leggi, tutti insieme communicarsi nel giorno ordinario della Pasqua di Resurretio (*Ibid.*).

are giving scandal by their heretical opinions, and begs the Republic to re-enact their former admirable provisions about religion, the only thing which this suggests to our critics is a bloodthirsty disappointment at the inadequate tribute of heads. The assassination clause had certainly *not* been strictly enforced. There is not a scrap of evidence to show that a single life was taken in accordance with the proclamation, or that the price of blood was even once paid in Lucca at this period.[23] But we may well believe that the other and more practical regulations affecting the daily lives of the little Luccan colony in Lyons had been observed at first and then come to be neglected. Charity and common-sense alike suggest that these were the opportune provisions which Pius IV and St. Charles wished to see re-enacted and carried into effect " in order that the evil and corruption of heresy might spread no further." [24]

It will be plain from what has been said that in the sixteenth century, as in the thirteenth, the dominant purpose which the Holy See had in view was to protect the faithful children of the Church from the infection of an heretical virus. Just as modern Governments are doing their utmost to stifle anarchist and Soviet propaganda by measures which those who are affected by their action stigmatise as iniquitous persecution, so the Popes employed, but on the whole with restraint and moderation, the means of repression universally practised in the age in which they lived. Elizabeth and her bishops burned heretics who denied the Trinity, hanged witches in scores and established a censorship of the Press just as severe as that of the Inquisition.

[23] I say with confidence that, considering the abundant official records still preserved in Lucca, the close examination to which they have been subjected, and the notoriety given to such a case as that of Burlamacchi, if any victim had been assassinated as a proclaimed heretic and the reward paid, we could not fail to have heard of it.

[24] Lord Acton not only wrote privately about this matter, as quoted above, *Letters to Mary Gladstone* (Mrs. Drew), p. 186, but he had previously referred to it in a letter to *The Times* in 1874 (see Acton ; *Correspondence*, I, p. 127). Pastor, *op. cit.* (Eng. Trans., 1928), Vol. XVI, pp. 347 *seq.*, devotes a very long footnote to the subject, endorsing what has been said above.

The banishment of teachers of false doctrine which the Popes enforced was a comparatively mild punishment and they were at all times ready to deal mercifully with those who recanted their errors and proved effectively that they would no longer be a source of infection to the healthy members of the fold.

But we are told that the real attitude of Innocent III towards heretics, not to speak of other Popes less worthy of respect, comes out in the triumphant satisfaction he manifested when he heard of the massacre at Béziers, one of the Albigensian strongholds. As Dr. Coulton puts it, " on receiving official news from his Legate to the effect that the Catholics had massacred nearly twenty thousand inhabitants without distinction of rank, or sex, or age, he wrote in warm congratulation to the Archbishop of Arles." Dr. Coulton appeals to the text of the letter, which is to be found in Migne (*P.L.*, Vol. 216, col. 158), and one might say of his account of it what he, as we have previously seen, asserts of Janssen's discussion of the medieval Bible, that " it is a masterpiece of the suppression of truth without too definite assertion of falsehood." The name of Béziers is not mentioned in the letter ; the whole emphasis falls on the capture of one stronghold after another. Three times over does the Pope clearly indicate that what he rejoiced at was the fact that the heretics has been driven out of the country they had infected. " In marvellous wise," he says, " the hand of God has compelled them to migrate from their tabernacles." He adds that " a dwelling-place is being prepared for the Holy Ghost in the abodes of the heretics who have been expelled " (*in locis expulsorum hereticorum*). He mentions that " Simon de Montfort has been appointed to rule in the land from which they have been evicted." Of these phrases our critic tells us nothing, but when the Pope declares that the faithful crusaders have acquired merit *ex ipsorum exterminatione*, Dr. Coulton, without a qualm, fastening upon this word, sets down as its correct rendering " by the extermination of these folk," and clearly conveys to his readers that it was the massacre of the Albigenses for which Innocent was thanking God.[25]

That anything like 20,000 people were put to the sword at Béziers is extremely improbable, though there was no doubt terrible carnage such as was always apt to occur, then and for many centuries later, in the sacking of a fortified town. The story of 7,000 people having perished in one church which was set on fire seems to be refuted by the fact that the building could not have held a third of the number. Also there is evidence that the town soon recovered and was in a position to defend itself once more against hostile attack.

The legend of Innocent's rejoicing over the " extermination " of the inhabitants of Béziers recalls a still more favourite theme of Protestant polemics, the massacre on St. Bartholomew's day and the coining of a medal by Pope Gregory XIII to commemorate this slaughter of the enemies of the Church. There can be no question that when the news was received at Rome of a blow which seemed to mean nothing less than the annihilation of the dreaded Huguenots the papal court exulted without restraint. What the normal English reader fails to realise is the political complications which formed the background of that portentous *coup d'état*, and also the well-founded fears to which these political complications had given rise. The menace of the Turks had by no means been eliminated by the naval victory of Lepanto. The Mediterranean shores were still exposed to attack, and the Holy See was besieged with appeals for help from the Emperor Maximilian, alarmed for his eastern frontiers.

[25] *Roman Catholic Truth*, p. 19. In view of such an example as this, there is a delightful irony about Dr. Coulton's title. In thorough accord with what has just been said above (that the purpose of the Crusade against the Albigenses was to expel rather than to slay), we may note two points which are emphasised in the short account of the expedition given by Roger of Wendover. He tells us that before the army reached Béziers they sent a formal demand to the inhabitants that they should either surrender the heretics among them or drive them out of the city. It was clearly implied that if they failed to do so the whole city would be held responsible. Secondly we learn that between Béziers and Carcassonne " more than a hundred " encampments of the heretics were found deserted, the occupants having fled to the mountains. This was the *exterminatio* of which Innocent speaks and with which he was satisfied. See Wendover (Rolls Series) II, 88.

It was the earnest desire of the new Pope to complete the work
so well begun by organising a great crusade against the Turk
which would give Christendom security from this ever-pressing
danger.   But the powerful monarchs in western Europe would
pay no heed to his warnings.   The rulers of France and Spain,
filled with jealous suspicions, continually kept watch on each
other's every movement.   Each felt that if the full strength of
his arms were diverted elsewhere he had a rival ready without
the least compunction to stab him in the back.   The French
King, Charles IX, was further embarrassed by the difficulty
of the Huguenots at home.   It was feared in Rome that under
the influence of his mother, the shifty Catherine de' Medici,
the fidelity to the Holy See which he professed was only skin-deep
and purely a matter of diplomacy.   In that particular summer of
1572 well-founded rumours were circulating that Charles was
in confidential communication with Coligny and that he was
deliberately encouraging the Huguenots to support the revolt
in the Netherlands in order to create difficulties for his Spanish
rival.

At the papal court, therefore, before the end of August,
apprehension had reached fever pitch.   News had recently
arrived from Holland of the martyrdom of nineteen priests
and religious, hanged and barbarously mutilated by the Cal-
vinists at Gorkum on July 9th without excuse or form of trial.
This was a fact which could not be gainsaid, and there were
many similar rumours more or less well-attested.   Stories of the
brutalities, the murders, the sacrileges, the violations of nuns,
the profanation of relics and shrines, the wanton destruction of
churches wrought by the Protestants, had long been current and
were coming in every day.   No doubt there may have been
exaggeration, indeed there was bound to be.   We who have lived
through an European War have reason to know that at times of
great popular excitement when strong patriotic feeling—and it
is the same with strong religious feeling—is evoked, accuracy of
statement is not much attended to.   What do we think now of
the report, endorsed even in the relatively cautious editorials

of *The Times*, that there was behind the German lines a " corpse-utilisation establishment "—it was thus that *Kadaververwertungs-anstalt* was unjustifiably translated—which turned the bodies of the slain to account by extracting the fatty matters they contained ? There was, however, plenty of foundation for the horrible tales which came to Rome of the outrages committed by the Huguenots both in France and the Netherlands.[26] No doubt the Huguenots also might have had their story to tell, but they had no representative in Rome to plead provocation, and so far as the Protestant excesses were concerned the Curia itself heard only one side. The result was that Pope Gregory, an emotional man, whose feelings were easily worked upon, had conceived an intense dread of the possibility of a Huguenot triumph in France. Two causes helped to accentuate this. The one was his conviction that the crusade against the Turk, which he had most at heart, could never be realised unless the monarchs of France and Spain laid aside their differences and made common cause against the enemies of the Church. So long as Charles IX coquetted with the Huguenots and left them to do more or less as they liked, all hopes of a cordial understanding between him and Philip II must be abandoned. But, besides this, there was a quite definite belief that the Huguenots had already made their plans to invade Italy. Pastor cites evidence of this persuasion from contemporary dispatches as early as March 1568 ; in particular he appeals to the report sent from Rome by Galeazzo Cusano to the Emperor Maximilian on September 6th, 1572, describing how the Pope had a *Te Deum* sung on the arrival of the first news of the attack made upon the Huguenots. His Holiness returned thanks to God, said the Emperor's envoy, because the Holy See was now relieved of the great danger which threatened them if the Admiral (Coligny) and his accomplices had been able to carry out the plan they had formed. Their purpose was to murder the King, and then to set Coligny himself upon the throne, in order thus to be the

[26] See the abundant evidence cited by Pastor, *op. cit.*, Vol. IX, PP. 372–374.

better able to help the rebels in the Netherlands and afterwards to invade Italy and make an end of the papacy itself. [27]

The mere fact that such a scheme appears to us now fantastic and incredible is no proof that the Roman Court did not honestly believe it. All the evidence (and Pastor in particular seems to have examined the diplomatic correspondence of the period very thoroughly) goes to show that up to. the end of August 1572 the Pope was in terrible anxiety as to how events in France would turn. When the news arrived a few days later that Charles had definitely taken his stand and that there had been a slaughter of the Huguenots, the relief must have been intense. It is surely intelligible that those whose minds were at last set at rest after years of apprehension would not in the first outburst of triumph over their dreaded enemies have considered very narrowly the means by which the result had been achieved. The supremely important fact was that the King of France was now the declared foe of the Huguenots. He had taken a step from which he could not go back. The main impediment to cordial co-operation among the great Catholic powers had been removed, and there seemed now good reason to hope that the great enterprise against the Turks might be successfully carried through.

How far Gregory when he ordered the medal to be engraved and a jubilee indulgence to be proclaimed was acquainted with the real nature of the blow which had been struck against the Huguenots in France is by no means clear. The special envoys of the French King pretended that the Huguenots were plotting the assassination of Charles and that he had merely anticipated them, exacting a just retribution before their schemes had matured. It seems, however, certain that Salviati, the papal nuncio in Paris, sooner or later assured the Pope that this was untrue, for there had been no plot. We cannot be sure how far Gregory had committed himself before he arrived at a full understanding of the circumstances of the massacre. But the documents cited by Pastor, Philippson, and others, make it

[27] See Pastor, *op. cit.*, Vol. VIII, p. 369, and especially note 4 ; Vol. IX, p. 373 and Appendix 7, p. 858.

clear that the Roman Curia regarded Charles's action as an astounding and wholly unexpected piece of good fortune. Probably the Pope was not anxious to learn the details of all that had taken place. If news suddenly reached this country that the entire Bolshevist administration of Russia had been wiped out by a party of Imperialist reactionaries, I fancy that a good many honest English people, even nowadays, would not wait to express their satisfaction until they knew exactly how the clearance had been effected, and even if it afterwards came to light that the Bolshevists had all been murdered in their beds, one may doubt whether the British Parliament would withhold political recognition from the authors of the massacre, always assuming that they had succeeded in establishing a new Government in the place of that which had ceased to be.

The one thing which now seems to be almost universally admitted by the many competent investigators who have occupied themselves with the massacre of St. Bartholomew is that the Holy See did not instigate it and knew nothing about it beforehand. In fact almost all are agreed, in spite of Lord Acton's contention to the contrary,[28] that the terrible slaughter in Paris on August 24th came about without any deep-laid design on the part of those who were responsible for it." There is no reason for doubting," writes Professor J. W. Thompson, " that the massacre of St. Bartholomew was unpremeditated. It was not plotted years before, or even many days before. The light of modern investigation has proved this to the satisfaction of every unprejudiced historian, whether Protestant or Catholic." [29]

The words of this History Professor of Chicago carry the more weight because Professor Henri Hauser, in his *Sources de l'Histoire de France*, recommends this book as the most reliable discussion of the subject. Another important fact, too often

---

[28] Lord Acton's longer article on the St. Bartholomew massacre was published in the *North British Review*, Oct., 1869. He reverts to the subject in his letter to *The Times* of 24 Nov., 1874.

[29] *The Wars of Religion in France* (1909), p. 451.

P

overlooked, is that the Pope, down to the very end of August, 1572, believed that both Charles IX and Catharine de Medici were playing directly into the hands of the Huguenots. His joy at this conclusive proof that his fears were not justified was proportionately great. Professor Thompson's opinion is supported by that of many other non-Catholic writers, notably by Philippson [30] and by Platzhoff [31], but the reader will naturally turn to the ninth volume of Pastor's *Geschichte der Päpste* (in the English edition Vol. XVII), in which chapter 7 provides an admirable sketch of the whole historical setting.

[30] " Die römische Kurie und die Bartholomäusnacht " in the *Deutsche Zeitschrift f. Geschichtswissenschaft*, VII, 1892.

[31] *Historische Bibliothek*, Vol. 28, 1912.

Chapter XII

GROVELLING TO THE POPE

For more than a hundred years—say from 1765 to 1870—the normal Englishman acquired such knowledge as he possessed of the history of his native land directly or indirectly from the pages of David Hume. Without charging the Scottish freethinker with exceptional anti-papal bias, we may say that Hume was ready enough to make appeal to national sentiment. Mistrust and defiance of Rome were, he knew, deeply ingrained in the heart of every true Protestant. Had not Shakespeare put into the mouth of King John, before his submission, this proud challenge ?

> Thou canst not, Cardinal, devise a name
> So slight, unworthy and ridiculous
> To charge me to an answer, as the Pope—
>
> So tell the Pope ; all reverence set apart
> To him, and his usurp'd authority.

When Hume, therefore, had to treat of John's surrender, he spares no detail in order to bring home more forcibly to his readers the ignominy to which that monarch was reduced :

In consequence of this agreement [he writes] John did homage to Pandulf as the Pope's legate with all the submissive rites which the feudal law required of vassals before their liege-lord and superior. He came disarmed into the legate's presence, who was seated on a throne ; he flung himself on his knees before him ; he lifted up his joined hands and put them within those of Pandulf ; he swore

fealty to the Pope ; and he paid part of the tribute which
he owed for his kingdom as the patrimony of St. Peter.
The legate, elated by this supreme triumph of sacerdotal
power, could not forbear discovering extravagant symptoms
of joy and exultation. He trampled on the money which
was laid at his feet as an earnest of the subjection of the
kingdom—an insolence, of which, however offensive to all
the English, no one present except the Archbishop of
Dublin dared to take any notice.[1]

Even Lingard, writing some fifty years later, felt that the
popular sentiment of those days would not allow him to defend
unequivocally such abject submission. He says, therefore :

> This transaction has heaped everlasting infamy on the
> memory of John. Every epithet of reproach has been
> expended by writers and readers against the pusillanimity
> of a prince, who could lay his dominions at the feet of a
> foreign priest, and receive them from him again as his
> feudatory. It was certainly a disgraceful act ; but there
> are some considerations, which, if they do not remove,
> will at least extenuate his offence.

The reasons which Lingard pleads in mitigation of judgment
have since his time been more powerfully set out, as we shall
see, by writers less under suspicion than he of holding a brief
for papal pretensions. But the sense of an outrageous national
humiliation still remains and is to this day exploited at every
turn by those who seek to accentuate the repugnances which
hold back the English people from any accommodation with the
papacy. Dr. Augustus Jessopp in *The Penny History of the Church
of England*, published by the S.P.C.K., the very bulk of which
(90 pages) is a sure testimony to its vast sale, reinforces his
italics with a note of exclamation when he tells his readers
how John " did homage for his kingdom to the Bishop of
Rome, and became no longer an independent king, but a
vassal of the Pope, *binding himself and his successors to pay a yearly*

---

[1] Hume, *History of England*, chap. XI. The story of Pandulf's trampling
on the money can by no means be taken as a fact certainly demonstrated.

tribute to the papacy for his kingdom ! During these shameful years," etc. Not less emphatically did Mr. J. R. Green, in a work which for its price and subject has enjoyed a popularity without parallel in modern times, insist that " England thrilled at the news [of John's submission] with a sense of national shame such as she had never felt before. ' He has become the Pope's man ' the whole country murmured ; ' he has forfeited the very name of King ; from a free man he has degraded himself into a serf.' " [2] In the same vein Dr. Percy Dearmer, issuing a handbook a few years ago in connection with the English Church Pageant, declared that " John, after much defiance, had grovelled to the Papacy as no other king ever did before or since," and he adds that " after Magna Charta had been signed Innocent III had the audacity to cancel it, to excommunicate the barons, by name and in the lump, and to suspend Stephen Langton from his archbishopric." [3]

How exaggerated, and indeed preposterous, all this language is, soon becomes clear to anyone who will study with a little patience the chronicles and correspondence contemporary with these events. J. R. Green, when better informed, had the honesty to own that what he had previously written could not be defended. In his larger History, published a few years later, instead of saying that " England thrilled with a sense of national shame," as quoted above, he expanded his paragraph thus :

> In after times men believed that England thrilled at the news with a sense of national shame such as she had never

[2] *History of the English People* (Edition 1876), p. 121.

[3] Dearmer, *Everyman's History of the English Church* (Mowbray, 1909), p. 62. This language is repeated in all sorts of educational manuals. See, for example, C. A. Lane's *Illustrated Notes on English Church History*, S.P.C.K., of which the 70th thousand was printed as far back as 1892, pp. 206–207. Similarly in Blackie and Son's *Complete History Readers, Book VII*, the young learner is told : " In sign that he [John] submitted, he even gave up his crown to Pandulf and received it back from him as a gift from the Pope. Every Englishman was ashamed of a king who could demean himself in this way," and again : " He [John] got the Pope to say that he was not bound by his oath, one of those pieces of papal interference that made Englishmen dislike the Pope," pp. 52–53.

felt before. . . . But this was the belief of a day still to
come. . . . We see little trace of such a feeling in the
contemporary accounts of the time. All seem rather to
have regarded it as a complete settlement of the difficulties
in which King and kingdom were involved.[4]

Following in this matter Mr. J. R. Green's excellent example,
our better-informed modern historians, with scarcely an exception, have had the honesty to set the matter in quite a different
light. For instance, Mr. G. B. Adams, who contributed the
volume on the Normans and Angevins to Longman's *Political
History of England*, writing in the more impartial atmosphere of
Yale University, where he was Professor of History, said :

We should be particularly careful not to judge this act
of John's by the sentiment of a later time. There was
nothing that seemed degrading to that age about becoming
a vassal. Every member of the aristocracy of Europe and
almost every king was a vassal. A man passed from the
classes that were looked down upon, the peasantry and the
bourgeoisie, into the nobility by becoming a vassal. The
English kings had been vassals since feudalism had existed
in England, though not for the kingdom ; and only a few
years before, Richard had made even that a fief of the
empire. There is no evidence that John's right to take
this step was questioned by any one, or that there was any
general condemnation of it at that time. One writer a
few years later says that the act seemed to many " ignominious," but he records in the same sentence his own judgment that John was very prudently " providing for himself
and his by the deed." Even in the rebellion against John
that closed his reign, no objection was made to the relation-
ship with the Papacy, nor was the King's right to act as
he did denied.[5]

Almost precisely similar is the tone of the late Regius Professor
of Modern History at Oxford, Mr. H. W. C. Davis, of Balliol :

[4] *History of the English People* (Library Edition), Vol. I, p. 235.

[5] Adams, *Political History of England*, 1066–1216. London, 1905, p. 424.

Innocent [he says], whose heart was set upon obtaining the assistance of John and the English for a new Crusade, had no wish to abuse his advantage ; nor is he to be blamed for the famous transaction of May 15th, when John made over his kingdom to the Holy See to be held as a fief for a rent of 1,000 marks. The idea was the King's, but it was no novelty to the statesmen of the age. Before John submitted, the sovereigns of the two Sicilies, of Sweden, Denmark, Aragon, Poland, had already become Papal vassals. Further, a perusal of the document containing John's profession of homage will show that, beyond the tribute, he incurred no obligations more onerous than those which all prelates undertook by their oath of fidelity at the time of consecration. He purchased the fullest measure of protection by a sacrifice of dignity to which neither he nor the great mass of his subjects attached much importance.[6]

Again, Miss Norgate, who devoted long years of study to this period, writes in her monograph on *John Lackland* :

One English chronicler (Wendover) says that John, in performing this homage, acted according to what had been decreed at Rome. Another, not less generally accurate and well informed, says that John " added it of his own accord " to the agreement already completed. On the whole, it is probable that this latter account of the matter is the correct one, at least thus far, that the scheme originated not at Rome but in England.

Without laying great stress upon it, Miss Norgate proceeds to note that the King in the charter of homage itself declares the act to be a voluntary one, performed with the counsel of his barons, also that no extant document contains any indication that the Pope had demanded anything of the sort. Finally, she concludes that John acted with a deep-laid design of attaching the Pope to his side. " There seems, in short," so she sums up

[6] H. W. C. Davis, *England under the Normans and Angevins*. London, 1905, p. 368. In quoting this passage I have incorporated in the text a sentence which in the original appears only as a footnote.

the matter, " to be good reason for believing that John's homage
to the Pope was offered without any pressure from Rome, and
on grounds of deliberate policy."[7]

Further on the same writer says :

> It was not till many years later that a great historian
> (Matthew Paris), who was also a vehement partisan, de-
> nounced John's homage to the Pope as " a thing to be
> detested for all time." The Barnwell annalist, writing at
> the time of the event, tells us indeed that " to many it
> seemed ignominious and a heavy yoke of servitude." But
> the action of all parties at the moment was a practical
> acknowledgemnt of their consciousness that, as the same
> annalist says, John by this act provided prudently both for
> himself and for his people ; for matters were in such a
> strait, and so great was the fear on all sides, that there was
> no more ready way of evading the imminent peril—perhaps
> no other way at all. For when once he had put himself
> under Apostolical protection, and made his realms part of the
> patrimony of St. Peter, there was not in the Roman world
> a sovereign who durst attack him, or invade them, inasmuch
> as Pope Innocent was universally held in awe above all his
> predecessors for many years past.[8]

It is surely a work of supererogation to quote further illustrations, but to show how little the view here protested against is
endorsed by up-to-date scholarship, I may venture to quote
one more passage, this time from Professor McKechnie's monograph on *Magna Carta*, now in its second edition.

> The surrender [he says] of the Crown to the Pope was
> embodied in a formal legal document which bears to be
> made by John " with the common council of our barons."
> Were these merely words of form ? They may have been
> so when first used ; yet two years later the envoys of the
> insurgent barons claimed at Rome that the credit (so they

---

[7] P. 182.

[8] Norgate, *John Lackland*, p. 183. Cf. Cardinal Manning in *Miscellanies*,
II, p. 251.

now represented it) for the whole transaction lay with them. Perhaps the barons did consent to the surrender, thinking that to make the Pope lord paramount of England would protect the inhabitants from the irresponsible tyranny of John ; while John hoped (with better reason as events proved) that the Pope's friendship would increase his ability to work his evil will upon his enemies.   In any case, no active opposition or protest seems to have been raised by any one at the time of the surrender.   This step, so repugnant to later writers, seems not to have been regarded by contemporaries as a disgrace.   Matthew Paris, indeed, writing in the next generation, describes it as " a thing to be detested for all time," but then, events had ripened in Matthew's day, and he was a keen politician rather than an impartial onlooker. [9]

It is interesting to note how readily those scholars who have made first-hand acquaintance with Matthew Paris admit that, monk though he was and possessed of a literary gift superior to all his rivals, he remained a vehement anti-papal partisan, and " a keen politician rather than an impartial onlooker." The idea that every monastic chronicler on account of his religious profession is to be regarded as an official apologist for the papacy and that his complaints of abuses and impositions have all the force of the admissions of an unwilling witness, is an utter delusion.   It was precisely because Matthew and others like him formed part of the system that they let their pens run on so freely.   Do we not all recognise that no critics of the army and navy are so violent, and generally speaking so untrustworthy, as those who themselves belong to the services which they attack ?

Not less curious is the fact that a similar infeudation of the kingdom to the Holy See seems to have taken place verbally some forty years before, in the time of that great law-giver and vigorous aggrandiser of the realm, Henry II.   The matter is not entirely clear, but in two letters of Cardinals Albert and Theodwin, they mention the conditions of the King's absolution

[9] McKechnie, *Magna Carta*, Glasgow, 1905, p. 32.

from his complicity in the martyrdom of St. Thomas, and after noting that he accepted readily the terms imposed, they add that he undertook to do more than this of his own free will, but they seem to consider themselves debarred from fuller explanations. Now Baronius (An. 1172, §5) prints from the *Acta Alexandri Papae III* another clause not mentioned in the conditions made public by the Cardinals, which runs thus : " Moreover I, and the King, my eldest son, swear that we will receive and hold the Kingdom of England from the Lord Alexander the Pope and his Catholic successors ; and we and our successors for ever will not account ourselves to be Kings of England until they shall recognise us as Catholic kings." There is also, as Lingard has pointed out, a letter of Peter of Blois, written in Henry's name, invoking the Pope's counsel and aid in the rebellion of his sons, declaring that England is under the Pope's jurisdiction and stating in explicit terms : " so far as feudal duty is concerned I am bound and pledged to you alone." [10] Almost equally puzzling is a curious entry in the chronicle of Roger Hoveden in the following words :

Richard, King of England, when held in captivity by the Emperor Henry, by the advice of Eleanor his mother, in order to secure his freedom, abdicated the realm of England and bestowed it upon the Emperor as Lord of the world, using the hat which he wore as emblem of the investiture. But the Emperor, as previously stated, at once, in the presence of the great lords of Germany and England, restored to him the said Kingdom of England, which was to be held from him for an annual payment of 5,000 pounds sterling by way of tribute. And thereupon the Emperor bestowed investiture by means of a double-barred cross of gold. But the said Emperor, at the time of his death, released both King Richard himself, and his heirs, from these, and all other obligations.[11]

[10] See Lingard, *History of England* (Edition 1883), Vol. II, p. 191. Peter of Blois, *Epist.*, n. 136, printed in Migne, *P.L.*, Vol. 200, col. 1389.

[11] Hoveden, *Chronica* (Ed. Stubbs), Vol. III, pp. 202-203.

This story, which hardly seems consistent with the documents which are copied in Hoveden's own pages, is at least worthy of attention from the fact that the chronicler records it without comment or protest. But a tribute of 5,000 pounds would have been seven times as great as the amount (1,000 marks) which John undertook to pay to the Pope for England and Ireland together. What is more, the stipulations agreed upon by both sides make it clear that the sum ultimately demanded for Richard's ransom was 150,000 marks, to raise which all the wool of the Gilbertines and the gold and silver vessels of the churches were to be sacrificed. The question of tribute might in certain cases be a serious matter, but so far as regards the mere feudal dependence upon the Holy See, not the least suggestion of ignominy attached to such a relation. As Luchaire remarks in speaking of the infeudation of Aragon to Pope Innocent at the same period : " We must never lose sight of the fact that the pious consciences of the Middle Ages, instead of seeing anything humiliating in this subjection to the Pope, regarded it on the contrary as a favour and a desirable privilege." [12]

The question of the alleged " audacity " of the Pope in cancelling the Charter is one that requires somewhat fuller treatment. And in the first place one might urge that the use of such a term as " audacity " is altogether out of place when we are dealing with the exercise of a perfectly legal and intelligible right fully recognised by the *jus gentium* which was generally prevalent at the time. Now, nothing can be plainer or more in accordance with common sense than the principle that an authority which is recognised as possessing the rights of an overlord may justly claim to exercise a veto upon any contract which the vassal enters into without the consent of the overlord when the contract is of a nature to modify substantially that vassal's constitutional position and his power of rendering service. Even supposing that the provisions of the great Charter had all been absolutely equitable and free from objection according to the received ideas of that age of

[12] Luchaire, *Les Royautés vassales du Saint Siège* (1908), p. 57.

feudalism, Pope Innocent would hardly have been worthy of his great position in history if he had allowed this clear infraction of his rights as overlord to pass unrebuked. People talk freely of the encroachments of the Papacy, but the difficulty for those who really understand something of the temper of feudal times is to know what would have become of religious authority, or indeed of religion itself, if the Papacy had *not* encroached. Nothing in the world is so impossible as to maintain a stationary position in the middle of a swiftly flowing current. Looked at in this light, the action of Pope Innocent in quashing the Charter was almost inevitable, even apart from the insidious representations submitted to him by John's envoys. Once the Pope's position as overlord was clearly recognised, and it *was* clearly recognised by the avowal of the barons themselves, it would have been pusillanimous to pass over this clear infraction of the rights which feudal law conferred upon him. This is a point of view, which though ignored by many who write in the interests of Anglican controversy, has impressed itself upon the less biassed students who represent the best and most recent developments of historical scholarship. Thus in the volume of the *Political History of England*, from which we have already quoted, Professor Adams wrote :

> By the end of September (1215) the news reached England of Innocent's Bull against the Charter itself, declaring it null and void, and forbidding the King to observe it or the barons to require it to be kept under penalty of excommunication. Doubtless John expected this from the Pope, and if his own view of the Charter were correct, Innocent's action would be entirely within his rights. No vassal had a right to enter into any agreement which would diminish the value of his fief, and John had done this if the rights that he was exercising in 1213 were really his.[13]

Miss Norgate, in her valuable work on *John Lackland*, evidently saw the matter from the same point of view. No excuse need be made for quoting her remarks at some length :

[13] *Political History of England*, Vol. II, p. 441.

The sixty-first article of the Charter enacted, as we have seen, that if the King should procure " from any one " a revocation or cessation of that document, such revocation should be accounted void. The only person, however, from whom such a thing could possibly be sought was, of course, the Pope ; and in so far as the Pope was concerned, the clause was itself in feudal law null and void from the beginning, owing to the action of the barons before the Charter was drawn up or thought of. Whatever may have been their real share in the surrender of the kingdom to the Pope in May, 1213, they had, at any rate, in February, 1215, if we may believe William Mauclerc (and there is no reason for disbelieving him), put on record their full con- currence in that transaction after it was accomplished, and even taken voluntarily upon themselves the whole respon- sibility, both for its accomplishment and for its initiation. Thereby they had deprived themselves of whatever legal pretexts they might otherwise have had for repudiating its consequences ; and foremost of those consequences was the fact that the Pope was now legally the supreme arbiter of political affairs in England, by a right which had been given him by the joint action of the King and the barons, against which no later reservation made between those two parties themselves, was of any force in feudal law. The framers of the Charter seem to have been conscious of this ; John, indeed, had pointedly reminded them of it before he consented to the Charter, telling the barons, in answer to their demands, that nothing in the government and constitution of England ought to be, or lawfully could be altered without the knowledge and sanction of the Pope, now that he was overlord of the realm, and he had publicly appealed to the Pope, as overlord, against them and all their doings. As soon as the Charter was sealed, he had despatched envoys to Rome to prosecute his appeal, and to lay before Innocent a statement of his case, together with such extracts from the Charter as were most likely to influence the Pope in his favour.   The result was that, on August 24th—two days before the papal denunciation of the " disturbers of the realm " was published by the English Bishops at Staines—Innocent, as temporal overlord of England, quashed the Charter, and as Pope, forbade its observance by either King or people, on pain of excommunication.[14]

This presentment of the case by a historian whose life, to speak broadly, was devoted to the study of that one particular period, inspires much more confidence than the rude epithets of Dr. Percy Dearmer or Mr. Lane.   But this is very far from summing up all that there is to be said on the subject.   I have assumed that even if the provisions of the Charter were in every way equitable, and even though John's grievances had been wholly factitious and illusory, Innocent would still have been justified in declaring it null and void on the ground that he had an unquestionable right to be consulted about a matter of such moment.   But *were* the provisions of the Charter wholly equitable ?   Had John no just cause to complain that his rights as a sovereign had been encroached upon ?   We have grown so accustomed to regard Magna Carta as the foundation of all our liberties that the very suggestion that this great monument of freedom was in any sense a one-sided compact seems to savour of impiety.   Similarly we have grown to regard King John as such a monster of cruelty and lawlessness, that the barons who were his bitter foes have undergone a kind of canonisation.   It never enters our heads to ask whether they may possibly have been hardly less tyrannous, vindictive, and dishonourable than the sovereign whom they so fiercely opposed. On both these points, viz., the equity of the provisions of the Charter itself and the character of the men who forced John to sign it, there is a great deal to be said which has a very important bearing upon the action of Innocent III in declaring the instrument null and void.

Several years ago a somewhat startling article appeared

14 Norgate, *John Lackland*, p. 246.

in *The Independent Review* [15] by a well-known jurist and Balliol College lecturer, Mr. Edward Jenks. Mr. Jenks's thorough first-hand acquaintance with the medieval system had been attested by an able work on *Law and Politics in the Middle Ages* and by a number of other books. His article bore the striking title, " The Myth of Magna Carta," and while undoubtedly it is not free from the reproach of paradoxical exaggeration, it directed attention to a number of important points too commonly ignored. " Mr. Jenks," says Professor McKechnie, " argues *with much force* that the Charter was the product of the selfish action of the barons pressing their own interests, and not of any disinterested or national movement ; that it was not by any means a great landmark in history, and that, instead of proving a material help in England's advance towards constitutional freedom, it was rather ' a stumbling block in the path of progress,' being entirely feudal and reactionary in its intention and effects." There is no need to identify ourselves with Mr. Jenks's extreme positions, but one may turn in preference to the already cited monograph of Professor McKechnie, which has been everywhere recognised as a sober work of high value.[16] Dr. McKechnie does not entirely endorse the views of Mr. Jenks, but he finds, nevertheless, that there is much truth in his general contention. Was the Charter a fair and satisfactory settlement ? That it contained the enunciation of many noble and just principles is undoubted. But there were also clauses in it which bore very hardly on the royal prerogative as hitherto recognised. Let us hear Professor McKechnie :

> The great weakness of the Charter lay in this, that no adequate sanction was attached to it, in order to ensure the enforcement of its provisions. The only expedient suggested for compelling the King to keep his promises was of a nature at once clumsy and revolutionary, and entirely

[15] November 1904.

[16] *Magna Carta, a Commentary on the Great Charter of King John.* With an historical introduction by W. S. McKechnie, LLB.., D.Phil., etc., Lecturer on Constitutional Law and History in the University of Glasgow. Glasgow, 1905, pp. xx, 608.

worthless considered as a working scheme of government. Indeed it was devised, not so much to prevent the King from breaking faith, as to punish him when he had done so. In other words, no proper constitutional machinery was invented to turn the legal theories of Magna Carta into practical realities. In its absence, we find what has sometimes been described as " a right of legalised rebellion " conferred on an executive committee of twenty-five of the King's enemies.[17]

If this is in any way a correct description of the provisions of Chapter 61—and the accuracy of the description, so far as one can see, allows of no dispute—Pope Innocent must have felt that he was in duty bound to come to the relief of the vassal, who after all had thrown himself upon his protection in taking the oath of homage and becoming his man. The Pope was not in a position to amend the document like a Parliamentary Committee. He must either accept or reject it as a whole. However much he might admire the principles laid down in other portions of the Charter, it was impossible to tolerate a compact in which, to quote Dr. McKechnie once more, " Civil war, levied on a warrant granted beforehand by the King, is treated as a constitutional expedient for the redress of particular grievances as they arise." [18]

There seems to be no need to travel any further in search of motives for Pope Innocent's action in annulling the Charter than what we may find in this one Chapter 61. No doubt there was no lack of other good reasons. The whole section, in particular, which deals with the forest laws, would probably have seemed to an impartial arbitrator of those days as a most unreasonable invasion of the Royal prerogatives. But Innocent in his Bull does not specify the precise points he objects to. He only describes the whole compact as disgraceful and derogatory to the Royal dignity. Neither is it to be forgotten that, when the Charter was frequently renewed in the next reign, with the full assent of the Pope and his legates, Chapter 61 and not a few

17 McKechnie, p. 150.   18 Ibid., p. 153.

other provisions which might have caused difficulty, had entirely disappeared. As a matter of wording, Innocent's Bull is a very dignified and worthy pronouncement. When we examine it, we find that he does not so much condemn the Charter on its merits, as denounce the whole course of action of the barons, whom he believed to be responsible for extorting it from the King. Hence we are led to ask : What kind of men were they ? What has recent investigation to say about them ?

The reader will perhaps recall the fact that, by the famous Chapter 61 of the great Charter, a committee of twenty-five barons, as executors, were appointed to see to the carrying out of the provisions of the document. There can be no practical doubt that these twenty-five, who were presumably not the least able and upright of their party, behaved both tactlessly and arrogantly, and also with an utter disregard of patriotic and popular issues. Professor Davis, who himself rather takes the barons under his protection, nevertheless owns that " the facts lend considerable colour to the indictment which modern writers have drawn up against them." On the other hand, if Mr. Jenks goes too far in attributing the hollow truce of Runnymede to " a conspiracy of self-seeking and reckless barons," Miss Norgate and Dr. McKechnie do not hesitate to denounce the behaviour of the twenty-five executors after the signing of the Charter in the strongest terms of reprobation. England, it was said at the time, was exchanging one King for five-and-twenty kings. The barons seem to have treated John with marked disrespect. For example, we learn from a French chronicle not too friendly to John, that the executors insisted upon seeing the King when he was seriously ill. They took advantage of his physical helplessness, and commanded that though he could not walk he should be carried into their presence in a litter ; and when he was brought in they did not even rise to greet him. But there were other grounds of complaint besides these.

> King and barons alike [writes Miss Norgate] knew that the " peace " had been made only to be broken. The barons were the first to break it. . . . All over the country

the barons were fortifying their castles. Some were even building new ones. A more scrupulous man than King John might well have deemed himself justified under such circumstances in doing what John did—following their example in preparing to fling the treaty to the winds and renew the war.[19]

Similarly Dr. McKechnie tells us :

Before the conferences at Runnymede came to an end, confidence in the good intentions of the twenty-five executors, drawn it must be remembered entirely from the section of the baronage most extreme in their views and most unfriendly to John, seems to have been completely lost.

At the end of August the barons had practically thrown off all restraint.

They were now [says Miss Norgate] taking upon themselves, in all those counties where their power was strong enough, to supersede both the sheriffs and the justices and to usurp their functions. . . . In their premature triumph they were even beginning to talk of choosing a new sovereign.[20]

Neither can it be said that the evidence for these and other statements is only a matter of inference. For example, we learn that whereas the Charter contained no provision for compelling the barons to fulfil their obligations towards John (though *vice versa* John was to be coerced as need arose), it was deemed necessary to elect a committee of thirty-eight to act as a check upon the twenty-five. These thirty-eight took an oath to compel both the King and the twenty-five to deal justly with one another. What is much more tangible and unmistakable, we have two formal protests against the barons' arbitrary rule preserved among the Patent and Close Rolls. They are signed by the Archbishops of Canterbury and Dublin, the Papal legate, and seven English Bishops. The first of these attests that when the barons were called upon to give John security for their performance of the conditions of the Charter, they absolutely

[19] *John Lackland*, p. 239. [20] *John Lackland*, p. 58.

refused, though their word had previously been pledged to do so when required.[21]   Similarly a protest was also signed against the encroachments of the twenty-five upon the royal prerogative in the matter of the forest laws.

> The Bishops [says Professor McKechnie] seem to have become alarmed by the drastic measures adopted or likely to be adopted, founded on the verdicts of the Twelve Knights elected in each county to carry into effect the various clauses of the Great Charter directed against abuses of the forest laws.   Apparently it was feared that reforms of a sweeping nature would result, and practically abolish the royal forests altogether.[22]

If we turn to the most recent discussion of the intricate and perplexing tangle of events which led up to and followed the signing of Magna Charta, it will be found that Professor Powicke, who has succeeded Professor H. W. C. Davis in the chair of Modern History at Oxford, does not notably diverge from the line of treatment adopted by his predecessor.   In the sixth volume of the *Cambridge Medieval History*, published in December 1929, Professor Powicke, who deals with the reigns of Richard and John, shows scant sympathy for the committee of twenty-five to whom the carrying into execution of the provisions of the Charter was committed.   " From the outset," he writes, " they showed an arrogant implacability which soon degenerated into the short-sighted egotism characteristic of earlier baronial revolts.   The twenty-five, if one prejudiced but generally reliable authority may be trusted, acted not as watchful guardians but as rulers of the Kingdom.   John's mercenaries styled them the twenty-five kings." [23]   And again in another place the same writer remarks :   " What wrecked the settlement from the outset was the rising temper of the King on the one hand, and of the rebels—many of whom were young and inexperienced men or ambitious *frondeurs*—on the other.   Robert FitzWalter and his companions had adopted in the name of God and the

---

[21] Rot. Pat. 181, Rymer, *Foedera*, i, p. 132 ; cf. McKechnie, p. 52

[22] McKechnie, p. 52.   [23] *Cambridge Medieval History*, VI, p. 248.

Church the programme which the Archbishop [Langton] had originally outlined for them, but they had no intention of following ecclesiastical guidance when power was once in their hands." [24]

There is every reason to believe that full reports of this intolerable behaviour of the twenty-five executors of the Charter must have reached Rome before the Pope issued his Bull of annullation on August 26th, 1215. There was at any rate plenty of time for the news to reach him. The Bull signed on August 26th was in England before the end of September. There is therefore no reason why Pope Innocent, when he signed the Bull, should not have had before him an account of all that had happened in England down to July 15th, or later. Consequently we need not for a moment suppose that the Pope acted only upon the *ex parte* statement of the King's envoys.

Surely after this exposition of the facts of the case, as they are set out in the narrative of our most modern and approved historians, none of whom own any allegiance to the Church of Rome, Dr. Percy Dearmer's comments upon the Pope's " tyranny " and his " audacity " in annulling the Charter must appear singularly biassed. The obvious purpose of these pronouncements, like so many of those we have encountered in the course of these chapters, is to make the Church of Rome odious and to deepen in his readers any feeling of distrust they may already entertain against the Papacy.

One curious point which may be noted here is the possibility that Innocent III in all this matter acted with a fuller understanding of the conditions which prevailed in England because he had himself in early life paid at least a flying visit to its shores. The evidence upon which this suggestion rests is the following. In 1207 a certain William, monk of Andres, an abbey some ten or twelve miles south of Calais, had occasion to go to Italy upon important business connected with the monastery to which he belonged. He tells us how he found the Pope at Viterbo, and how, largely owing to the influence of Cardinal Stephen

[24] *Ibid.*, p. 246.

Langton, he met with a gracious reception. His account of his successful negotiations, which contains one or two graphic touches, runs as follows : [25]

> Finding at last my opportunity, I who write these things, one day when the Pope had awakened after his mid-day siesta and was for the time at leisure, came to him when he was alone (*solus ad solum accessi*) and saluted him on my knees. Afterwards, being invited to kiss him (*ad eius osculum invitatus*) and much encouraged thereat, I sat down by his direction at his feet and showed him the privilege of Pope Alexander formerly granted to our church.

We need not go into the business discussed, but Pope Innocent was very gracious, and finally replied :

> At the proper time and place we will hear you read your despatches, and whatever our duty to God allows, that we will gladly do for yourself and for your church ; for at the time when we were residing at Paris and following the schools (*tempore quo Parisiis in scholis resedimus*) we went on a pilgrimage to St. Thomas. On that journey we received hospitality at your church, and, under the rule of some venerable old man, we found it, as it seemed to us, in an excellent state of discipline.

This is a very clear and explicit statement recorded by a reliable witness, who had heard it from the Pontiff's own lips. In support of it we may notice that in August of the year 1179 King Louis of France came on a pilgrimage to Canterbury, an almost unprecedented event, duly registered by such English chroniclers as Ralph de Diceto and Matthew Paris, who dilate upon the honour paid him by the English King and on the offerings made by Louis. Now it is certain that the young Italian of noble family, Lothario di Segni, the future Innocent III, was at this precise time a student in Paris. He probably left for Bologna the next year. The example given by the French King is bound to have found many imitators. Lothario may even have attached himself to some of

[25] See *Willelmi Chronica Andrensis* in M.G.H. ; SS. xxiv, pp. 737, 738.

the *magnates*,[26] who formed Louis's retinue on that occasion. It is highly probable that King Louis stayed near Andres on his way, for the Abbey Chronicle records his journey at some length.

What lends further countenance to this idea is the special interest which Innocent always took in England and his intimacy with several distinguished Englishmen, notably Stephen Langton and Robert de Curson, who probably had been his contemporaries at Paris. Both these two were certainly made Cardinals by him and entrusted with affairs of the highest importance. Moreover, it would seem from the detailed account of his own missions, given by Giraldus Cambrensis, that Innocent was on extremely easy terms with the Englishmen whom business took to Rome. This impression is confirmed by a very interesting narrative which Thomas de Marleberge, of Evesham Abbey, compiled, after making more than one journey to the eternal city. The case between Marleberge and his opponents, representing the Bishop of Worcester, was argued before Innocent in person, and one of the Bishop's counsel advanced the plea :

" Holy Father, according to what we learnt in the schools and to what was laid down by our professors, no prescription can run against the rights of a bishop." Whereupon the Lord Pope interposed, " Certainly you and your professors must have drunk copiously of your English beer when you learned such principles as these."[27]

This sounds distinctly like the remark of one who had had some personal experience of English fare. English beer, it must be admitted, does not seem to have been altogether popular with travellers from the South. That very elusive satirist, Hugo Primas, who is apparently the true author of many of the ribald " Golias " verses attributed by error to Walter Map, has a charming quatrain preserved to us in the *Distinctiones Monasticæ* of an anonymous English Cistercian.

---

[26] Cf. the *Chronicon Angliæ Petriburgense ;* " 1179. Peregrinatio Ludovici regis Franciæ et aliorum magnatum ejusdem regni ad S. Thomam Cant."

[27] *Chronicon Abbatiæ de Evesham* (Rolls Series), p. 189.

Hugh Primas [says this compiler] when he found himself in England, and humorously complained in verse that he was compelled to drink beer, wrote, between jest and earnest, the following lines :—

> Est labor hic esse, quum sit potare necesse
> Potum de messe, quam nos consuevimus esse.
> Poto, sed invite ; probo pocula gentis avitae,
> Vinum de vite, quia vitis janua vitae.[28]

Pope Innocent III, like Hugo Primas, seems to have preferred the beverage of his forefathers.

---

[28] " It is wearisome to be here, since it is necessary to drink draughts of the grain that *nous autres* are accustomed to eat. I drink, but reluctantly ; the cups I favour are those of my forefathers—wine from the grape—for the vine is the gateway of life." See *Spicilegium Solesmense*, III, 472. It is impossible in a translation to preserve the play upon words in the original. As for the metre, Hugo evidently allows himself great liberties, *e.g.*, in lengthening a short *e* before a cæsura. This quatrain seems to have escaped the notice of Wm. Meyer when he wrote on Hugo Primas in the Göttingen *Nachrichten* for 1907.

CHAPTER XIII

PAPAL RAPACITY AND THE ECCLESIA ANGLICANA

IF the Papacy as an institution has incurred the antipathy and mistrust of our Protestant fellow-countrymen, no small part of that aversion is due to the popular histories which represent the Popes, at the climax of their power, as abominably misusing the authority they enjoyed in order to fill their coffers and further their political ambitions. " The Pope," we are told by so respectable a student of the past as the late Dr. Augustus Jessopp, " flooded the country with foreign ecclesiastics, extorted incredible sums of money on various pretexts and provided for bishoprics and other preferments before they fell vacant." " It makes one blush," he says, " to think or read of it all." " The King's weakness," writes Dr. Percy Dearmer of Henry III, " led also to the Pope's barefaced encroachments " ; and again : " the real result of Henry III's misgovernment was the development of English nationality in opposition to King and Pope alike. Constitutionalism was established ; and once more it was the English Church that secured the liberties of England." " There seems," we learn from Mr. Lane, " to have been something like a conspiracy between King and Pope to *denationalise* the English Church and realm." " The first clause of Magna Charta," declares Mr. J. H. Fry,[1] with a lavish use of italics, " is as follows : ' *The Church of England* '—not the Roman Church in England but the Church of England—' *shall be free* ' . . . The independence of the Church of England is the alpha and omega of Magna Charta. The freedom of the

---

[1] *The Church of England : ever a true branch of the Catholic Church, and never a part of the Church of Rome*, by J. H. Fry (Skeffington, 1913), p. 65.

232

Church of England forms the golden clasp of this precious bracelet which is the symbol and pledge of the freedom of *the English nation*. . . . The Magna Charta is a standing proof that in 1215 England would submit to no papal domination."

Without for a moment seeking to deny that there were glaring abuses in the matter of papal provisions to benefices, or that the demand for money contributions from the English clergy was carried during the thirteenth century to quite unjustifiable extremes—on both these points something must be said further on—the first topic which calls for attention is the manner in which the *Ecclesia Anglicana*, the Church of England, is spoken of as something existing independently of the Church of Rome. One would have thought that after the publication of F. W. Maitland's epoch-making volume on the *Roman Canon Law in the Church of England* it would have been impossible for anyone to use such language as that adopted by Mr. Fry above. The most striking testimony to the conclusiveness of the arguments which Maitland urged was the fact that Bishop Stubbs, whose position was assailed, never attempted any reply and indeed told a friend that he was not prepared to dissent from the view propounded by his critic.[2] Now among the many points established in Maitland's famous volume no one is more important than his recognition of the truth that there never was, properly speaking, any such entity as the *Ecclesia Anglicana*. " Too often," he remarks, " we speak of ' the Church of England ' and forget that there was no ecclesiastically organized body that answered to that name. No tie of an ecclesiastical or spiritual kind bound the Bishop of Chichester to the Bishop of Carlisle, except that which bound them both to French and Spanish Bishops." It we want to obtain right views of the ecclesiastical life of the Middle Ages, it is hardly possible to lay too much stress upon the fact that the position of the Church in England differed in no substantial way from the position of the Church in France or in Spain, or even in the more isolated States of

[2] See A. T. Carter, *A History of English Legal Institutions* (4th Edition, 1910), p. 232.

Central Europe, or in Ireland, or in Scandinavia. It is true that the term *Ecclesia Anglicana* was occasionally used, and that we meet it from time to time in the pages of Lyndwood's digest of the constitutions issued by Archbishops of Canterbury at their provincial councils. But for all that the phrase *Ecclesia Anglicana* was not a doctrinal but a geographical expression, a compendious way of referring to that portion of Christ's Church which lay within the dominions of the King of England. It would no more have occurred to Lyndwood to speak of " Anglicanism " as a distinct abstraction, representing the complexus of the doctrines or practices of English Christians, than it would occur to anyone nowadays to speak of Cambrianism as an abstraction representing the complexus of the doctrines and practices of the Church of Wales. All the world admits that the Roman Communion in modern times is cosmopolitan. But the cosmopolitanism of the Church in the thirteenth and fourteenth centuries was even more pronounced. No doubt the centralising tendencies at work have very much developed since the Council of Trent. Communications have become indefinitely easier, the Holy See has exercised a much more watchful control over the proceedings of provincial councils, the observance of the periodical visits *ad limina* has been strictly enforced upon the whole episcopate, a certain proportion of the clergy in almost every country in the world have spent some years of study in Rome. But it may be questioned whether these and other causes have been more efficacious in drawing together the different groups and units of the modern Catholic Church than were certain other influences which were at work throughout Christendom in the later Middle Ages. In particular, we are much inclined to doubt whether any historian has yet adequately estimated the effect of the study of one common ecclesiastical law, and secondly, and even more notably, whether anyone has done justice to the incredibly important part played in this assimilating process by Religious, especially those of the mendicant Orders, who journeyed from country to country and from province to province to an extent which has been little investigated or understood. Of course, all this intercourse was facilitated enormously by the fact that Latin was still universally a spoken language among all who had any pretensions to education. If we find a great number of foreigners, as we do, who were provided to English benefices, it must not be forgotten that we also find a vast crowd of Englishmen who secured for themselves more or less lucrative posts abroad, and that there were a still greater multitude of students who poured out of the country to attend the lectures at Paris and Bologna, at Padua and Vercelli. The obstacle of language which in later centuries became so real a check upon migratory habits, practically did not exist. A professor would lecture in turn at Oxford and at Paris, at Bologna or Cologne, at Basle or Padua, at Heidelberg or Valladolid, at Prague or at Coimbra, and his audience, if he were a man of any fame, would maintain its numbers quite irrespective of the fact that he was not a native of the country in which he was for the first time residing.

And since we have touched upon this matter of Universities, let us note how ill the whole history of such institutions accords with the idea that there was in those days anything of the nature of a national English Church. To begin with, in practically every case an University was constituted by a Papal Bull, in other words, by a charter from the Holy See. Here are the terms in which one such Roman document, addressed to Cambridge by John XXII in 1318, is described by Mr. Bliss :

> Ordinance at the King's request addressed to the University of masters and scholars in the *studium generale* at Cambridge, establishing there a *studium generale* in every faculty, and confirming all privileges and indults hitherto granted by Popes and Kings.[3]

Surely on Anglican principles this was a matter for the

---

[3] Bliss, *Calendar of Entries in the Papal Registers*, Vol. II, p. 172. The first Bull addressed to Oxford is calendared in Vol. I, p. 306. It is printed in full with other documents in *Munimenta Oxon*, I, p. 26. The Papal Bull by which the University of St. Andrews was founded in 1413 is facsimiled in Vol. II of the *National Monuments of Scotland*.

Archbishop of Canterbury or a national synod to concern themselves with, not for the Pope. But the same held good at Oxford, for besides what might be called a foundation Bull emanating from Innocent IV in 1254, we have a most important document, issued in 1300 by Boniface VIII, and thus summarised in the *Munimenta Oxoniensia*, of the Rolls Series.

Boniface has received a petition from the Chancellors, Masters, Doctors, and Scholars of the University of Oxford showing that the Kings of England from time to time have granted them divers privileges and, among others, that the Chancellor should have the cognizance of all contracts and the punishment of crimes done within the boundaries of the University, in all cases wherein a scholar or his servant or other person subject to the Chancellor's authority is a party (except cases of homicide, mutilation, and freehold ; in which by the King's breve the delinquent may be brought before another tribunal), and praying for the confirmation of these privileges. He (Boniface) therefore exempts the University from all ecclesiastical authority of Archbishops, Legati nati, Bishops, and other ordinary judges, and pronounces null and void all previous sentences of excommunication, etc., which may have been fulminated against them.[4]

In 1368, Pope Urban V issued a Bull determining that for the valid election of the Chancellor of the University the confirmation of the Bishop of Lincoln, the diocesan, was not needed. In the same year statutes were passed by the University to regulate appeals, in which the following clauses occur :

Also, that the right order of the tribunals belonging to the University in their proper subordination may be more clearly known, the University has enacted and decreed, that next above the weekly Official should be the Chancellor, or his Commissary General, and immediately above this last the Congregation of Regents, and next above that again the University of Regents and non-Regents, and immediately

[4] *Munimenta*, pp. 79-80.

above this, in any civil cause, our Lord the King, but in any spiritual cause only our Lord, His Holiness, the Pope.[5]

It will be observed that neither the Archbishop of Canterbury nor the diocesan are so much as mentioned ; while the fact that the supreme authority thus accorded to the Holy See was not a mere formality is attested by numerous documents which may easily be found in the *Calendars of Papal Registers* edited by Messrs. Bliss and Twemlow.[6] What sort of a national Church was this in which the Pope, by a stroke of the pen and without even the pretence of saying by your leave, excluded the Archbishops and other dignitaries of that Church from any sort of jurisdiction over, or interference with, their own leading University ?

To return, however, from this digression, the argument is that every antecedent consideration would incline us to the belief that throughout Christendom the religious life and thought of each country, small or great, centred in Rome. It was from the Pope that all jurisdiction was derived as well as all spiritual favours, whether of the nature of dispensations or privileges. It was he who, as Maitland has so convincingly demonstrated, was the Universal Ordinary. He could interfere anywhere, and often did so of his own *mero motu*, taking things into his own hands, without apology, over the heads of Archbishops, Bishops, and all intermediate authorities. His action might sometimes be resented, but the principle was recognised, and in practice no resistance was made. Again, it was to the Pope that every Archbishop, after having made humble petition for the pallium, took an oath of obedience in the most ample terms. And throughout the length and breadth of these Christian lands, all recognising Papal authority, there was, as stated above, a constant coming and going of students, pilgrims

---

[5] *Munimenta*, p. 232 and cf. p. 460.

[6] See for example as early as 1312, Vol. II, pp. 111 and 167, where the Pope settles a protracted dispute between the University of Oxford and the Dominican Order. See also in the same volume, pp. 472, 492, 493, 495. And in the volume of *Petitions*, in the same series, pp. 385, 386, 460, 504, 526.

and friars, more particularly of the last-named in the special capacity of preachers and professors.

Now, one may ask : of the many hundreds and thousands of strangers, who in this manner found their way into England, whether from motives of curiosity, or devotion, or study, or again, in the quality of official visitors, or even legates representing the Holy See, is there a single recorded instance of an observer who has left it upon record that England differed from the rest of the world in the fact that it possessed a national Church ? Has any one of the many capable clerks and casuists of foreign birth who were provided to English benefices expressed his surprise that " the English Courts Christian held themselves free to accept or reject, and did in some cases reject the Canon Law of Rome " ? Or *vice versa*, has a passage ever been discovered in the writings of any of the innumerable Englishmen who went on legal business to Rome, or studied at foreign universities, which implied that he found the religious atmosphere strange and missed the independence of his own national Church institutions ? In any case, it does not seem rash to conclude that if any such testimony were forthcoming, we should soon hear of it. Evidence of this sort would be far too valuable to our Anglican friends as a controversial asset for them to allow it to be forgotten.

Passing on, then, to the matter of the intrusion of foreigners into English livings, which figured prominently among the grievances of that age but which seems to be even more bitterly resented by the Anglicans of the present day than by those who actually suffered from it, I venture to call attention to a letter of 1318 which touches upon the point. Reviewing the volume of the Winchester Episcopal Registers in which this document was printed, the *Athenæum* commented upon the " striking combination of the phrase *Ecclesia Anglicana* with the humble attitude of the English prelates." As the letter is long, it seems worth while to italicise one or two outstanding phrases, but unless the whole substance of the document were given, it would hardly be possible to judge of the respectful tone in which a palpable grievance is pressed upon the notice of His Holiness. The occasion which led to the drawing up of this remonstrance was the issue of a very stringent Constitution by Pope John XXII, at the beginning of the year 1318, through which he revoked all the dispensations for plurality granted by his predecessors, and commanded pluralists, under threat of excommunication, to surrender all their benefices save one. Every Bishop was required to make a return of the livings vacated and their value, together with the names of the former incumbents. The Register, printed by Mr. Baigent, as editor, lets us know that the Bishop of Winchester eventually forwarded to the Pope a list of over thirty such benefices which had been actually surrendered. As might have been expected, the working of the new Constitution was not unattended with difficulties, and all the Bishops of the Province of Canterbury who were then in England, wrote a collective letter to the Pontiff to explain to him the condition of affairs. The document was authenticated with the seals of all of them, and is found transcribed in the Register which Mr. Baigent is editing. After the usual formal introduction, in which the Archbishop and fourteen suffragans [7] who are ennumerated in order of seniority, " devoutly kiss the blessed feet of His Holiness with all submission and reverence," the epistle proceeds as follows :

The whole English Church applauded, when lately it had learnt assuredly that the Creator and Redeemer of the whole world, who maketh the rough ways plain and by His just judgment exalteth the just, had been pleased by His Divine Providence to promote your Holiness to the summit of the Apostolic dignity. *And we, though unworthy, being included in your pastoral charge, and ourselves derived, as rivers from their fountain-head, from the exalted throne of the Holy Apostolic See,* are moved to action by keener incitements, and that unweariedly, from the fact that you are known to have entertained, always, an intense desire and a noble zeal for the

[7] The Bishops of St. Asaph and Landaff, Mr. Baigent tells us, were abroad, the see of Rochester was vacant. All the others affixed their seals to the document.

salvation of souls and the reform of the Universal Church, as, indeed, is clearly evidenced by the gracious fruits of your works manifest to all ; and we have determined, therefore, to have recourse to your Holiness, our matchless refuge, on behalf of ourselves and our churches, and the clergy and people committed to our charge, touching all that appertains to the stability of the English Church and the salvation of the people. Be it known then to your Blessedness, that in our common country, in which we are passing the days of our pilgrimage, dignities, parsonages, parish churches, and other benefices, having the most extensive cure of souls, like cities that were full of people, sit all solitary ; whereas others, already void, as an effect of the stringency of your Constitution, directed against pluralists, with salutary forethought, for the edification and salvation of the souls of the faithful, are suffered to remain without curates, and in the case of others the parsons are men of foreign nationality, instituted in the times of your predecessors, who bear indeed the name of pastor, but know nothing of the sheep of their flock, and pay no heed to their bleating, being themselves unknown to all, since rarely, if ever, have they visited, neither have they any intention of visiting, the places committed to their rule ; [8] so that the three-fold food, the food of the word and of a good example, and the bodily food of the poor, wherewith parsons who dwell among their flocks are wont to refresh them, is taken away ; the service of God is everywhere diminished, the cure of souls is neglected, and no hospitality of any kind is kept up ; and the benefices themselves, bereft of the succour

[8] In 1324, there were only nine aliens beneficed in the diocese of Winchester, as certified in a return made by Bishop John de Stratforde, viz. : Giles Anglicus, R. of Bramdean ; Bertrand de Asserio, R. of Freshwater ; Stephen de Claro Monte, R. of Bentworth ; Nicholas Fighino, R. of Havant ; Ricardin Justini, V. of East Meon ; Reymund Pelegrini, R. of Arreton ; Robert Sweof, R. of Monxton ; Stephen Lupart, R. of Buckland ; and Peter de Columbariis, R. of Chipstead. (*Register of John de Stratforde*, fol. 193.—Mr. Baigent's Note.) [It will be observed that the stress of the Bishops' complaint falls, not on their being foreigners, but on their being absentees.]

of those who should defend them, are in countless ways
stripped of their rights and liberties, while the noble buildings
raised by the munificence of those now dead, are falling
into ruin ; and, bitterest thought of all, in these our days, the
devotion of the lay people to the Church, in consequence of
these evils, is growing utterly lukewarm, or rather, vanish-
ing altogether ; for as soon as we begin to exercise our office
against them, in defence of those rights of the Church which
have been filched away through the prevailing irreligion,
they cast the aforesaid abuses in our teeth.   Forasmuch, then,
as from the sweet odour of your fame, both preceding and
following your elevation to the Apostolic dignity, you are
publicly proclaimed as directly intending chiefly this,—
that in the Lord's vineyard throughout the world the service
of your tender care, bestowed alike on the blossoms and the
fruit, may produce the sweetest odours and fertilise it
abundantly ; we on our part, and on the part of the other
prelates, both secular and regular, and the clergy of the
Province of Canterbury lately assembled with us, to treat,
in so far as we lawfully may, concerning the condition of the
Church and Kingdom of England, surrounded as we are,
on all sides, by the snares of our enemies, but with full
trust in the clemency of your Blessedness, *cast ourselves at
your feet who hold the highest Apostolic office, and humbly beg that
you will deign, in your two-fold office of affection, to make salutary
provision for these English churches*, now widowed, as it were,
through the loss of the personal presence of their Rectors ;
vouchsafing to grant both to us and to other clerical patrons,
if it please you, in the case of all the churches of our patronage, and those of all other patrons within the Province of
Canterbury, now void by reason of pluralists through the
operation of the said Constitution promulgated thereunto,
authority to provide, collate, and even present, with the
acknowledged right of patrons, approved men, able to
build and to plant, through whose means the aforesaid
perils may be happily counteracted, having becoming

R

regard to the standing of the men ; or otherwise, that you
will yourself be pleased graciously to confer such benefices
on the approved clerks, whose names contained in separate
schedules, will be presented to your Blessedness, whenever
it shall please you to receive them, by the bearer of this
letter. We also humbly ask, most loving Holy Father, that
in accordance with your most holy intention, the powers
of your holy office may be employed in making provision
against the aforesaid difficulties, in such manner that to
the English Church (wherein indeed the harvest is great,
but now the labourers are few) a worthy restoration may
hereafter result and continue. We, also, earnestly and
again and again beseech your Holy Eminence of dignity
Apostolic, to regard with your wonted kindness Master
Andrew de Bruges, clerk, the bearer of this letter and in this
business our special messenger, to whose worth, assuredly, his
merits rather than any exalted dignities and honours bear
witness ; and ourselves also, your servants and the servants
of your Church of the Province of Canterbury, who are ever
ready to obey your Apostolic behests. And forasmuch as,
till now, we have not reported to your Apostolic dignity
the names of the benefices of pluralists who have been
ejected in accordance with the requirements of your said
Constitution as, indeed, it was not in our power to do,
seeing that up to this time we have been continually hin-
dered by our constant endeavours to secure internal peace,
and by our own journeyings hither and thither, not without
great fatigue, through divers countries, may it please you
of your kindness, in the bowels of your paternal affection,
to have us excused and to admit our said clerk to a gracious
hearing, touching these and other matters concerning the
state of the English Church when, according to the instructions which we, in our humility, have given him, he shall
deem it right, with becoming reverence, to communicate
to the Apostolic ear, giving unquestioning credence if it
please you to what he shall say. Again we pray that what

we have written may not exasperate the kindly mind of our most loving Father against us, or cause it to turn away from us ; for as the Most High God knoweth, we have undertaken to bring these things to the knowledge of your Holiness with, as we have said before, no other intention than this,—our sincere desire for the succour of the Church which we know is ever present to your mind.   Farewell in Jesus Christ, and long may the Papal dignity, reverenced above all others, flourish under your governance of the Universal Church, in peace and joyfulness.   Given in London, under our Archiepiscopal Seal and the Seals of all our fellow-Bishops, your ministers aforesaid, on the third before the Kalends of June, in the year of our Lord one thousand three hundred and eighteen.

Now the first thing which strikes us about this important document is that it is not only a century later in date than Magna Charta, but that fifty years have passed since that era of extortions and provisions was inaugurated by Gregory IX and Innocent IV which Matthew Paris represents as straining the loyalty of the English clergy almost to breaking point. Nevertheless the entire episcopate of the Province of Canterbury, in the very act of pressing a grievance, declare in most humble wise their complete dependence upon this new French Pope. Their recognition of the submission due to the Supreme Pontiff, in virtue of the office which he holds, has in no respect been impaired by the excesses of which his predecessors may have been guilty in their deplorably human ambition to make themselves masters of the Italian peninsula.   This, at any rate, was the least discreditable of the motives which Matthew Paris attributed to Innocent IV, the subject of his never ceasing invectives.   Although the Bishops reflect not obscurely upon the abuse of Papal provisions which had led in so many cases to the appointment of foreigners to English benefices, it is equally plain that as a matter of principle they do not dispute the Pope's right to provide.   Moreover, it may be said that the general impression left by a perusal of the Episcopal Registers is not so unfavourable as might be expected to the results of this system of Provisions. Not only do they bear witness to a certain moderation and tact on the part of the Popes in the exercise of their prerogative, but they bring before us the names of more than one good and capable ecclesiastic who owed his career of usefulness in England to the direct intervention of the Holy See, in the form of letters of provision. A conspicuous example of both facts may be seen in the career of Bishop Grandisson of Exeter (1330–1360). Prebendary Hingeston Randolph, with the fairness and candour which everywhere distinguishes his work, calls attention to the good sense displayed by Pope John XXII when, on having provided John de Grandisson, then Archdeacon of Nottingham, in 1326 to the vacant See of Exeter, he discovered that another candidate had already been elected by the Chapter and was favourably looked upon by the King. The Pope, " with a very good grace indeed, however reluctantly," transferred his Reservation to the Bishop-elect, thus saving the principle, but removing all cause for friction. The new Bishop, John de Beverley, occupied the episcopal throne for little more than three months, and on his death in the June of 1327 the see was once more vacant. This time the Pope held firmly to the reservation he had again made in favour of John de Grandisson.

Whatever may be thought of these proceedings [writes Prebendary Randolph] by those who have no sympathy with Papal claims, they were, at any rate, justified by the result. It was a good and wise choice, and gave to Exeter the most devoted and illustrious of her Bishops. The new Bishop found his whole diocese distressed and disordered. . . . He plunged into his work bravely and eagerly, without a moment's delay that could be avoided, grudging even the few days that were occupied by necessary formalities and spurning the attractions of the Court and the flattery and praise of men. He could not rest until he was united to his " spouse " ; and when he had once taken possession of his diocese, it was found almost impossible to induce him to leave it again through all his long episcopate, and he devoted his days with untiring energy, unflinching self-sacrifice, and conspicuous success to its reformation and good government.

Bishop John de Grandisson, who was probably born in this country, may fairly be accounted an Englishman, but his father [9] was a Burgundian of distinguished family, and a foreigner according to our modern acceptation of the term. The fact is that a good deal of misconception prevails about the " foreigners " supposed to have been introduced by the Popes into our national Church at this period of English history. The whole state of European politics and of Christian society was so utterly different from anything which is now familiar to us that the attempt to establish parallels is quite illusory. As has been already noted in an earlier chapter, we must remember that long after this time—the latest registers now under consideration are of the reign of Edward III—the language commonly spoken by the educated classes in England was French, and that Latin was conversationally familiar to almost all who could read and write. In the Register of Bishop Sandale of Winchester, who was a Yorkshireman, though the vast majority of the entries are in Latin, two or three documents are found in French. In the Register of Bishop Grandisson, who lived on until 1360, the number of private letters in French is considerable, though they alternate with the Latin epistles which he usually addressed to ecclesiastics and men of learning. But in none of these volumes, so far as I have seen, is there any single document or memorandum couched in English, although the vast majority of the Bishops and their officials were Englishmen born and bred.[10]

---

[9] His mother Sibilla, daughter of John de Tregoz, seems, in spite of her family name, to have been an Englishwoman. So, at least, the Bishop himself states in writing to Pope Benedict XI (*Register*, I, p. 111.)

[10] In an appendix to the Register of Bishop Stafford (1395–1419), Prebendary Hingeston Randolph gives an analysis of sixty wills proved in the Bishop's court. All these seem to be in Latin, with the exception of one in French, printed *in extenso*. Of course some wills exist in English of earlier date than this, but they are at least extremely rare. The very small number of wills drafted in English before the fifteenth century is made plain in the volume of *Early English Wills* printed by the Early English Text Society.

At this epoch pretty well half the soil of France was for a hundred years in the occupation of Englishmen, who spoke and wrote the language of the natives as their own mother tongue. The pleadings of the English law-courts, the proceedings of the English Parliament, were all conducted in French. If we want a true analogy for the state of things during the fourteenth and part of the fifteenth century, we must think, not of England and an " Italian mission," but of some such condition of affairs as now prevails in Wales, where the appointment of an Englishman, an Irishman, or a Yankee as parson, while not an ideal nomination, would still be a matter of comparative indifference. No doubt the acceptable candidate will ordinarily be a Welshman, born in the country. Also there will at times be an outcry in Wales against the Saesneg (Sassenach) holders of livings, just as there was an outcry against the foreign favourites of Henry III or Edward II, and against the thrifty Scots who came flocking to London in the train of King Jeamie. But the root of such ill-feeling will lie rather in the jealousy of the disappointed than in any real impossibility of an alien discharging the duties which belong to his official position. Few Bishops in English history have done more for their dioceses than the Burgundian, St. Hugh of Avalon, the great Bishop of Lincoln. Yet it seems certain that he habitually wrote and spoke in Latin or French, and if he understood English at all, which is doubtful, to the end of his life he required an interpreter whenever he wished to converse with the peasantry in rural districts.

It is, therefore, absurd to suppose that the foreign ecclesiastics, mostly French-speaking, provided by the Pope to English benefices were marked off from the body of the people by any such line as separates a Frenchman from an Englishman now-a-days. Very significant are the terms of a letter of remonstrance addressed by Bishop Grandisson to Pope Clement VI about the Papal provisions. What the Bishop complains of is not that foreigners were appointed to English livings, but that all patronage was taken out of the hands of himself and his colleagues in the Episcopate.   The letter implies that the clergy thus provided by the Pope were very generally of English birth, and this Mr. Bliss's extracts from the Vatican registers fully bear out, but as Bishop Grandisson complains, the English clerks who rushed off to Avignon to sue for benefices, did not represent the highest type of candidates for promotion, and were far less worthy than those who remained at home.   In any case, the real abuse was not the sending of foreigners to England, but the naming of foreigners who never came to England at all.   This same protest sent off by Bishop Grandisson in November 1342 began with the words, which symbolise well the tone of the appeal : " *Quidquid servus suo Domino et filius Patri pio,*" (with all the good wishes that a servant may offer to his master and a son to a fond father). The occasion of that letter was, after all, quite exceptional. Clement VI on succeeding to the Papacy, seems to have made the astounding promise that he would grant benefices to all poor clerks who should come to Avignon and claim them within two months of his coronation.   " As many as one hundred thousand," writes Mr. Bliss, " are said to have come, and the register for the first year of his pontificate consists of no fewer than twelve volumes." [11]   The significance of this latter detail will be appreciated, when it is added that in the reign of his predecessor Benedict XII, one volume usually sufficed to contain all the grants of benefices and other documents emanating from the Papal Chancery in the course of a year. No wonder that the Pope's generosity only whetted the appetite of the needy clerics, and that we find him a few months afterwards launching anathemas against the petitioners, in a Bull, the terms of which can hardly be read without a smile.

Whereas certain persons, as We have frequently learned from experience, casting from them their regard for decent manners and the reverence due to Ourselves, have presumptuously dared and still do dare, when We are in consistory, and at other times when We are riding, to cast

[11] *Calendar of Entries in Papal Registers relating to Great Britain,* Vol. III. Preface, p. vi.

before Us and sometimes upon Us, their petitions, in which
they even wrap up stones to Our perturbation, We . . .
do by these presents strictly forbid all and singular to cast
down petitions in Our sight. . . . Moreover, those who
shall presume to the contrary, if they be clerks, We render
incapable of holding ecclesiastical benefices, but if they be
laymen, We will that they thereby incur sentence of excommunication, &c.

From what has been said it would hardly seem that the charge
of attempting to " denationalise " the Church of England
amounted to very much. The unfortunate feature of the case
is, however, that these imputations are scattered broadcast in
countless popular histories and especially in school-books for
children. The prejudice against the Popes is to a large extent kept
alive by misrepresentations which seem to the uncritical learner to
be just as authoritative and unassailable as the facts of botany
or chemistry which are put before them in their science lessons.

But what of the statement which in various forms is repeated
in many books of this class, that Englishmen revolted against
the Church of Rome and the Popes because they had so often
wrung money unjustly from the people ?

To discuss this question adequately would require a volume
to itself. It must be sufficient here to point out that while there
can be no thought of denying the existence of grave abuses or
of disputing the fact that the alleged rapacity of the Roman
Curia was the subject of general complaint, it was impossible
that a vast organisation like that of the Universal Church could
be maintained without some sort of taxation, while a demand
for money is what every man in all places and at all times is
most prone to resent. The papal taxation fell almost entirely
upon the clergy, and the clergy, most of all the monastic clergy,
in their chronicles and correspondence, have supplied us with
nine-tenths of the information we possess about medieval times.
The influence of such a writer as Matthew Paris upon posterity
has been enormous ; and yet what is the opinion formed of
him by an authority who more than any scholar of our genera-

tion has studied this chronicler, not by any means without sympathy, but critically and dispassionately ? The late Mr. A. L. Smith, who at the time of his lamented death was Master of Balliol, writes thus :

> Instead of being representative of his age on this question of submission to the Papacy, Matthew Paris represents an extreme position. He is like that millionaire who said " merely to be *asked* for money makes me feel positively ill." The one constant quantity in all his charges against the Papacy is extortion of money or money's worth. Historians have been somewhat too ready to assume that his attitude was the typical and normal one, whereas, when viewed in its proper environment and background, we can see it was (1) extreme, perhaps unique, in its vehemence ; (2) perfectly natural in a man of his views ; (3) perfectly illogical. For even he admits that one or two precedents (*ne ad consuetudinem traheretur*) admitted will rivet the Pope's claim for ever ; that is, one or two practical instances will deprive the Englishman of his favourite blundering refuge, the power of saying : " The theory holds good of course, but in practice . . . ? " That is, Matthew Paris really admits the theory, but hopes to raise objections to each proposed application of it.[12]

So again of Matthew's complaints of the submissiveness of Henry III to the papal demands and of the King's willingness to take a share of the spoils, Mr. A. L. Smith remarks :

> A King of Henry's position and necessities, and above all, of his character and convictions, could have done nothing to stay the hand of the Pope. He was reminded that it was no use his kicking against the pricks. The hopelessness of the situation lay not in the pusillanimity of a regulus, but in the futility of setting up a tribunal of God upon earth, and then expecting that it could live without a revenue and administer the whole world without taxing it.[13]

[12] A. L. Smith, *Church and State in the Middle Ages*, p. 178.

[13] *L.c.*, p. 166.

What is quite certain is the fact which has been pointed out above, that after fifty years of Provisions and endless demands for money, the Bishops of England had not changed their attitude of respectful submission to the Holy See, neither is there any unequivocal sign of insubordination on the part of the clergy, as a body, right down to the time of Henry VIII's break with Rome. And yet, as has already been said, it was the clergy—not the people, except very indirectly—who suffered from the papal exactions. Undoubtedly they grumbled among themselves, just as it is the dearest privilege of subordinates in our own fighting services to grumble and to leave behind them memoirs and correspondence which cannot be printed without much editing, but when it came to the point they did as they were bidden. The same high authority whom we have just quoted, and he by no means stands alone in these views, points out how completely Matthew Paris has misrepresented the attitude towards Pope Innocent IV of the great Bishop Grosseteste, particularly in the account which he gives of Grosseteste's last days.

The dying bishop is made to castigate just the very things and persons that were the objects of Matthew Paris's perennial animosity, the violations of Magna Charta, the *non obstante* clause in papal bulls, the usuries of papal money-lenders in England, the exaction of legacies from the dying, the intrusion of unfit papal presentees, the postponement of episcopal ordination. He is made to denounce the Roman Curia as the home of avarice, usury, simony, rapine, wantonness, licentiousness, gluttony and pomp ; to denounce the King as its accomplice and sharer in rapine ; and, most startling of all, to denounce the Dominicans and Franciscans, for whom in life he had nothing but eulogy and the highest esteem. These two orders he had held up as models, from them he had drawn his best friends, and without them he said his work would be impossible. Now they are picked out as object lessons in a fierce indictment of heresy for failing in their duty to preach against papal provisions, and the Pope himself becomes the arch-heretic.[14]

The late Master of Balliol makes it clear that in his view the document upon which these statements were based was a fabrication, though possibly Matthew Paris did not know it was. Similarly the famous letter cxxviii, in which the Bishop refuses to institute the Pope's nephew to a Lincoln canonry, appears in none of the manuscripts which contain the collected letters of Grosseteste, though the St. Alban's monk and whole generations of English historians after him have accepted it as genuine, because the wish was father to the thought. Even Bishop Stubbs " is content to observe mildly that Grosseteste's view of the Papacy seems to have altered at the end of his life." Strongly as Grosseteste resisted certain papal provisions and other ill-advised measures for raising money, there is not in all his undisputed correspondence a word which would suggest that he ever showed disrespect to the Holy See or faltered in his recognition of the Pope as God's vicegerent upon earth. But with such an example before us, how can we put confidence in the denunciations of medieval chroniclers, unless there is a consensus of testimony which eliminates the personal bias of the partisan, a bias often little less blindly unreasoning in the ardent reformer than in the rebel against convention and constituted authority?

Finally it should be noticed that the thorough investigation of the papal system of finance which has been undertaken of recent years by Göller, K. H. Schäfer, Paul Fabre, G. Mollat, and many others, has proved highly to the credit of the Holy See as compared with that of the secular administrations of the same period. It is true that very considerable sums flowed into the *camera apostolica* and that an unhappily large proportion of revenue was apt to be spent in military undertakings in defence, it was alleged, of the patrimony of St. Peter. But the investigation taken as a whole has dissipated the legend of systematic extortion and vast pontifical hoards.

[14] *L.c.*, p. 115.

How wildly extravagant were the assertions of the chroniclers, even of those who enjoy a certain credit, such men for instance as Matthew Paris and Villani, may be judged from a case in which the latter has over and over again been cited in denunciation of pontifical avarice. Even so sound a scholar as Dr. Workman was betrayed some years ago into writing as follows :

> The son of a shoemaker of Cahors, James D'Ueza,[15] was a worthy native of a city so famed through the Middle Ages for its usurers that Dante specially singles them out for punishment in his lowest Hell. At John's death a banker, the brother of Villani, the historian of Florence, was ordered to take an inventory of his hoard. It amounted to eighteen millions of gold florins in specie and seven millions in plate and jewels. "The good man," satirically adds Villani, "had forgotten the saying, 'Lay not up for yourselves treasures upon earth'; but perhaps he intended this wealth for the recovery of the Holy Land." [16]

It would hardly be possible to find a better illustration of the unreliability of all medieval testimony, especially as regards numbers. "What stronger evidence could you have?" the reader will be tempted to exclaim, "it comes from the brother of the man who made the inventory." But even in recording the matter as above, Dr. Workman adds in a footnote : "The sum seems to me incredible and I suspect error." His suspicion was fully justified, as we shall see, but meanwhile this portentous example of papal avarice continues to be cited. Mr. Turberville gives references to Dr. Workman, Dr. H. C. Lea describes John XXII as "extremely avaricious," and Mr. Dudley Wright informs the readers of *The Freemason* (September 14th, 1918) that he "amassed the enormous sum of 25,000,000 of florins," as before. But Dr. H. C. Lea is, as usual, the worst offender.

---

15 M. Albe has proved that this is quite untrue, Jacques Duèse was not the son of a shoemaker but of a wealthy burgher. See Mollat, *Papes d'Avignon*, p. 43 note.

16 *The London Quarterly*, April, 1903, pp. 321–322.

Referring to the avarice of John XXII, the historian begins by saying :

> His quenchless greed displayed an exhaustless fertility of resource in converting the treasures of salvation into current coin. He it was who first reduced to a system the "Taxes of the Penitentiary" which offered absolution at fixed prices for every possible form of human wickedness, from five grossi for homicide or incest to thirty-three grossi for ordination below the canonical age.

We may leave this question of the taxes of the penitentiary aside, as an examination of the evidence would take much space. Let it only be said that a substantially complete refutation of this baseless and preposterous charge has long ago been provided in the book of Father T. L. Green, *Indulgences, Sacramental Absolutions and the Tax Tables;* but let us pass on to another count in Dr. Lea's indictment which requires less explanation. The whole charge here turns on a bare point of fact :

> After John's death [so he continues], when an inventory of his effects came to be made, there was found in his treasury eighteen millions of gold florins, and jewels and vestments estimated at seven millions more. Even in mercantile Florence the sum was so incomprehensible that Villani, whose brother was one of the appraisers, feels obliged to explain that each million is a thousand thousand. When we reflect upon the comparative poverty of the period and the scarcity of the precious metals, we can estimate how great an amount of suffering was represented by such an accumulation, wrung as it was, in its ultimate source, from the wretched peasantry, who gleaned at the best an insufficient subsistence from imperfect agriculture. We can, perhaps, moreover, imagine how, in its passage to the papal treasury, it represented so much of simony, so much of justice sold or denied to the wretched litigants in the curia, so much of purgatory remitted, and of pardons for sins to the innumerable applicants for a share of the Church's treasury of salvation.

One notes how Dr. Lea, with the righteous indignation of the anti-clerical fanatic, dots the *i*'s and crosses the *t*'s so that no one should overlook the sufferings of " the wretched peasantry " whom he chooses to set before us, without one shred of evidence, as the principal victims of this unscrupulous papal greed.

Well, in all this there is much that may be matter of opinion and that will be interpreted according to the preconceived views of the critic. But the question of fact stands out. Did John XXII leave behind him in the papal treasury a sum of eighteen millions of gold florins ? The papal account-books, still in existence, provide the means of making the calculation, and G. Mollat, the editor of John XXII's Regesta, with E. Göller, have undertaken the task. They find that the actual sum in the treasury was somewhere about 750,000 florins ; it certainly did not amount to a single million.[17] Can any further comment be necessary ?

Another point in which the misconceptions of the last century have been corrected by fuller investigations, is the matter of the Statutes of Provisions and *Praemunire*. In the older history books we were commonly told that all this legislation was prompted by the desire of the people of England to suppress appeals to Rome, mainly because the country was in this way drained of vast sums of money which went to fill the papal coffers and to line the pockets of Roman officials. A better understanding of the problem has shown that this conception was in many ways erroneous. It was not the people who were interested in the passing of the Acts of Provision, but the royal officials and the lay patrons. Moreover, there never was any attempt made to enforce them systematically. The real purpose and effect of the Statute of *Praemunire* were for the first time made clear in the *English Historical Review* for April 1922 by Mr. W. T.

---

[17] See G. Mollat in the *Revue d'Histoire Ecclésiastique* V (1904), pp. 525-530. The whole article, which is entitled *Jean XXII fut-il un avare ?* deserves careful reading. It is continued in the number for the following January. Compare also E. Göller, *Die Einnahmen*, pp. 122-124, as well as some earlier papers by Sägmüller and Cardinal Ehrle.

Waugh, whose conclusions seem to have been generally accepted. His final summary statement runs thus :

The wording of the Act itself, the circumstances in which it was passed and the general disregard of it for so many years point alike to the conclusion that it was originally a measure of but limited purpose, intended by those who framed it to protect ecclesiastics from punishment for executing the sentences of secular courts and to prevent the arbitrary translations of bishops.

CHAPTER XIV

THE POPES IN PROTESTANT TRADITION

THERE seems to be a curious lack of information regarding the extent to which the two Books of " Homilies appointed to be read in Churches " remained in actual use during the seventeenth and eighteenth centuries. " The Constitutions and Canons Ecclesiastical " of 1604 distinctly enjoin that every Sunday the parson or his curate " shall read some one of the homilies prescribed, or to be prescribed, by authority " ; but unless he is a duly licensed preacher he " shall only study to read plainly and aptly (without glossing or adding) the homilies already set forth." [1] Further, we know that numerous editions still continued to be published down to modern times and this may probably be accepted as evidence that the practice of reading them aloud had not yet entirely fallen into desuetude. The Thirty-nine Articles of Religion, to which every ordained clergyman of the Church of England was required formally to profess adhesion, declared in Article XXXV that the Second Book of Homilies, like the First, " doth contain a godly and wholesome doctrine," adding : " and therefore we judge them to be read in churches by the Ministers, diligently and distinctly, that they may be understood of the people."

There can be little doubt that many generations of Englishmen were accustomed to listen Sunday after Sunday to these discourses, and must have formed their opinions regarding the practices of popery and the facts of papal history in accordance with what was read to them. If they desired to pursue the subject they had in many churches the opportunity of consulting

[1] Cardwell, *Synodalia*, Vol. I, pp. 273 and 275.

that authoritative and very detailed work, *The Acts and Monuments*, more familiarly known as " Foxe's Book of Martyrs." Although it is not correct to say, as has sometimes been stated, that an order of Convocation enjoined that a copy should be set up in every parish church, still the Convocation of 1571 did require every bishop and archdeacon to possess this book ; which should, they recommend, be made accessible to the public. Moreover, in very many churches copies were provided by the zeal of the parishioners, which copies were commonly left exposed, but secured by a chain, for all men to read therein. Thus, as we learn from the Vestry Minutes of St. Michael's, Cornhill, " it was agreed, 11 Jan., 1572, that the booke of Martyrs of Mr. Foxe and the paraphrases of Erasmus shal be bowght for the church and tyed with a chayne to the Egle bras." Foxe's volumes, by the way, cost the parish the not inconsiderable sum of £2 2s. 6d. Similarly, the Churchwardens' Accounts of St. Nicholas, Warwick, in 1633, record the expenditure of 10d. for " mending the Churche booke and setting on the chainis to ye Bookes of Martirs." Copies still exist, or existed until recent times, in such out of the way churches as those of Apethorpe (Northants), Enstone (Oxon), Lessingham (Norfolk), etc. Of Foxe's book we shall have something to add later, but meanwhile we may note what was said of it very truly in a former edition of the *Encyclopedia Britannica :* " More than any other influence, it fanned the flame of that fierce hatred of Spain and the Inquisition which was the master passion of the age. Nor was its influence transient. For generations the popular conception of popery has been derived from its melancholy and bitter pages."

But to return to the Book of Homilies. At the recurrence of each Whitsunday, or on the Sundays following, a large proportion of our English forefathers, sitting in their pews, had read to them an edifying discourse upon the Gifts of the Holy Ghost in which they were incidentally invited to express their opinion of " the Popes' intolerable pride." After certain citations from Scripture and the Fathers, the question was again

asked : " Do not these places sufficiently convince their outrageous pride in usurping to themselves a superiority above all
other, as well ministers and bishops, as kings also and emperors ? "
And thereupon follows a little historical excursus, which deserves
to be quoted at some length :

But, as the lion is known by his claws, so let us learn to
know these men by their deeds. What shall we say of him
that made the noble King Dandalus to be tied by the neck
with a chain and to lie flat down before his table there to
gnaw bones like a dog ? Shall we think that he had God's
Holy Spirit within him, and not rather the spirit of the
devil ? Such a tyrant was Pope Clement the Sixth. What
shall we say of him that proudly and contemptuously trod
Frederick the Emperor under his feet, applying that verse
of the Psalm to himself : " Thou shalt go upon the lion and
the adder ; the young lion and the dragon thou shalt
tread under thy foot " ? Shall we say that he had God's
Holy Spirit within him and not rather the spirit of the
devil ? Such a tyrant was Pope Alexander the Third.
What shall we say of him that armed and animated the son
against the father, causing him to be taken, and to be
cruelly famished to death, contrary to the law of God and
also nature ? Shall we say that he had God's Holy Spirit
within him, and not rather the spirit of the devil ? Such a
tyrant was Pope Paschal the Second. What shall we say
of him that came into his popedom like a fox, that reigned
like a lion, and died like a dog ? Shall we say that he had
God's Holy Spirit within him, and not rather the spirit of
the devil ? Such a tyrant was Pope Boniface the Eighth.
What shall we say of him that made Henry the Emperor
with his wife and his young child to stand at the gates of
the city in the rough winter barefooted and barelegged,
only clothed in linsey woolsey, eating nothing from morning
to night, and that for the space of three days ? Shall we
say that he had God's Holy Spirit within him, and not
rather the spirit of the devil ? Such a tyrant was Pope

Hildebrand, most worthy to be called a firebrand, if we shall term him as he hath best deserved.

Many other examples might here be alleged ; as of Pope Joan the harlot, that was delivered of a child in the high street, going solemnly in procession ; of Pope Julius the Second, that wilfully cast St. Peter's keys into the river Tiberis ; of Pope Urban the Sixth, that caused five cardinals to be put in sacks and cruelly drowned ; of Pope Sergius the Third, that persecuted the dead body of Formosus, his predecessor, when it had been buried eight years ; of Pope John the Fourteenth of that name, who, having his enemy delivered into his hands, caused him first to be stripped stark naked, his beard to be shaven, and to be hanged up a whole day by the hair, then to be set upon an ass with his face backward towards the tail, to be carried round about the city in despite, to be miserably beaten with rods, last of all to be thrust out of his country and to be banished for ever. But to conclude and make an end, ye shall briefly take this short lesson : wheresoever ye find the spirit of arrogancy and pride, the spirit of envy, hatred, contention, cruelty, murder, extortion, witchcraft, necromancy, etc., assure yourselves that there is the spirit of the devil, and not of God ; albeit they pretend outwardly to the world never so much holiness.

It hardly need be said that the history here recounted is of the most fantastic description. Some of it is sheer romance without any sober authority in its favour, but even where the facts are in substantial accord with the truth, as seems to be the case with the Hildebrand incident at Canossa, no hint is given that the Pope, wearied out and disgusted by a long series of duplicities, had every reason to subject the sincerity of King Henry IV's repentance to the severest test, and in the event was once more deceived. The first episode alluded to in the Homily is a fitting specimen of the rest. The writer speaks of " the noble King Dandalus." Now Francesco Dandolo, though he belonged to a distinguished Venetian family, was never a king. It was not until more than eighteen years after the event referred to that he was elected Doge. When he came as the special envoy of the Republic to the papal court at Avignon to sue for peace, the reigning sovereign Pontiff was not Clement VI but Clement V. It seems to be true that Francesco presented himself before the Pope with a chain round his neck and that his countrymen ever afterwards nicknamed him, " Cane " (the " dog "), but these servile trappings were no more than an example of that extravagant symbolism which the Middle Ages delighted in. When some little time later in the same century the town of Calais after a year's siege was starved into surrender, Eustache de S. Pierre, the wealthiest burgess of the town, as Mr. Green recounts in a picturesque passage, volunteered to lead the party of hostages demanded by Edward III. " For me," he said, " I have great hope in the Lord that if I can save this people by my death, I shall have pardon for my faults, wherefore will I be the first of the six, and of my own will put myself barefoot in my shirt and with a halter round my neck in the mercy of King Edward." All the rest of the Dandolo story about the lying flat down under the table and gnawing the bones like a dog is pure fiction. Even John Foxe, though he refers to the episode three times in illustration of the overweening pride of the papacy, makes it clear that the chain was voluntarily assumed by the Venetian envoy in order to propitiate the Pontiff.

So again the description of Alexander III treading Frederick Barbarossa under his feet is just such another invention of a later age and has no sort of contemporary authority to support it, but Foxe refers more than once to this " treading upon the neck of Barbarossa " and improves the occasion with the reflection : " Consider moreover the behaviour, manner, condition and property of almost all the Popes who have been there six hundred years, and what dragon or serpent could be more viperous than their own doings and words can speak and give testimony against themselves." [2]   There is of course no question

[2] This refers of course to the supposed use by Alexander of the words, " the young lion and the dragon thou shalt tread under thy foot."

that a reconciliation took place between Frederick and the Pope at Venice in July 1177, but the picture of the interview drawn quite recently in the *Cambridge Medieval History* is very different from that with which the Homilies and Foxe present us :

> There in front of St. Mark's, amidst a reverent and deeply moved assemblage, the two champions met after a struggle of eighteen years for the ideal supremacy which each deemed granted to him by God. The moment was full of solemnity. The Emperor, overcome by sentiments of reverence for the aged man who received him, threw off his imperial mantle and prostrated himself before him. The Pope, in tears, raised and embraced him, and leading him into the church gave him his benediction. The next day the Pope said Mass in St. Mark's, and on his quitting the church the Emperor held his stirrup and made ready to conduct his palfrey. The Pope, however, gave him his blessing, at the same time dispensing him from accompanying him to his barge.[3]

It would be useless to go through the whole series of charges and to meet each with a refutation in form. No one now believes that the Emperor Henry IV was starved to death or that it was Pope Paschal who instigated his worthless and treacherous son to rise against him. So again, however barbarous may seem the ignominious punishment inflicted by John XIII (*not* " John the Fourteenth of that name ") upon the Prefect Peter, after grievous provocation, it is to be noted that this culprit, whom Otto I surrendered to the Pope to deal with as he pleased, was not put to death. He was banished, but his life was spared, whereas the twelve " decarcones," his abettors in the insurrection, were hanged by Otto without more ado.

It is upon misrepresentations and exaggerations such as these, derived for the most part from sources long subsequent to the events they chronicle, and taking no account of the medieval tendency to favour always the more bizarre and blood-curdling

[3] *The Cambridge Medieval History*, Vol. V, p. 450.

story in preference to a tame narration of facts, that the edifice
of anti-papal prejudice has been built up ; but it is now so
firmly compacted and so deep-seated that it can hardly be
overthrown. No doubt it may be pleaded in excuse that
shocking charges were indisputably made, and that in some cases
the men who made them were contemporaries who professed
to be loyal sons of the Church. It requires some little first-hand
acquaintance with such writers as Liutprand, Matthew Paris,
Petrarch or Giraldus Cambrensis to realise how extraordinarily
incontinent of speech the censor was apt to be when his prejudices were deeply involved. He was prepared to believe
anything of an opponent, and what he believed, or thought other
people might believe, he spoke out ; indeed, when a little
reiteration had hardened him he was prepared to swear to it.
If John Foxe could have been asked why he depicted Pope
Boniface VIII as such a monster of infamy, he would no doubt
have replied that he had said no more than was to be found in the
articles charged against him by William de Nogaret and William
de Plaisians, which are set out at large in his own Book of
Martyrs. Nevertheless all this testimony is now rejected *en bloc*
by the saner scholarship of the present day. In such works as
Gregorovius's *Rome*, the Protestant *Realencyclopädie*, and Hauck's
Kirchengeschichte Deutschlands, the Pontiff is acquitted of the
extravagant charges made against him of licentiousness, sorcery,
heresy and flagrant simony, however severely the writers in
question may condemn his theory of the papal power and the
doctrine of the two swords. Indeed, it is difficult to read through
the articles of accusation submitted in the posthumous trial of
Boniface without reaching the conviction that they are utterly
untrustworthy. But for all that, John Foxe still survives in his
progeny, in such writers as Mr. Hugh Stutfield, Mr. Joseph
McCabe, and Dr. Rappoport. For example, the first-named
informs us that " the high-water mark of papal pretension was
reached at the jubilee of A.D. 1300, when that unmitigated
scoundrel and libertine, Boniface VIII, seated on the throne of
Constantine, arrayed with the sword and sceptre, shouted aloud

to the assembled pilgrims : ' I am Caesar ; I am Emperor ' " [4]
The story is an idle tale and the epithets applied to the Pontiff
merely reflect the venom of the writer. Similarly, Mr. McCabe
expresses himself in terms that are hardly less unparliamentary.
In 1916 this gentleman published a book (*Crises in the History
of the Papacy*) with Messrs. Putnam, primarily an American firm
of high standing, who are also well aware that in the United
States the Catholic Church is influential and cannot be outraged
with impunity. Having occasion in that work to refer to
Boniface VIII, Mr. McCabe describes him as " the last great
representative of the papal ideal in its earlier and more austere
medieval form." [5] No word of disparagement is added with
regard to the Pope's personal character. A few years later,
however, the same writer compiled another and smaller book
under the title of *The Popes and their Church, a Candid Account*.
In this work, which was brought out by Messrs. Watts and Co.
(Johnson's Court, Fleet Street), who act as publishers to the
Rationalist Press Association, Mr. McCabe presumably felt
more at liberty. Consequently in a reference to the posthumous
trial of Boniface we read :

> " Clement was forced to hold a Consistory and for days
> the most astounding evidence about Boniface was put
> before him. Boniface had been addicted to natural and
> unnatural vice, blasphemy, scepticism, simony and all
> species of corruption. Now we cannot check this evidence
> . . . Yet the witnesses were of such a character that we
> cannot admit more than exaggeration. The man at whose
> feet thousands had grovelled in 1300 was stained with
> every vice from paederasty to murder." [6]

Mr. McCabe also states in the same work that Boniface VIII
was " a thorough blackguard and despised those whom he duped
and fleeced." But the fact is that the whole case against the Pope's
moral character rests upon the testimony of his unscrupulous

[4] H. Stutfield, *Priestcraft*, p. 69.

[5] McCabe, *Crises in the History of the Papacy* (1916), p. 203.

[6] McCabe, *The Popes and their Church ; a Candid Account*, pp. 58–59.

and bitter enemies. Mr. McCabe thinks that the witnesses were so respectable that " we cannot admit more than exaggeration." Ernest Renan was not less sound a Rationalist than Mr. McCabe and he was a man who was respected at least for the fact that he never tried to court popularity or to make money by flinging dirt at the Church which he had quitted. Those who may consult his articles in the *Revue des deux Mondes* 1872 and in the *Histoire littéraire de la France*, Vol. XXVII, or his book on *Philippe le Bel*, will find a very different estimate of the trustworthiness of Nogaret and Philip's other satellites. And with this agrees the view of M. Charles Langlois, whose special research in connection with this very matter is well known. Even Dean Milman and Gregorovius range themselves on the same side. But such bitter prejudice as that imbibed for generations from the Homilies and from John Foxe does not easily die. The volume on *Medieval Rome*, in the " Story of the Nations " series, calmly sets before its readers this account of the Pope's death :

> Rome sent an escort to bring him safely to the Vatican, where he shut himself up like a prisoner, a prey to fury, mistrust and disgust, without a friend, without a hope. The prophecy of the poor hermit whom he had shut up in that solitary tower now came true. " Boniface," he had said, " shall come in like a fox, reign like a lion, and die like a dog." He refused all nourishment, dashed his head against the wall in accesses of passion, and a month after his release from Anagni, was one morning found dead in his bed. His enemies, and they were many, saw in his end a judgment of Heaven." [7]

But all this is based upon data that are utterly unreliable. If we may quote another sober and competent medievalist, Samuel Berger declares without hesitation that " Boniface has been very unjustly treated by historians of more than one school " ; and as for the story that the Pope after he was taken prisoner at Anagni went out of his mind and died tearing his

[7] Miller, *Medieval Rome*, pp. 105–108.

own flesh, Berger simply remarks : " This was not the case," [8]
adding that " history has been merciless to his memory."
Similarly, Hauck, however little in sympathy with the principles
and motives by which the Pope's action was guided, does not
hesitate to declare that : " an impartial criticism must entirely
reject the accusations repeatedly hurled against him by his
opponents of leading an immoral life abandoned to the most
shameless excesses. Such a charge is supported by no witnesses
worthy of credit. It is just as unfounded as the accusation of
heresy of which he is equally the object." [9]

Another Pope, or at any rate another papal claimant, who has
fallen under the lash of Mr. McCabe's righteous zeal against
ecclesiastics who have been unfaithful to the vows by which they
have pledged themselves, is Baldassare Cossa, who in 1410 was
elected by a party of the Cardinals and took the name of John
XXIII. In accordance with the indictment laid before the
Council of Constance, " this Holy Father," says Mr. McCabe,
" was described as wicked, irreverent, unchaste, a liar, dis-
obedient and infected with many vices." He secured his
election " by violence and fraud." As Pope he was " an op-
pressor of the poor, a persecutor of justice, a pillar of the wicked,
a statue of simoniacs, addicted to magic, the dregs of vice,
wholly given to sleep and carnal desires." He practised sacrilege, adultery, murder, spoliation, rape and theft. Further,
we learn that Dietrich von Nieheim describes him as " a man of
unbounded sexual license, of ferocious cruelty, a bandit all his
life, utterly irreligious, absolutely devoid of moral scruple." [10]
It is quite true that language of this sort was freely used during
the fierce animosities engendered by the great Schism of the
West, and it is also true that such authorities as Gregorovius and
Krüger seem to think there was foundation for it. We cannot
altogether deny the possibility that Cossa's life may have been

---

[8] Lichtenberger's (Protestant) *Encyclopédie des Sciences Religeuses*, Vol. II,
p. 355.

[9] *Realencyclopädie f. Protest. Theologie*, III, p. 299.

[10] J. McCabe, *The Popes and their Church*, p. 69.

as scandalous as his enemies said ; but it ought at any rate to be pointed out that the case against him all depends upon the extravagant utterances of witnesses so blinded by prejudice as to be quite unreliable. If this Pontiff had happened to be a sympathiser with Huss, instead of Head of the Church which claimed to sit in judgment on heretics, Krüger and Gregorovius would in all probability have declared that the allegations made to Cossa's discredit were malicious fictions, and, as evidence, absolutely worthless. Even as it is, Dr. B. Bess in the *Realencyclopädie* identifies himself with the carefully pondered judgment of G. Erler,[11] and declares that John XXIII was probably neither better nor worse than his contemporaries. The whole case turns upon the credibility of Dietrich von Nieheim. Yet certain gossip of Dietrich's regarding Cossa's relations with the ladies of Bologna, which, of course, Dr. Rappoport sets down as history, is ridiculed as preposterous by Gregorovius himself.[12] The contemporary historians of Bologna know nothing of such scandals. At any rate it is interesting to find that a modern student of this period, a non-Catholic scholar, whose pages bear continual witness to the diligence with which he has studied Dietrich von Nieheim and all the original sources, expresses himself in the following terms upon the charge of debauchery brought against Baldassare Cossa :

It must [he says] be remembered that chastity was not then a virtue greatly in vogue, that the moral feeling of Italy was lower than in other countries and that most of the mighty ones of the earth were monsters of immorality. . . . One of Cossa's greatest friends, as one of his greatest enemies, bear alike witness, though indirect, to the comparative purity of his life. Carlo Malatesta, an upright and honourable man, was a friend of Baldassare Cossa. He respected him, and even when in later years at Constance he bore witness against him, he never said anything tending to accuse him of sensuality. Pope Gregory XII [one of

[11] Erler, *Dietrich von Nieheim*, pp. 341–344 and cf. 225.

[12] Gregorovius, *History of Rome* (Eng. Trans.), VI, p. 614.

the rival Popes], on the other hand, was one of Cossa's worst and most inveterate enemies. He fulminated a bull against him, in which he enumerated every charge known to him against Cossa, but he also never accused him of immorality. The evidence of these two men far outweighs that of Nieheim. Furthermore, all the Popes for more than a century back, with the single exception of Clement VI, had been men of clean lives, and it is in the highest degree improbable that Cossa would ever have worn the triple crown had he been the prodigy of sensuality described by Dietrich von Nieheim.[13]

Always and everywhere we find ourselves confronted by the same sort of difficulty. On the one side a malicious accuser, or a band of accusers, who set no limits to their passionate invectives, and pile up a catalogue of indescribable abominations which it seems incredible that anyone could have committed whose position required him to retain in some measure the respect of his fellow-Christians. On the other side we have men of repute who soberly commend the integrity of the Popes attacked, or at any rate leave no hint that they were suspected of misconduct. The extravagance of the accusers shows itself in every phrase. They are nearly always people in the pay of the declared enemies of the papacy, and their own lives for the most part are stained with notorious scandals. It is a discreditable campaign, carried on with poisoned weapons, and there is no sign that the original authors of these charges, though they professed to be the champions of order and decency, were animated by any higher motive than base malevolence.

The real problem in all these cases is the attitude of medieval chroniclers. They recount, without any indication of doubt as to the facts, the most astounding scandals of Popes and ecclesiastics in high places. From the thirteenth century onwards, there is hardly a single annalist that does not retail the story of Pope Joan ; and, as we have seen, a really pious and spiritually-

[13] E. J. Kitts, *In the Days of the Councils, a sketch of the Life and Times of Baldassare Cossa* (1908), pp. 169–170.

minded monk like William of Malmesbury launches anathemas against the estimable Pontiff Sylvester II because he believed that he had sold his soul to the devil. The explanation is to be found, I think, partly in the extreme credulity of the age, partly in the fact that the monks and friars were often the most violent of political partisans. Even now we are not so far removed from a period when the simpler-minded were prepared to believe any fantastic tale because " they had seen it in print." It seems likely that at a period when the ability to read a manuscript, or to write it, was the distinction of a very small proportion of the population the reverence for the *litera scripta* was intense to a degree impossible for us now to realise. On the other hand, the readiness of all classes, clergy and laity alike, to believe in the existence of countless papal irregularities did not shake the people's faith in the Pope's leadership or his right to teach the Church. They probably did not argue about it. The papacy was a fact, an institution as stable as the sun, but like the sun it did not greatly trouble them because it was occasionally eclipsed or had spots on it.

Again, once people were familiar with the idea of the necromancy attributed to Pope Sylvester or with the horrors of the Roman court during the tenth century, it is easy to understand that in the agitated politics of medieval Italy, under stress of papal exactions either unjust or believed to be such—not to speak of ecclesiastical censures which were not the less bitterly resented because they were often richly merited—those who were aggrieved set absolutely no bounds to the violence of the language they employed. Men in those days were extravagant in act and extravagant in speech. The virtue of moderation only comes to be appreciated as society attains a certain level of culture. Both the earlier and later Middle Ages tended toward excess, just as the savage loves garish colours and the child loves noisy games. You do not expect nowadays to find a king of England, however much he might dislike the policy of an Archbishop of Canterbury, suborning assassins, as Henry II did, to compass the prelate's death. Neither does a ruling prince with his own hands stab to the heart a guest who had come to his court protected by a safe-conduct under the privy-seal, though this was what King James II of Scotland did in 1452 to William, the eighth Earl Douglas. On the other hand one does not hear or expect to hear, in these times in which we live, of kings baring their shoulders and submitting to be scourged by ecclesiastics in punishment of their misdeeds. Bishops do not now command an army in the field or maintain publicly a family of illegitimate children ; but neither do bishops —at any rate not Anglican bishops—wear perpetual hair shirts and fast on bread and water throughout the forty days of Lent. Speaking generally, it was always the tendency of medieval censors of morals to pile up the agony. The descriptions of the pains of the lost which occupy so large a place in early literature from the " Apocalypses " of St. Peter and of St. Paul down to Dante's *Divina Commedia*, or again to the Vision of the Monk of Eynsham and the accounts of St. Patrick's Purgatory, beggar imagination in their attempts to describe the horrible. The main object is to inspire terror, just as the war-paint of the savage or the ghastly helmets which formed part of the equip-ment of the Japanese warriors less than a century back, were seemingly devised with a similar purpose. We note the same crude feeling at work in the hideous punishments—breaking on the wheel, burning at the stake, flaying alive, drawing and quartering, boiling in a cauldron, pressing to death with weights—which were inflicted on criminals in every country of Europe long after the revival of learning and in the full tide of the " glorious Reformation." True to this spirit, ex-travagance of language in the denunciation of moral excesses, was looked upon as a virtue. The sweeping accusations made by even sainted prelates and earnest reformers (for example, by St. Peter Damian or St. Bernardine of Siena) cannot be accepted too literally. They often need to be severely dis-counted, precisely because of the extreme zeal and the very high ideals of those whose feelings were outraged.

My point, then, is that if vile things have been said, and

spread broadcast, and have even been believed by many in good faith, regarding the Popes of the nineteenth century, without a shadow of justification, we must expect to find even more atrocious calumnies of the same kind written down and circulated during the Middle Ages. The mere fact that the Pope was the spiritual head of Christendom in no way rendered him immune from slander. In a thousand ways it is made clear to us that, while medieval chroniclers and others respected the office of the supreme Pontiff, they by no means necessarily respected his person. No Catholic ever held that the Pope was impeccable. It has been one of the results of that welter of conflicting creeds which since the sixteenth century has distracted the greater part of Europe, that we have all now become extremely sensitive about the reputation of our ecclesiastical representatives. In the bosom of a family, unrestrained criticism of its head, or heads, often runs rampant. It is only when a stranger is present that the flow of tongues is checked. When all Christendom knew but one creed and recognised one spiritual chief, everyone felt free to express his views, often with quite alarming frankness, knowing in reality that his utterances would be discounted by hearers who understood the situation just as well as he did and were aware that he was only letting off steam. Now, each denomination maintains, as far as possible, company manners, and is painfully self-conscious, realising that anything given away will be utilised to its own prejudice by its rivals. It is in this consideration that we may find at least a partial explanation of the unmeasured invectives and the appalling want of reticence of so many medieval chroniclers and preachers.

Moreover in the Middle Ages there was no law of libel, and relatively speaking no publicity such as our newspapers and our postal service provide nowadays. The writer of the most violent outbursts in a monastic chronicle might feel reasonably sure, even though he were a Matthew Paris, that the chances were a thousand to one against any copy of what he wrote ever coming into the hands of those against whom his denunciations were directed. His public was his own community and possibly a little local circle. He was likely to be a man with strong prejudices, for it rarely happened that he was in a position to hear both sides of any public matter under debate. He was also apt to be credulous and fond of the sensational and at the back of it all there was the feeling that the scandals reported of great ecclesiastics constituted a sort of palliation of the everyday shortcomings in monastic observance to which he himself might plead guilty or which were charged against his fellow religious.

From these and similar influences it resulted that in the days before the invention of printing, the wildest accusations and the most extravagant stories were freely circulated, even though they were directed against no less august a personage than the Sovereign Pontiff himself. There was no critical sense as to the value of evidence, and there was intense partisanship. The Popes, as temporal rulers, were constantly entangled in the fierce political disputes of the times. Moreover the unrestrained passion and self-seeking which led to the perpetration of so many cruelties and deeds of blood are not likely to have been confined to acts alone. The man who so freely murdered or stole, would be sure to back up these atrocities by perjuries, calumnies and lies. A malicious story once invented, or elaborated from some relatively trivial foundation in fact, would circulate readily and would find many honest believers amongst those who, through nationality, accidental circumstances or motives of interest, found themselves arrayed in the camp opposite to the pontiff so impugned. On the whole, the wonder seems to be that the contemporary literature preserved to us which attacks the personal character, the administration and the finance of the medieval popes, is not more acrimonious and lurid than it is.

Chapter XV

DARKENING THE SHADOWS

For the denunciations of the chroniclers in the Middle Ages we may feel a certain sympathy. For the most part they really believed what they wrote. The abuses they attacked, supposing them to have been as represented, were real abuses and were a very proper subject for indignation. Moreover, once a story had been told them, it would have been very difficult to control the facts by further inquiry. There were no newspapers or telegrams in those days, and but little correspondence. Communications were very restricted as compared with the standard of our own times.

No excuse of the same kind can be made for the type of literature of which Dr. Rappoport's *Love Affairs of the Vatican* is the most disreputable example known to me. He claims to be a scholar and a historian who works in great libraries and is familiar with many languages. A long list of previous publications stands to his name. What is more particularly nauseating in the work in question is its profession of a high moral purpose and its claim " to do justice to the Popes who were worthy Vicars of Christ." [1] Even if we classed it as a work of fiction, it would be beneath contempt on account of its vapid style and the methods by which the narrative has been pieced together. And yet it was a high-priced book, alleged by its publishers to be a " best seller " and to be found at all the libraries. If any curious person should take the trouble to attempt the

---

[1] It would, I think, be true to say that there is not one word of commendation or approval expressed for any Pope from the first page of the book to the last.

investigation, and to trace the text of the volume to its sources, he will, before long, begin to doubt whether beyond a few interpolated phrases, introductory paragraphs and connective passages, Dr. Rappoport can really be regarded as the author of the book at all. It seems in fact to be little more than a mosaic of translated extracts, taken from vile or utterly worthless originals, which serious scholars have long ago cast aside. As already hinted, the author has borrowed largely from the German original of Griesinger's *Mysteries of the Vatican.* The whole long account, for instance, of the poisoning of Alexander VI, a story to which we will return further on, is taken over from this source [2]; but let us take another passage from the beginning of Chapter VII, printing on one side the existing English translation of Griesinger and opposite to it that of Dr. Rappoport's new and " original " work.

GRIESINGER, 1861.	RAPPOPORT, 1912.
A worthy successor followed Sixtus in Innocent VIII. (1484-1492) ; he had no less than sixteen recognized illegitimate children, of whom he exhibited no little paternal pride. His favourite, a certain Franceschetto, was one of these, and to provide him with land and lieges, Girolamo Riario, the son of the last Pope, and possessor of Imola and Forla, had suddenly to depart this life 14 Ap. 1488. Innocent trusted, after the murder, to transfer the cities without difficulty, and not only incited the Forlians to rise against their ruler,	Pope Innocent VIII. was a worthy successor to Pope Sixtus. He had not less than sixteen illegitimate children, in whom he publicly showed pride. His favourite was Franceschetto ; and in order to provide him with land and people, Jerome Riario, son of the late Pope, who possessed Forli and Imola, had to leave this earthly state quite suddenly, April 14, 1488. Innocent hoped to make himself easily master of the said cities after this murder, and to this end drove the people of Forli to revolt against their lawful rulers, supporting

[2] See Pastor, *History of the Popes* (Eng. Trans.), VI, p. 135.

T

but provided them with a considerable armed force for the purpose. But though Girolamo was killed, his son Octavio, and his widow, the famous Catarina Sforza, who was as lovely and able as she was courageous and energetic, had survived, and she, mustering her adherents, completely routed the papal troops. Catherine even captured six of the enemy's generals, and had them at once put to death, finally obliging the Forlians to lay down their arms, acknowledge her son as his father's heir, and herself as regent during his minority.[3]

them with an army. But Jerome had left, besides his young son under age—a widow, the beautiful, clever, brave, and energetic Catherine Sforza, who put the Papal army to flight ; she took six officers prisoners, whom she promptly executed, and then forced the people of Forli not only to do homage to her son, but also to accept her as Regent.[4]

Or let us take another work which our author affects, an anonymous book on the Papacy by " Anti Romanus."

ANTI ROMANUS, 1838.

Das zehnte Jahrhundert ist die schmachvollste Epoche in der schmachvollen Geschichte des Pabstthums. Das ganze Regiment der Statthalter Gottes war in die Hände lasciver, herrschsüchtiger Damen gerathen. Diese baten die päbst-

RAPPOPORT, 1912.

But it is especially the tenth century which is rich in gallant intrigues of the Bishops of Rome and the clergy. Without exaggeration one may say that the government of the Popes in those days was in the hands of lascivious and ambitious

---

[3] *The Mysteries of the Vatican* (Eng. Trans.), I, p. 331. Allen and Co., 1864.

[4] Rappoport, *The Love Affairs of the Vatican*, p. 224. 1912. The allegations made in this passage are quite unreliable. For example, it is certain that Girolamo Riario was the nephew and not the son of Sixtus IV. See Pastor (Eng. Trans.), IV, 232 ; Creighton, *Hist. of Papacy*, III, 68. Innocent VIII had two illegitimate children born before his ordination to the priesthood, but we have no certain knowledge of any others. (Pastor, V, 240, etc.)

liche Krone an die Meistbietenden ihrer zahllosen Liebhaber feil oder gaben sie ihren unehelichen Kindern. Die schändlichsten und verworfensten Abenteurer drängen sich während dieses Hurenregiments der Braut Christi als Bräutigame auf. Es gibt kein Verbrechen, kein Laster, was damals nicht am römischen Hof ausgeübt worden wäre. Der päbstliche Palast war in ein wahres Hurenhaus verwandelt und in Rom herrschte eine völlige Anarchie.[5]

women. Like the Prætorian guards once in the time of the pagan Emperors of Rome, these ladies held the papal power in the hands, offering the pontifical crown to the dearest and cleverest of their many lovers, or placing it on the head of one of their many illegitimate children. The most disreputable and corrupt adventurers imposed themselves as bridegrooms of the Church. There was scarcely a crime or an abomination which was not committed at the court of Rome, and whilst the city was a prey to anarchy, the palace of the Popes was being changed into a very house of ill fame.[6]

Let me add also one brief illustration to show Dr. Rappoport's use of the notorious book of Chavard, *Le Célibat, le Prêtre et la Femme*. Speaking of such women of degraded character as Theodora and Marozia, M. Chavard says—and it will be seen that Dr. Rappoport closely follows him—

CHAVARD, 1894.

Tous ces pontifes pratiquent les mœurs des Sarrazins, auxquels ils payent tribut, et meurent presque tous ou empoisonnés ou étranglés, ainsi qu'il convient à des héros de sérail. L'un d'eux, Jean XII.,

RAPPOPORT, 1912.

All these Popes were imitating the mode of life of the Saracens, to whom they were paying tribute, and like Oriental rulers, true heroes of a seraglio, these chiefs of Christendom died either by

[5] Anti Romanus, *Das Pabstthum*, I, 426.   [6] Rappoport, p. 49.

le petits-fils de Marozia, homme couvert d'incestes et d'adultères, ordonnait des prêtres dans une écurie et invoquait Vénus et Bacchus, en franc païen qu'il était.[7]

poison or strangulation. They committed follies worthy of Oriental despots, and vied in their debaucheries with the emperors of pagan Rome. John XXII. (*sic*) ordained priests in a stable and swore by Bacchus and Venus.[8]

Then follow in both and in the same order the same quotations from Baronius (in Rappoport it is spelled Beronius, p. 12), Bernard de Morlaix, Honorius of Autun, and Matthew Paris. But here again Dr. Rappoport distinguishes himself:

Honorius, prêtre d'Autun, s'exprime avec plus d'énergie encore ! " Regardez," s'écrie-t-il, " ces évêques et ces cardinaux de Rome, ces dignes ministres qui entourent le trône de la Bête."

And Honorius, priest of Antrim (*sic*), expresses himself even more energetically. " Look," exclaims this author, " at the prelates and the cardinals of Rome, those worthy ministers surrounding the throne of the Beast."

This is the sort of thing which extends apparently right through Dr. Rappoport's work, always, of course, without any other indication of indebtedness than the general indication of " sources " in the bibliographical appendix. I have not spent sufficient time on the inquiry to pretend to trace all the author's borrowings. For example, eighty-six pages, which make up a full quarter of the bulk of this sixteen-shilling book, are devoted to the story of Olimpia, the sister-in-law, and, according to Rappoport, the mistress of Pope Innocent X.[9] Whether this fictitious narrative is in part the author's composition or the whole is a mere translation, does not clearly appear. The only thing that is certain is that it is based, so far as its main incidents go, upon the *Life of Olimpia*, written

---

[7] Chavard, *Le Célibat, le Pretre et la Femme*, Paris, 1894, p. 328.

[8] Rappoport, pp. 11, 12.   [9] See pp. 253 and 329.

by Gregorio Leti, under the pseudonym of the "Abbate Gualdi." A hundred years ago von Ranke told the world that this pretended biography was "nothing but a romance spun out of fabulous anecdotes and the chimeras of a poetic imagination." There was not, he added, the slightest trace of any improper relations between Innocent X and his sister-in-law.[10]

A single specimen in parallel columns will suffice to render Rappoport's dependence on Gualdi's abundantly clear.

"GUALDI" 1666.

Dès qu'il eut reçu le chapeau, il lui abandonna la direction de sa vie. On le savait si bien en ville que ceux qui voulaient obtenir quelque grâce de lui, s'addressaient directement à elle . . .

Lorsque quelqu'un essuyait un refus du Cardinal, loin de se désespérer, il se retirait en murmurant : " Il n'en a sans doute pas encore parlé à sa belle-soeur ; je reviendrai."

Ce fut Donna Olimpia qui apprit au Cardinal l'art de la dissimulation. . . . "Votre mérite, non l'amour d'Urbain vous a créé, mais si le talent est capable de conduire au cardinalat, croyez-moi, il est insuffisant pour mener à la papauté . . . Sixte Quint dissimula sa science et son génie

RAPPOPORT 1912.

Gradually His Eminence let the whole burden of his business and affairs rest on the shoulders of his sister-in-law. All requests, all documents were addressed directly to Donna Olimpia and often when people, coming to solicit a favour, had received a negative reply, they were heard to observe : " Perhaps the Cardinal has not yet spoken to Donna Olimpia."

Donna Olimpia continually endeavoured to impress her brother-in-law with the fact that if a Cardinal could be appointed on the strength of his personal merit, intrigues were absolutely necessary in the election of the Pope. And she always gave him as example Sixtus the Fifth, who had feigned imbecility in order

[10] Ranke, *Die Romischen Päpste*, 6th Edit., Appendix, in his *Sämmtliche Werke* (1874), Vol. XXXIX, pp. 172*, 173*.

tant qu'il ne fut que Cardinal, convaincu qu'il atteindrait plus facilement ainsi au pontificat ; que sa conduite vous serve de leçon.[11]

to be elected Pope by the Conclave.[12]

How incredibly worthless Dr. Rappoport's compilation is from any scholarly standpoint may be illustrated by one or two examples. In Chapter V the author discusses the papacy at Avignon, and makes some extracts from the *Epistolae sine titulo* of Petrarch, to illustrate the moral depravity of the papal court. Of course Dr. Rappoport does not go to the original ; he has consulted, as one may eventually discover, a scandalous little publication called *Les Courtisanes de l'Eglise*, by B. Gastineau, which in 1870, under the Empire, was not allowed by the French police to be advertised by placard, on account of its name and subject.[13] The passage, as transcribed by Rappoport, contains some portentous misprints (Rhadamantë for Rhadamanthus, Pasiphahus for Pasiphaë, etc.), but the point I wish to emphasise lies in what professes to be an original comment by Dr. Rappoport at the close :

Thus [he says] writes Petrarch, the sincere Christian. . . . His letters are not dated, but in his fifteenth epistle he admits that the two Clements (VI. and VII.) had done more harm to the Church than the seven first Georges.[14]

Seeing that Clement VII (the French Antipope, of course, is meant), only began his pontificate in 1378, four years after Petrarch's death, it is plain that the passage at least contains a ridiculous anachronism. But the real puzzle, of course, is the " seven first Georges." It was only after much waste of

---

[11] " Abbate Gualdi " (*i.e.*, Gregorio Leti), *Vie de Donna Olimpia*, edited by A. Dubarry, Paris, 1878, pp. 48–50.

[12] Rappoport, *Love Affairs*, p. 256.

[13] Gastineau, *Les Courtisanes de l'Eglise*, Paris, 1870. This fact is attested by a letter published in the 2nd Edit., p. xvi. Amongst the other *courtisanes de l'eglise* the author includes St. Mary Magdalen, accusing her of being a temptress to her Master Christ.

[14] Rappoport, p. 153.

time that I stumbled upon the book just mentioned, *Les Courtisanes de l'Eglise*. There I found in the same position a remark that " *les deux Clément avignonais avaient fait plus de mal d l'Eglise que les sept premiers Grégoire.*" But this was equally puzzling. Why should the seven first Gregorys be supposed to have done so much mischief. Eventually, through another channel, I obtained a correct reference to the original letter of Petrarch,[15] and then the mystery was explained. Petrarch says that " our two Clements (*i.e.*, Clement V and Clement VI), have done more mischief to the Church in a few years than your seven Gregorys (he is writing presumably to some one in Rome) would be able to repair in many centuries." [16]

But blunders of every kind simply swarm in Dr. Rappoport's pages. On p. 39 we are told that Pope Gregory V wrote a letter of reprimand to the Bishop of Liège, Henry de Gueldres. Considering that Pope Gregory V died in 999, and Henry of Gueldres was Bishop of Liège in the thirteenth century, this would be difficult to accomplish. The letter of course emanated from Gregory X. On the other hand, when we read of " Bishop Ivo of Chartres, known as the Holy One " (p. 34), or of " the canonic law being trampled under foot " (p. 50), or of John X " reading the Holy Mass " (p. 68), we become aware that Dr. Rappoport is simply translating some one of his French or German " sources." The simplest Latin phrases are frequently transfigured. For example, we have *nudatus ad iguen* (p. 16), *plebs Romanum* (p. 114), *dummodo illa suo concede retur arbitrio* (p. 154), etc. Of course, this may be due to mere carelessness in correcting proofs, but no other cause than ignorance can have led Dr. Rappoport to speak of " *Contemporary authors* like Baluzius and Mézeray, who have left minute descriptions of the lives of the popes of Avignon " (p. 148). Baluzius and Mézeray, of course, were not fourteenth century writers, but scholars who lived in the reign of Louis XIV.

[15] Letter numbered xvii. in the edition of Lyons, 1601.

[16] " *Neu me forsan veri inscium aut diversae sententiae arbitreris, duos Clementes nostros, plus attrivisse Ecclesiam paucis annis quam septem Gregorii vestri multis saeculis restaurare possent,*" p. 642.

The reader will have learnt from the first chapter of this book that no attempt is here made to deny or excuse the dreadful scandals of the pontificate of Alexander VI. If Dr. Rappoport had contented himself with denouncing the licentiousness of Rodrigo Borgia before and after his election to the papacy, there could have been no occasion for protest. But there were many stories circulated concerning that Pontiff which are devoid of all foundation, and these Dr. Rappoport, faithful to his principle of painting everything connected with the Roman Curia in the blackest possible colours, has made a point of retaining and embellishing with more lurid tints. The story of the death of Alexander deserves to be quoted as a case in point. As presented in *The Love Affairs of the Vatican*, the narrative runs thus :

Alexander VI died ; succumbing to the poison of which he had so often availed himself in perpetrating his numerous crimes. The poison he had so often mixed for others, he drank himself. They say that his son Cæsar, desirous of possessing himself of the estates of several rich Cardinals, had invited them to one of his dainty suppers *à la Borgia* in the gardens of the Pope. The wines destined for the guests had been scrupulously prepared according to the formula. But the butler made a fatal mistake ; and instead of the guests, the Holy Father and his son quaffed the cups of Spanish and Sicilian wines into which the poison had been mixed.

The necessary invitations had been sent out ; it was summer time, and the Pope was to meet his friends in a vineyard not far from the Vatican. All the arrangements for the little feast were entrusted to Cæsar, who also had to prepare the poisoned cups. In order that the poisoned wine should not be mistaken for the other wine, Cæsar sent a faithful servant of his to the vineyard with an order to place the poisoned wine in a particular place and to watch over it, that none should drink it except those whom he himself should point out. The servant did as he was ordered, but when the Papal cellarer asked why that particular wine was placed apart, he replied laughing that it was a wine of extraordinary strength, and therefore must only be handed to the most highly honoured guests. This answer the cellarer naturally found quite plausible. The Pope arrived rather earlier than the other guests, for he had to talk things over with Cæsar. It was the Pope's misfortune to have left a small amulet (a consecrated Host in a little gold case, which he always carried with him, because it had been foretold that he should not die as long as he was not parted from it) behind in his apartment in the Vatican, and he sent his son's faithful servant, the same who was watching the poisoned wine, to fetch it. Scarcely was the servant gone when the Pope, calling to his cellarer, asked if everything was in order. As the weather was so oppressively hot and he felt very thirsty, he wished to drink a goblet of wine immediately. The cellarer, not daring to give the Pontiff inferior wine, and really believing what the servant had told him, that this wine was the best, filled a decanter and placed it on the bench on which Alexander was seated. Without suspicion, the Pontiff filled a goblet with the wine and drank it quickly. In the moment Cæsar arrived ; and as he was thirsty, he, too, filled the goblet and emptied it as his father had done. A quarter of an hour later supper was served, but before he had taken a mouthful the Pope fell to the ground, writhing like a worm, suffering great bodily pains. Cæsar Borgia almost immediately showed the same symptoms, and the two noble sufferers were hastily carried to the palace. The doctors recognised signs of poison and prescribed antidotes. The drug was very strong. Cæsar, young and strong, escaped death, although he suffered seriously for ten months before he was reinstated in health, but the Pope died in a few days, on August 18, 1503.

It was a tragic death—as tragic as that of any of those emperors who had ruled in pagan Rome—a death full of infernal visions. Legend relates of seven demons who had come to visit the dying Pontiff in the supreme moment, demanding the fulfilment of a pact he had contracted with Satan in the moment of his election. For twelve years of his pontificate he had sold his soul to the Spirit of Darkness. But the inventors of this legend scarcely understand the psychology of Borgia. Alexander was no Faust and no Titan, declaring war to the Ruler of the Universe. Familiar with all the most abominable vices, crimes, and debaucheries, he nevertheless naïvely imagined that he believed in God. His sins would be forgiven unto him, and, the tiara on his head, he would sit among the cherubim and seraphim in glorious Paradise, contemplating in the azure of Infinity the Mother of Christ—her face, perhaps, reminding him of Julia Farnese. He had no hallucinations and no visions, this Pontiff of the sixteenth century. Doubts and questionings about the invisible world only trouble the thinking brains of a self-torturing philosopher, not those of a Borgia.

In this gratuitously offensive association of the Mother of Christ with Julia Farnese, the Pope's mistress, the bad faith of the writer stands revealed. He classes himself with Léo Taxil and the most infamous of the contributors to the *Bibliothèque Anti-Cléricale*. But what of the truth of this story of Pope Alexander's death ? Though founded upon the *History* of Guicciardini, who was a contemporary, it is universally rejected at the present day by serious historians, whatever their creed. For example, in the *Cambridge Modern History*, Dr. Richard Garnett, of the British Museum, who had previously devoted special attention to this subject, writes as follows :

On August 5 Alexander caught a chill while supping with Cardinal Corneto ; on the 12th he felt ill ; and on the 18th a fever carried him off. The suddenness of the event, the rapid decomposition of the corpse, and the circumstance that Cæsar Borgia was simultaneously taken ill, accredited the inevitable rumours of poison, and his decease became the nucleus of a labyrinthine growth of legend and romance. Modern investigation has dispelled it all, and has left no reasonable doubt that the death was entirely natural.[17]

The same view is held by Bishop Creighton, who remarks :

It was said that a scheme was devised by the Pope and Cesare to poison a wealthy Cardinal ; but owing to a mistake of the server the poisoned wine was given to themselves. This story was readily believed and in some form or other is repeated by all the historians of that time, but it rests on no authentic basis. There is nothing to confirm it in the description of the Pope's illness as given by eyewitnesses. Rome was in a pestilential condition and a supper in the open air was not unlikely to lead to an attack of fever. It is not surprising that two men living under the same conditions and in the same place should suffer from fever at the same time. Contemporaries saw a proof of the effects of poison in the rapid decomposition of the Pope's body, which grew black and swollen. This has been repeated by more modern writers who ought to have known that it was evidence only of the condition of the atmosphere. There is no real reason for attributing the death of Alexander VI to other than natural causes.[18]

With this view Gregorovius, the Protestant *Realencyclopädie*, and von Pastor, who has gone into the case in great detail, are in full agreement. Moreover, the stories current in Rome which attribute the Pope's death to poison all contradict one another. For example, while Guicciardini declares that Alexander and Cesare had plotted to poison ten Cardinals, Sanuto speaks only of one who was to be made away with by this means. The best-informed contemporary writers like Giustiniani, the Venetian ambassador, and Burchard, the Pope's Master of Ceremonies, say nothing of poison. Alexander assuredly has enough crimes to answer for without attributing to him those for which there is no evidence.

[17] *Cambridge Modern History*, Vol. I, p. 241.
[18] Creighton, *History of the Popes*, Vol. IV, p. 44.

It is rarely that Dr. Rappoport thinks fit to give any verifiable reference for the allegations which he makes. But occasionally he is guilty of this indiscretion, and the result of an attempt in one case to follow up the trail thus indicated is so curious that it seems worth while to put it on record. Speaking of Queen Joanna of Naples, who had been, so he assures us, the mistress of Clement VI, he goes on to declare that her friendship with Pope Urban V, his successor, was of the same character.

> Some whitewashers of Joanna [he says] have pointed out that the friendship existing between the Pontiff and the Queen must have been a pure and holy one, considering that Urban has become a canonised Saint of the Church. But there are, nevertheless, indications that the favours which Urban V showed to Joanna, and the honours he heaped upon her—honours which had never before or since been lavished on any other woman—were marks of a more than platonic friendship.

In justification of this Dr. Rappoport tells us a little further on :

> At the beginning of May 1368, the Pope left Rome and retired to his delightful villa at Montefiascole (*sic*), there to inhale the pure country air. He was accompanied by the Queen of Naples, who shared the pontifical *villegiature*. Did she compensate in those rural and pastoral surroundings the friendship of the pastor of the Catholic Church, as she had compensated Clement VI. for the interest he had shown in her ? " If one considers," says an impartial historian, " the character of Joanna and the general morality prevalent at the Roman Court in those days, one can scarcely doubt these assertions."

And then we are given a reference to Joudou, *Histoire des Souverains Pontifes*, Vol. I, p. 107. The reference, of course, is inaccurate. It should be Vol. II, p. 107 ; but that is a trifle. Turning to the page indicated we find the following which, as some doubt might arise as to the correct translation, it will be better to copy in French :

" Urbain," [writes M. Joudou] " avait pris si chaudement

les interêts de la reine de Naples, que *ses détracteurs ont dit* que Jeanne l'accompagna à Montefiascone, et que là elle recompensa Urbain comme elle avait recompensé Clément VI. *Ces assertions ne sont appuyés sur aucune authorité*, et cependent si l'on considère le charactère de Jeanne et les mœurs de la cour romaine, on serait tenté à ajouter foi à de pareils faits.''

The last clause is perhaps ambiguous, but in view of the words I have italicised and of another passage to be quoted immediately, it is impossible to believe that Joudou meant more than that the marks of favour shown by Urban (*e.g.*, the conferring upon Joanna of the golden rose) and the supposed visit to Montefiascone may have been authentic facts. Anyway, it is certain that, some few pages further on, Joudou, when passing judgment upon the moral character of Urban V, uses the following language :

As a priest he was one of the most virtuous pontiffs that ever governed the Church ; the truly priestly spirit inspired all his actions. Humble and modest, he referred to God, the Creator of the Universe, all the marks of respect shown to His Vicar. He said in his heart : '' Not to us, O Lord, but to Thy Holy Name alone all glory is due.'' Urban always wore the habit of St. Benedict which he never laid aside even during sleep.

How this eulogium can be consistent with the belief that Urban V, a Pontiff who has been beatified (not canonised) by the Church, was during the last years of his life the lover of Queen Joanna, one entirely fails to see. In any case, it is certain that Dr. Rappoport, in pretending to quote his printed authority, not only transforms the words before him, but leaves out an important qualification which must essentially change its whole character. Bishop Creighton describes Urban V as '' a man of sincere and earnest piety,'' and this represents the unanimous verdict of all historians except virulent detractors of the type of Dr. Rappoport.

But as a final example of this libeller's readiness to throw mud, a brief reference may suffice to the repulsive story of Petrarch's younger sister whose name is said to have been Selvaggia and who is described as a maiden only sixteen years old. Dr. Rappoport relates this fiction in much detail alleging that his narrative is based upon the biography of the poet, written by Jerome Squarciafico. It is much more likely that the account, the offensive features of which the reader will be glad to be spared, is taken at second or third hand from some more accessible modern source probably in French or German. One might suspect the influence of Griesinger's *Mysteries of the Vatican*, to which the author of the *Love Affairs* is frequently indebted, translating long passages without any indication that he is borrowing from a modern original. But Griesinger has not here directly supplied the material. He duly mentions the scandal, but his account is shorter and runs thus :

> The Avignon age seems to have reached its zenith under Clement VI (1342-1352). Of the two previous Avignon Popes, John XXII had been remarkable for little else than his love of gold, and Benedict XII for his love of women and wine. From him dates the favourite proverb, *bibere papaliter* (drink like a pope). Among the inmates of his harem was a sister of Francesco Petrarch, who had refused the Pope's solicitations concerning her, though supported by the offer of a Cardinal's hat. Her other brother, Gerardo, proved less scrupulous and in exchange for a heavy purse, delivered her over to His Holiness.[19]

Now here is a story which, depending as it does upon the sole authority of ribald gossip recorded a century after Benedict's death, can hardly claim to be seriously discussed. But it is worth while to point out that the tale is absolutely inconsistent with the data furnished by the most authoritative modern biographers of Petrarch, notably by Gustav Körting[20] *Petrarca's Leben und Werke*. According to Körting, Petrarch's only sister, Selvaggia, was married in the year 1324 to a Florentine gentle-

---

[19] Griesinger, *Mysteries of the Vatican* (Eng. Trans.), Vol. I, p. 319.
[20] Körting, *Petrarca's Leben und Werke*, p. 54.

man, named Giovanni Summofante, and from that day forth passed entirely out of Petrarch's life. Now as Benedict only became Pope in 1334, *i.e.*, ten years later, it is plain that the details given by Squarciafico are irreconcilable with this historically attested fact. But what renders the circulation of so odious a story the more indefensible is the character of the Pontiff himself. By Bishop Creighton, Benedict was judged to be " an upright but feeble-minded monk." [21] It is not enthusiastic commendation, but such language excludes belief in the possibility of horrors such as that described. Hauck's estimate of the Pope's character, which may be found in the Protestant *Realencyclopädie*, is more favourable. Benedict, he notes, " planned to restore the strict discipline of the Benedictines and Cistercians, as well as of the mendicant orders." In the work which enjoyed the editorial revision of Dr. Rappoport himself the *Times Historian's History of the World*, we read of Benedict XII :

Historians allow him the praise of being an upright and honest man, no less free from avarice than from lust of rule. He saw the existing evils in the Church and some of them, as far as he could, he removed. . . . Overlook superstition, which was the common fault of his age, and we shall find nothing to prevent our declaring this Pontiff to have been a right-spirited man. [22]

To Gregorovius also Benedict was " simple, rough and upright," and he adds that " almost all biographers call him ' *justus et durus, constans* '." [23] Dr. Karl Jacob comes to a similar conclusion. There may have been, he thinks, some slight deterioration of character, owing to the luxurious surroundings of the papal court at Avignon. Benedict may as Pope have given up something of the austerity of his former life as a Cistercian Abbot, " but we are forced to the conclusion that he never in any way transgressed the limits of what was then permitted." [24]

---

[21] Creighton, *History of the Papacy* (Edit., 1897), I, p. 48, Vol. II, p. 567.

[22] Vol. VIII, p. 628.   [23] *Rome in the Middle Ages* (Eng. Trans.), VI, p. 224.

[24] Jacob, *Studien über Papst Benedikt XII*, p. 155.

This last statement was penned in full view of the charges brought by Petrarch and Squarciafico to which reference is made on the same page. It would be tedious to multiply testimonies further, but we may notice that Fierens, who studied and edited the Pope's letters for the Institut belge de Rome,[25] describes him as an austere monk who remained faithful to his ideals to the end of his days, while to Carl Müller he was " a man of the strictest integrity of life and of considerable learning." [26]

It is plain, then, that unless we are prepared to set aside the unanimous verdict of every modern historian of repute, we must believe Squarciafico's circumstantial story to have been just the same sort of impudent fabrication which we have already encountered in the case of Pius IX. Of course it does not follow that Petrarch's biographer invented the tale himself, but an invention it surely is, begotten of that fatal medieval recklessness of speech and readiness to believe evil of those to whom for political and other reasons the listener was opposed.

Even apart from Dr. Rappoport's deliberate falsifications of history, nothing could be easier than to compile, as he has compiled, a scandalous chronicle of any institution whose record stretches back into those past ages when the majority of mankind were little removed from barbarism and when every ruler, being a law unto himself, was unaffected by the fear of adverse public opinion. One would only have to omit all reference to the good done or attempted, and to show a little ingenuity in exhibiting what is evil in the most offensive light. By such means an indictment can always be made out which will seem plausible to the outsider so long as he knows no more of the conditions of life in those days than it is found convenient to tell him. Let it be admitted, as I for one would readily admit, that the standard of moral conduct among the clergy of the Church of England during the past hundred years is worthy of all respect, it would nevertheless not be difficult for anyone who

<hr/>

[25] Fierens, *Lettres de Benoît XII*, Introduction, pp. xxviii and xliv.
[26] Carl Müller, *Der Kampf Ludwigs des Baiern mit der Römischen Curie*, Vol. II, p. 3.

kept an eye upon the scandals chronicled week by week in some of the less self-respecting of our Sunday journals, to frame an appalling catalogue of ecclesiastical misdemeanours. If Dr. H. C. Lea, or Dr. Rappoport, or Dr. Coulton, had employed their flair for the unwholesome in compiling a " History of Clerical Wedlock since the Reformation," instead of concentrating upon the irregularities of the Catholic Church, no one of them would have failed to produce a record which would be not less repellant to British respectability than anything they have written in condemnation of sacerdotal celibacy.

Chapter XVI

WHAT PREJUDICE IGNORES

ARGUMENT must always be to some extent a personal matter. What convinces me will not necessarily convince my next-door neighbour. It may be that he sees difficulties that I do not see. His experience has been different from my own. Things appeal to him, that do not appeal to me, and on the other hand he may not feel the need of certain demonstrations which appear to me to be vital if the basis of the argument is to be firm and its conclusions logical. My own line of study has brought me into contact with much of the seamy side of medieval Christianity. Often I have found myself hesitating for a moment and asking myself: "If these charges are true, if these abuses were tolerated, was the Church after all a purifying and spiritualising influence in the life of the people?" But by giving myself time and weighing the matter fairly, I have felt able to affirm with conviction, that even at the worst of periods the clergy and their teaching as a whole made for good.

If I were to try, then, to put in a very few words the point I want to bring out in this chapter, I might say that my object is to show the tremendous vitality that may be latent in a sickly Church. There is a story in Boccaccio of a Jew who came to Rome and who after witnessing and being appalled at the corruption that he saw there ended by becoming a Christian, because, he said, no institution that was not divine could have failed to go to pieces when it was so honeycombed with decay. This is something more than a paradox. There is really force in the argument. Now in recent years a great effort has been made by a certain school of historians to paint in the blackest colours the ecclesiastical and social life of the Middle Ages. There is in particular Dr. Henry Charles Lea, an American author who died some years ago, who wrote a *History of the Inquisition*, a *History of Sacerdotal Celibacy*, a *History of Confession and Indulgences*, a book on *Superstition and Force* and some other similar works. Again there is Dr. G. G. Coulton, a writer who has been persistent in his attacks upon Cardinal Gasquet, Father Gerard, Mgr. Moyes and every prominent writer on the Catholic side. I need not mention others. These historians have made it their business to rake together horrors and scandals, examples of avarice, debauchery, superstition and cruelty ; and a very terrible picture they set out. " Clerical morals in the middle ages," says Dr. Coulton, compendiously, " were such as no civilised modern country could tolerate."[1] Similarly, Dr. Lea comes back again and again to such statements as these : " Under such (clerical) influences it is no wonder that Rome had become a centre of corruption whose infection was radiated throughout Christendom," [2] or " Society was thoroughly corrupt—the world has rarely seen a more debased standard of morality than that which prevailed in Italy in the closing years of the Middle Ages," [3] with much more to the same effect.

Now, without entering into details about the horrors of those days, or touching upon the scandals connected with the name of such a pontiff, for example, as Alexander VI, since it is necessary to give some more definite idea of what is said, I may cull a few characteristic passages. For instance, the same Dr. Lea writes ·

In fact, one of the most urgent symptoms of the necessity of a new order of things was the complete divorce between religion and morality. There was abundant zeal in

[1] *Friar's Lantern*, p. 248.

[2] Lea in *Cambridge Modern History*, Vol. I, p. 672.

[3] *Ibid.*, p. 673. I take my illustrations for convenience sake from this one chapter in the *Cambridge Modern History* ; but similar passages abound in Dr. Lea's other writings.

debating minute points of faith, but little in evoking from
it an exemplary standard of life. The sacerdotal system,
developed by the dialectics of the Schoolmen, had constructed a routine of external observances through which
salvation was to be gained, not so much by abstinence from
sin as by its pardon through the intervention of the priest,
whose supernatural powers were in no way impaired by the
scandals of his daily life. Except within the pale of the pagan
Renaissance, never was there a livelier dread of future
punishment, but this was to be escaped, not by amendment,
but by confession, absolution and indulgences. [4]

Similarly in the opinion of the same historian,

the denunciation of clerical vices and abuses, in the
satires of the time, show how completely these books (of
Brant, Faber, Erasmus, &c.), responded to the popular
feeling, how dangerously the Church had forfeited the
respect of the masses and how deeply rooted was the aversion
it inspired. The priests hated Rome for her ceaseless
exactions and the people hated the priests with perhaps
even better reason. So bitter was this dislike that Erasmus
tells us that among laymen, to call a man a cleric or a
priest or a monk, was an unpardonable insult. [5]

I will add one more brief extract from the same source.

A priesthood trained in this formalism which had practically replaced the ethical values of Christianity, secure that
its supernatural attributes were unaffected by the most
flagitious life, and selected by such methods as were practised
by the Curia and imitated by the prelates, could not be
expected to rise above the standards of the Community.
Rather, indeed, were the influences to which the clergy
were exposed, adapted to depress them below the average. [6]

It may be noticed that these strictures reduce themselves to
three or four heads. We are assured that there was widespread
moral corruption among both clergy and laity and, many

[4] *Cambridge Modern History*, I, p. 673.

[5] Lea, *Ibid.*, p. 676. [6] Lea, *Ibid.*, p. 674.

would add, in monasteries and convents as well. Further, that what religion there was, consisted of a mere veneer of superstition and mechanical observances which exercised no practical restraint upon conduct; and thirdly, that the Church was universally despised and detested on account of the evil example of its representatives. Now we may reply to these accusations in two ways. They might in the first place be met by a flat denial. This has often been done, and indeed no thoughtful student can doubt that Dr. Lea's picture of the evils of the times is overcharged. None the less, I consider, with all possible deference to some distinguished authorities who think otherwise, that there has been too pronounced a tendency among our Catholic apologists to ignore and to deny these unwelcome facts. I would rather myself take up the position that while it is indisputable that very serious corruption existed, and while it is impossible after the lapse of years to determine how far the mischief really went, we have at the same time the most striking manifestations of a healthy and vigorous life battling with the evil and destined in the end to gain the upper hand. In everything that lives and grows there is a certain element of corruption. The capacity for vital development seems to be inseparably united with the possibility of disease and decay. Even in the physical life of our fellow men we say that a robust constitution is shown not so much by its immunity from ailments, as by its power of resistance to the strain and exhaustion of disease and by its recuperative energy. It is when a man is stricken down by fever and a complication of disorders, and those mysterious benignant agencies, which build up tissue and repair waste, steadily gain the mastery over the virus with which he has been infected that we say that his constitution is sound or that his vitality is great. And this is the sort of vitality that the Church has displayed when it has been sick unto death, weakened by foes within and without. It must be remembered that He who said to His disciple " Thou art Peter " (the rock) and " the gates of hell shall not prevail," was also Himself to prophesy and bear witness to the fall and recovery of that very apostle.

It is a common assertion with those carping writers to whom I have previously referred, that the Catholic Church in the sixteenth century was reformed not from within but from without. Luther, Calvin, and the other leaders, they tell us, brought such pressure to bear upon the Emperor, Charles V, that through his menacing appeals, the Pope and the Curia at last awoke from their lethargy and by convening the Council of Trent, began, very tardily, to set their house in order. No doubt there is an element of truth in this, but what I want to insist upon here is that the motive power of the spiritual reform came from inside. If that vital energy had not been there, external stimulus would only have brought about disruption and collapse. All efforts at resuscitation must have proved as ineffectual as the attempt to galvanise life into a corpse. It follows, then, that where I absolutely and entirely disagree with Dr. Lea and his sympathisers is in their contention that the religion of the Reformation period had ceased to be more than a religion of forms. It is utterly untrue, as I hope to show in the remainder of this chapter, that the thought of amendment of life and the ideal of moral purity had gradually succumbed under a sacerdotal system in which absolutions, indulgences, and the purchase of Masses were held to supply the place of all other acts of virtue.

And to begin with, although we must recognise that it is hard in the case of the greater number to decide whether the love of God existed in the hearts of clergy and people, or whether their piety was only skin-deep, still there are certain tests that cannot well mislead us. Love consists in deeds not words. Were there any willing to suffer, and still more, even to go to meet suffering, for the sake of the Faith they professed? I do not know that, tried by such a test, the state of religion in these islands comes out particularly well. We are all familiar with the noble death of Blessed Thomas More and Cardinal Fisher, and of the fate of the London Carthusians and of the Observantine Franciscans of Sheen and of the five Benedictine Abbots. And then there was the great " Pilgrimage of Grace " from the northern counties, and we know of the many hundreds of clergy who elected to be deprived of their benefices and to be cast adrift on the world in Elizabeth's day rather than give up the Mass, and we know of eighty Scottish Observantine Franciscans who preferred to be deported abroad rather than surrender their habit and community life, and there is always, at the back of all, the glorious and consoling example of Ireland. There is abundant proof both here and in a multitude of other details, upon which I cannot touch, that the religion of clergy and people in England had not been a mere form or a dead creed. But on the other hand it cannot be maintained that, taken as a whole, the behaviour of the monks and friars in England under stress of persecution was remarkably heroic. There is much to be pleaded in extenuation, and I do not for a moment believe that they were generally corrupt and dissolute, as Dr. Coulton, for instance, pretends, but we cannot establish the fact of their fervent observance in the years before the suppression by any conspicuous achievement or by any example of heroic sanctity like that of St. Bernardine of Siena in Italy, of St. Vincent Ferrer in Spain, of St. Collette in France, or St. John of Capristrano in Hungary.

But, whatever may be the case in England, there is by God's Providence one important country in which we are able to show by a test of the most conclusive kind that at the very lowest ebb of this period of decadence the Catholic faith was a living reality, inspiring men with apostolic zeal and the courage of martyrs. It was in 1492 that Columbus discovered the New World. True to the profession which he had always made, that one of the main objects of his explorations was to win new territories for Christ and His Church, he took out with him on his next voyage a band of religious to act as missionaries. This was only the beginning. From that day forward as the invaders pushed their conquests from the islands to the mainland, occupying first the whole of Central America, and then making themselves masters of Mexico, or New Spain as they called it, on the north, and of Venezeula, Peru and Chile on the south, the work of evangelisation went on continually hand in hand with the occupation of the soil. It was not a fitful effort, but a systematic creation of permanent missions over the whole country, while the missionaries everywhere formed the one powerful barrier that stood between the natives and the rapacity of their conquerors. A missionary's life is not an easy one at any time, but it was a thousand times more arduous then than in our own day. The discomforts of the voyage, the expatriation from home and friends, the incredibly long delays which attended all appeals to the central administration in Europe, the tyranny and in many ways the active hostility of the lawless officials, who saw in the missionaries and with reason, the great check upon their greed and brutality, the absence of any organised system of supplies, the difficulty created by languages and races of an entirely new type, all these were things to daunt the stoutest heart. It often took a missionary a year of travel before he could reach the district assigned him for his labours. And yet, even in this age of relaxation and decay, when the work for God and souls had to be done, the labourers pressed forward to do it, and they offered themselves in such adequate numbers, that an ecclesiastical settlement was effected in these vast regions upon a scale which has not its parallel elsewhere in history. It was a stupendous moral miracle. Can we escape the conclusion that in spite of all the signs of decay and dissolution in the Church, the vital spark, kindled and fanned by the Spirit of God, had never been extinguished ? Can we doubt that the faith was a reality and not a mere form to the Spanish friars who in the first fifty years of the sixteenth century, while Europe was seething with religious strife, accomplished all this ?

I will not ask my readers to accept these facts upon my bare word or upon the assurance of over-partial Catholic chroniclers. Let me quote something of what we read about this missionary work in standard Protestant historians such as Helps, Prescott, Winsor, and Hubert Howe Bancroft.

Sir Arthur Helps, after telling how the first Dominican missionaries died off in New Spain, speaks with deep respect of the enthusiasm which prevailed among their brethren in Europe, and the eagerness to supply their places. He quotes with approval the words of Remesal :

> With the news that came every day to Spain of the many nations of those parts, and how new ones were continually being discovered, the Lord disposed the minds of many saintly men belonging to the glorious Order of St. Dominic that they should freely offer themselves to leave their native towns, provinces, and religious homes, to go to the Indies to preach. . . . These good and worthy desires seized grave and elderly fathers of wisdom and prudence, old in the practice of the honourable offices of the Divine Service, reverenced in their communities, punctual in the choir, constant in prayer, learned men, masters in theology and examples to youth, because at first only men of this kind went to the Indies.

Of the many who offered themselves in 1528, forty were chosen, and more than twenty of these set sail together to start a mission on the coast of Venezeula.

Again, when Las Casas, in spite of his own reluctance, was in 1544 made Bishop of Ciudad Real in Chiapas, he took out with him from Spain no less than forty-five Dominican friars. After a voyage which lasted six months in all, ten of the friars were despatched to Tabasco by sea, and nine of them perished when the vessel foundered in a storm. The remainder were exposed to the most bitter animosity of the colonists on account of their support of Las Casas in his uncompromising denunciation of slavery. At Ciudad Real, as Hubert Howe Bancroft attests, things got so bad that :

> alms were refused them, and their supplies soon becoming exhausted they abandoned their temporary convent and proceeded to the native town of Chiapas, whence, having

fixed upon this point as their base of operations, they
gradually extended their labours over the province. The
settlers placed in their way every obstacle that self-interest
and ingenuity could devise, but the energy and devotion
of the friars overcame all opposition, and when in 1549
Cerrato came to their support they had already established
several convents, including that of Ciudad Real, and had
visited and carried their teaching into the remotest parts
of the province.[7]

From the same neutral authority we may learn of the wonderful success of the mission to Tuzulutlan, a district of Guatemala,
which had been known to the Spaniards as the Tierra de Guerra
(the Land of War), but which was afterwards deservedly re-
christened by the name of Verapaz (true peace). There for
once Las Casas had been allowed a free hand. Fray Luis
Cancer, O.P., had gone there in 1541 with one or two companions, and all Spanish officials and colonists had been forbidden to set foot in the district. In 1545, Las Casas was enabled
to revisit this province, which had hitherto been regarded by the
Spaniards as absolutely untameable. To quote Bancroft again,

Las Casas found the condition of affairs to be so satisfactory that he caused the depositions of six Spaniards to be
taken for the purpose of reporting to the Emperor the true
nature of the conquest of this formerly warlike region.
From the statements of these deponents it appears that
previous to the entrance of the Dominicans the inhabitants
of these regions resisted all attempts to subdue them, but
that by infinite labour and care the friars had overcome their
ferocity and exasperation. In his progress through the
country, the bishop everywhere met with a kind welcome.
Escorted by Don Juan (a native chief), a son of the Lord
of Coban, with many of his subjects, he proceeded from
town to town, receiving offerings and presents at each
place.[8]

[7] H. H. Bancroft, *Central America*, II, p. 339.

[8] H. H. Bancroft, *Central America*, II, p. 364.

It appears that the number of Dominican friars who in little more than four years had wrought this change was eight.[9]

Fray Luis Cancer, who had been the leading agent in this result, shortly afterwards paid a visit to Europe along with Las Casas. Together the two friends persuaded the Emperor, Charles V, to allow Fray Luis to undertake the conversion of Florida upon the same plan that had proved so successful in Tuzulutlan. With this design Brother Louis set out for Seville accompanied by two other Dominicans. Writing to Las Casas before his departure, he says : " All Seville is surprised at this undertaking. Those who most fear God approve of it ; others think that we are going like sheep to the slaughter." In Mexico he was joined by another Dominican Father and a lay brother. They then set sail for Florida, but contrary to their express instructions, the captain of the vessel landed them at a point of the coast where the Spaniards had previously committed depredations. As a result they had hardly set foot on shore when they were set upon by the Indians and beaten to death with clubs.[10] It is interesting to note, again under the guidance of Mr. Bancroft,[11] that " between 1566 and 1600 four unsuccessful attempts were made by Jesuits, Dominicans and Franciscans to christianise Florida. In these efforts nearly all the missionaries lost their lives. Finally, in a second attempt made by the Franciscans, they gained a foothold in the country, and in 1612 a province called Santa Elena was founded by the chapter general at Rome."

But what I want specially to insist upon is that these efforts at conversion, begun in the very earliest years of the discovery of the new world, were not desultory attempts. They were utterly and entirely different from the tardy advances made by the English in North America and Hindustan, or the Dutch in Batavia or Ceylon. In this province of Guatemala of which I have been speaking, though relatively of no great extent, no less than sixty-six Franciscans arrived between 1571 and

[9] *Ibid.*, note 52.   [10] H. H. Bancroft, *Central America*, II, p. 356.

[11] *Ibid.*, note 58.

1573, and in the year 1600 there were in Guatemala twenty-two Franciscan houses and fourteen houses of Dominicans. Or let us turn to Mexico, where the Franciscans predominated :

There [says Bancroft] the Order established a regular government at an early date, and under its direction systematic measures for the conversion of the natives gradually supplanted the doubtfully productive efforts of erratic missionaries. The instruction of children in Christian doctrine throughout the subjected provinces was carried out with unrelaxed zeal, while the adults listened to the words of salvation in their own language.[12]

The proficiency acquired by the friars in the native languages [he adds in a note] was in many cases remarkable. Among great numbers may be mentioned Pedro de Castillo, who acquired the Mexican and Otoni dialects to perfection. This friar's religious enthusiasm was unyielding. Crippled and blind, he caused himself to be borne from town to town in a chair, preaching and teaching on every occasion possible.

Fearless friars pushed forward into remoter regions and dauntlessly entered the haunts of tribes untamed as yet by sword and arquebuse. Whether it was Guzman's explorations into unknown lands or a voyage of discovery undertaken by Cortes into unknown seas that offered an opportunity of carrying the tidings of joy, there were ever ready at hand priests ready to risk their lives to extend the spiritual conquest. We cannot but admire the courage with which they penetrated alone into the country of the barbarous Chichimecs. In 1539, two friars went from Michoacan into that region and baptised many.[13]

Neither, according to Bancroft, were the Dominicans less zealous and active than their rivals, and he speaks with equal respect of the Augustinians.

With regard to Peru, the historian Prescott, treating of the beginnings of the Spanish dominion there in the year 1534, the

[12] *Mexico*, II, p. 394.   [13] *Mexico*, II, p. 395.

very date when our English King Henry VIII was taking the
last steps in the breach with Rome, explains how " Pizarro was
required by the Crown to bring a certain number of these
holy men in his own vessels, and every succeeding vessel brought
an additional number of ecclesiastics."

They were [he goes on] men of singular humility who
followed in the track of the conqueror to scatter the seeds
of spiritual truth and with disinterested zeal devoted themselves to the propagation of the Gospel. Thus did their
pious labours prove them true soldiers of the Cross and
showed that the object so ostentatiously avowed of carrying
its banner among the heathen nations was not an empty
vaunt.

And then follows a very fine and very just tribute from
this Protestant historian.

The effort to Christianise the heathen is an honourable
characteristic of the Spanish conquests. The Puritan, with
equal religious zeal, did comparatively nothing for the
conversion of the Indian, content, it would seem, with having
secured to himself the inestimable privilege of worshipping
God in his own way. Other adventurers who have occupied
the New World have often had too little regard for religion
themselves to be very solicitous about spreading it among
savages. But the Spanish missionary from first to last has
shown a keen interest in the spiritual welfare of the natives.
Under his auspices, churches on a magnificent scale have
been erected, schools for elementary instruction founded,
and every rational means taken to spread the knowledge
of religious truth, while he has carried his solitary mission
into remote and almost inaccessible regions, or gathered his
Indian disciples into communities like the good Las Casas
in Cumana or the Jesuits in California and Paraguay. At
all times the courageous ecclesiastic has been ready to lift
his voice against the cruelty of the conqueror and the no
less wasting cupidity of the colonists ; and when his
remonstrances, as was too often the case, proved unavailing

he has still followed to bind up the broken-hearted, to teach the poor Indian resignation under his lot, and light up his dark intellect with the revelation of a holier and happier existence. In reviewing the bloodstained records of Spanish colonial history, it is but fair and at the same time cheering, to reflect that the same nation which sent forth the hard-hearted conqueror from its bosom sent forth the missionary to do the work of beneficence, and spread the light of Christian civilisation over the farthest regions of the new world.[14]

And now there are two or three considerations upon which it seems well to insist before we turn to other matters.

First, it is not to be supposed that the monks and friars of Spain had maintained a higher level of fervour than the religious of the rest of Christendom. At the very time that these things were happening, we hear incessant complaints of the relaxation of discipline and the decay of piety. The same Dr. H. C. Lea whom I quoted at the beginning maintains that the corruption of the Church in the Spanish peninsula was such that it had completely forfeited the respect of the people. For example, he says :

> In the petitions or cahiers of the Spanish Cortes we find an uninterrupted expression of hostility towards the Church unrelieved by any recognition of services, whether as the guardians of religious truth or the mediators between God and man. To the Castilian of the 14th and 15th centuries, it was simply an engine of oppression. . . . In short, it seems to have been regarded as a public enemy.[15]

May we not fairly draw the inference that the language of fierce denunciation, the prevalence of grave and shameful scandals, and the existence of a spirit hostile to all ecclesiastical authority, are far from proving that religion is dead or that it has degenerated into more unprofitable formalism. No doubt those splendid examples of self-sacrifice, courage and

[14] Prescott, *Peru* (Ed., 1850), II, pp. 174–175.

[15] *Cambridge Modern History*, I, p. 675.

faith that we have been considering came almost entirely from the reformed communities of the Franciscan and Dominican Orders. But this reform itself had sprung from within. It had been worked out in loyal and respectful subordination to ecclesiastical authority—an authority often sadly lacking itself in the desire for moral perfection which it sanctioned in others. It was the spirit of God, breathing where it listed, which inspired first one and then another to rise above the lethargy and self-indulgence into which the greater part of the world was sinking. These reformers were more, not less, devoted sons of the Church than their fellows ; and it is noteworthy that in that age of extreme decadence, I mean between 1400 and 1530, there are sixty-five or sixty-six Saints or Beati who have been separately raised by the Church to the honours of the altar.

Again it is noteworthy that this work of evangelisation was not a spasmodic effort ; it was sustained and it was carried out by many bands of missionaries and on a large scale. Take Mexico for example. Twelve Dominicans and twelve Franciscans set out for New Spain in 1525. Three of the Dominicans died before they got there, while they were waiting for transport at San Domingo. Thomas Ortiz, obtaining recruits from the island, eventually reached Mexico with his Dominicans in 1526. There were twelve in all, but five died, four went back and three remained. One of those who went back to Europe appealed for recruits among his brethren in Spain. His appeal was well received and he started once more for Mexico with twenty-four companions, but from sickness and other causes only six actually arrived there. None the less we know that only two or three years later, *i.e.*, in 1539, there were twenty-two Dominicans labouring in that country. Of the Franciscans there is evidence that in 1536 (that is less than a dozen years from the beginning), they numbered about eighty in Mexico, and were recognised as a separate province. In 1542, Brother James of Testera, Commissary General of the Franciscans, brought to the same country as many as a hundred and fifty friars of his Order.

Now we can best appreciate the significance of all this by turning our eyes for a moment to missionary effort outside the Church. I do not want to say unkind things about our Protestant fellow-countrymen, but here are one or two striking facts which I have recently had occasion to investigate carefully. Down to the beginning of the nineteenth century there were only two missionary organisations belonging to the Church of England, the Society for the Propagation of the Gospel and the Society for Promoting Christian Knowledge. The S.P.G. took over as its special province the English plantations in North America and the West Indies. After fifty years of work and the expenditure of large sums of money, this is what an eye-witness of high character who lived in the midst of it all said of the S.P.G. missionaries :

> Any indifferent man could not avoid imagining that by propagating the Gospel in foreign parts was meant the conversion of natives in those parts in which the Royal Charters and proprietary grants of our plantations enjoin the civilising and conversion of the Indians by doctrine and example. . . . There is not one missionary (the Albany and Mohawk excepted) that takes the least notice of the Indians . . . The practice of the missionaries is to obtain a mission to our most civilized and richest towns, where there are no Indians, no want of an orthodox Christian ministry, and no Roman Catholics, the three principal intentions of their mission . . . The missionaries are not stationed in such poor out-towns as the Charter supposes, but in the most opulent, best-civilized and Christian towns in the provinces. . . . I have a very great regard for all good ministers of the Christian Gospel, and have no private or particular resentment against any missionary, but as an impartial historian, I could not avoid relating matters-of-fact for the information of persons concerned, who by reason of distance and other business cannot be otherways informed.[16]

16 See *The Month*, October 1909. The writer was Dr. Douglass, who published his account at Boston in 1750. He bears the reputation of a deeply-religious man, though he was not an Episcopalian.

So far as my investigations enable me to control the statement, this expresses the simple truth. There were about sixty missionaries who received a substantial salary from the Society. They were nearly all settled among the English planters in populous districts—the majority in towns like Boston and New York. They made hardly any pretence of labouring for the conversion of the Indians, and what they did even for the christianising of the negro slaves was incredibly little. It was made a matter of great congratulation in the official Reports of the Society that the efforts of one missionary, specially set aside to provide for the spiritual needs of the negroes in New York, had been singularly blessed. In eight years he had baptized two hundred and nineteen negroes of whom twenty-four were adults, or, in other words, an average of three adults a year ; the rest of the converts were children.

No wonder the Anglican Bishop Berkeley, who had lived in the colonies, wrote on the subject with feeling.

> It must be owned our reformed [*i.e.,* Protestant] planters, with respect to the natives and the slaves, might learn from those of the Church of Rome how it is their interest and their duty to behave. Both French and Spaniards have intermarried with Indians to the great strength, security and increase of their colonies. They take care to instruct both them and their negroes in the popish religion, to the reproach of those who profess a better. They have also bishops and seminaries for clergy and it is not found that their colonists are worse subjects or depend less on their mother country on that account.

Seven years earlier than this, Bishop Berkeley had not hesitated to write :

> Now the clergy sent over to America have proved, too many of them, very meanly qualified in learning and morals for the discharge of their office. And indeed, little can be expected from the example or instruction of those who quit their native country on no other motive than that they are

not able to procure a livelihood in it, which is known to be often the case.

And when we turn our eyes to the other Anglican organisation, the S.P.C.K., we find that things were no better. The S.P.C.K. took over for its own special province the mission of Hindustan. But all that it did was to accept the charge of a few missionary stations founded by the Danes. These stations were now carried on by Danish clergy as the paid servants of an English Society.

Here are a collection of the names—*all* the names I could discover in several years of Reports—of those to whom the S.P.C.K. paid salaries to undertake the conversion of the people of Hindustan. Messrs. Schultze, Gneister, Sartorius, Kiernander, Dol, Bosse, Obuch, Wiedebrock, Kolhoff, Fabricius, Zeglin, Walther, Diego, Cramer, Sichterman, Aguiar, Pressier, Aaron, Rajanaiken, Schwartz, Gericke, Jaenicke, Pohle, and Poezold. These fine old English surnames must surely suffice to show how deeply the cause of missionary enterprise in the East was taken to heart by devout Anglicans at home. Moreover, the following passage from Messrs. Allen and McClure's official *History* of the S.P.C.K., speaks eloquently enough.

In 1789 (ninety years after its foundation), the Rev. A. T. Clarke was appointed this mission *and it seemed as if at last the English Church was about to find clergymen of its own willing to become missionaries to India.* He was sent forth with joy from the Society's house, and great expectations were raised. But in 1791 Mr. Clarke suddenly threw up his charge and accepted a chaplaincy in the Company's service.

Let me repeat that I do not say these things with any wish to cast a slur upon much devoted and earnest work that is carried on by Anglican missionaries nowadays. But there are other causes operative now, which it is not part of my province to go into here.

Finally, there is another point of contrast between the missions of the degenerate and superstitious Catholicism of the declining Middle Ages and those of the English Church in the eighteenth century. In commemoration of the 200th anniversary of its foundation, the S.P.G. published a very self-laudatory record, which fills 1,500 pages and was, I think we may assume, most carefully compiled. Now on p. 931 D. we find a list headed : *The Society's Roll of Martyrs*, which is introduced with the text : " These are they which came out of great tribulation." The roll numbers nineteen names, of which seven are names of natives. But the point upon which I would lay stress is the question of date. The first martyrs of the S.P.G., according to its own official list, were three clergymen and two catechists who perished in the Indian Mutiny in the year 1857, one hundred and fifty-six years after the Society was founded. I do not wish to be ill-natured in questioning the title of these martyrs to the name, but the same record informs us that they perished like other Europeans in the massacre, not because they were missionaries, but because they were associated with the English rule in India.

It seems to me, then, that we are not going too far if we claim for the Catholic Church of this much maligned period of corruption and decay a vital force which Protestantism has never shown. After all, life manifests itself primarily by growth and renewal, a growth and renewal subordinated to one vivifying principle. Speaking generally, most of the energy shown by religious organisations outside the Catholic Church has been spent in disintegration, in a breaking away from unity. But not to press these metaphors unduly, we can at any rate assert that no more conclusive proof could be given that religion at the Reformation period had not degenerated into what Dr. Lea calls a mere routine of external observances than the heroic efforts made to extend a knowledge of the Gospel to the pagans of far distant lands.

And there is just one other piece of evidence of the same tendency, but of a quite different nature, to which I should like to appeal. All those abuses and scandals and hideous forms of crime can never lend themselves to the control of statistics. Those who recount them, whether they are satirists or pulpit orators, are equally prone to exaggerate. They had no possible object in reminding us of the existence of earnest men and women, who amid all the corruption around them led devout lives, gave themselves to works of charity and tried unostentatiously to do their duty. But that these good Christians, men of education moreover, for it is not a question here of the ignorant peasantry, formed a very considerable class, can be convincingly proved by a searching test—I mean the books that they read. Printing was invented in the middle of the fifteenth century, but the output of printed books was inconsiderable until the year 1470. For the next thirty years, which we are accustomed to regard as a period of extreme relaxation of morals and piety, the diligence of bibliographers has accumulated for us the most minute statistics regarding the various editions which then began to be dispersed through the world by the printing press in very considerable numbers. Now it does not follow, because the general tone of all this output wears a pronouncedly religious cast, that therefore the people who bought these books were very devout. That certainly would not follow. The man who purchased a *Horae*, the popular prayer-book of those days, did not necessarily spend much of his time in using it. It was the proper and decent thing for men of a certain position to own a *Horae ;* and the possession of one no more proved that he was a devout man than the fact that he carried, as most men then did, a short rosary at his girdle, proved that he said his rosary. Neither perhaps can we argue so very safely from the fact that one hundred editions of the Latin Bible were printed before the year 1500. The Bible was a book wanted, for professional reasons by many students, by most ecclesiastics and by all preachers who had sermons to prepare. The same also is probably to be said of the large number of editions issued of certain collections of sermons like the *Promptuarium* of Herolt. These in like manner were used by preachers to take their sermons from ready-made, and further they often contained collections of anecdotes and little stories which readers found entertaining. But besides these, there were a very large number of more serious works the sale of which can in no way be explained on the principles just suggested. No man who recalls the simple earnest piety, the sublime moral lessons, which are contained in *The Imitation of Christ*, can for a moment doubt that the men who bought and read that book were not attracted to it for any adventitious or unworthy reason. They did not buy it because it amused them, or because it promised them great indulgences, or a short way of getting to heaven without effort or suffering, or because it made their flesh creep by recounting the gruesome torments of the lost. They bought it simply to do good to their souls, and they must have had some kind of appreciation of what was meant by moral discipline and the service of God to be attracted to it at all. Now of this *Imitation* or *Following of Christ*, a hundred different editions are known to be in existence printed between 1472 and 1500. Of these, fifty-nine editions are in Latin, eighteen in Italian, seven in German, nine in French, seven in Spanish and Portuguese. In the British Museum Collection alone, forty-five of these editions are to be found, all issued before the year 1500. But you may say : after all the *Imitation* is a very small book. So it is, but I only appeal to it as a specimen of the sort of religious literature which men were buying at the end of the fifteenth century, simply because they were in earnest in wanting to do good to their souls and for no other possible reason. There is quite a vast literature of books of this type and of all sorts and sizes. Take for example the *Life of Christ* by Ludolfus the Carthusian. That is a big folio which when closely printed occupies seven or eight hundred pages. Of this there were seventeen different Latin editions, printed before 1500, besides three or four in French and four in other languages. I cannot conceive anyone being led to take up Ludolfus's *Life of Christ* unless his motive was that he wanted to know more about the works of our Blessed Lord and to learn to be a better man. Or take the spiritual treatise *De Ascensionibus mentis ad*

Deum of a quite out-of-the-way author, Brother Gerard of Zutphen—I mention it here because it happens to have been translated into English. It is a religious work of the severest character, especially interesting because St. Ignatius utilised it, and followed its arrangement in his *Spiritual Exercises*. But this *De Ascensionibus* again, though it is not in any way famous, went through ten editions before 1500, *i.e.*, in about fifteen years, one of these editions being a translation into Low German. And there are countless other examples of the same kind. Now men did not buy books in those days simply for the sake of furnishing a room. They were costly things, and if anyone did not mean to read what he bought, he soon found that he had a better use for his money than to accumulate lumber. Again we may be still more sure that the booksellers did not print these multiple editions simply for the sake of edification. They printed them because they were able to sell them. And so it seems to me that we have the most conclusive evidence for the existence of a large class of educated men even at the close of the Middle Ages who were intent upon learning how to serve God better, to train themselves in solid virtue and to do good to their neighbours. These were not the men whose lives we read about in the scandalous chronicles of the times. They lived and prayed and did penance in obscurity, but they were all most loyal sons of the Church, and it is among them as I conceive that we find the secret of that vitality which showed itself so wonderfully in the missions to the heathen of the New World.

I do not think, then, that Catholics need allow their faith to be perturbed by the very serious falling away from high ideals which no doubt found its climax in that revolt from Roman authority which we call the Reformation. Grievous abuses and scandals there undoubtedly were, but when writers like Dr. Lea, in that superior tone and quasi-philosophical language which they affect, tell us of the formalism which had practically replaced the " ethical values of Christianity," we may take up that little volume of the *Following of Christ*, which is after all the most world-renowned book that the fifteenth century produced, and ask ourselves whether Dr. Lea and his friends, with all their pompous talk about the ethical values of Christianity, have anything higher or nobler to teach us than Thomas à Kempis, or whether that talk has prompted one disciple to travel to the other end of the world in order to bring benighted pagans to the knowledge of a higher moral law.

There must be some among my readers who will be able to recall the extraordinary sensation produced a quarter of a century ago by the revival of the mediæval morality play of *Everyman*. Not much is known for certain about its author or the country of its origin ; but whether it was first written in English or in Dutch, it unquestionably belongs to the close of the middle ages and it was then printed several times both in this country and in Holland. We hear a good deal in that play about Confession, but nothing about indulgences or the " purchase of Masses." When Everyman, warned of his approaching end, has turned at last to heavenly influences, he finds that only " Good Dedes " is able to pass with him into the presence of the great Judge, and " Knowledge " is left without to announce to the audience :

> Now hath he suffered that we all shall endure,
> There " Good Dedes " shall make all sure ;
> Now hath he made endynge.
> Me thynketh that I here engelles synge,
> And make great joye and melodye,
> Where Every-mannes soule shall receyved be.

I think one may say that no " complete divorce between religion and morality " is perceptible here.

INDEX